Life In The Wild Blue Yonder

Jet Fighter pilot stories from the cold war.
Second Edition

John Lowery

ISBN-10: 1515195791
EAN-13: 9781515195795

To the memory of Major Kermit L. Haderlie, USAF, the talented cowboy from Freedom, Wyoming. He reached for the stars and almost made it. But fate had other plans.

Contents

Foreword

John Lowery is a highly regarded writer in several genres: aviation, flight safety, hunting, and wilderness survival. I first met him when we were flying maintenance-quality-control functional test flights in F-86Fs at Williams Air Force Base (AFB), Arizona. John was a Fourth Fighter Interceptor Wing veteran of the Korean War, while I was a fledgling learning at the master's feet. Over time, I too became a functional test pilot in the F-86, working under Captain Lowery as the chief of flight test. Subsequently, he went on to fly the F-105D in combat, and command an F-4C Wild Weasel Squadron based out of Okinawa, Japan. During his career, he also flew a plethora of other air force aircraft prior to his retirement. Following retirement from the air force, he established a successful business as a flight instructor and FAA-designated pilot-proficiency examiner for corporate flight departments, specializing in the corporate jet Sabreliner and several turboprop aircraft. His span of operations in this endeavor was global. Concurrently, he authored five aviation books dealing with multiengine and transport-category aircraft performance and general aviation accident prevention.

John's roommate in the Fourth FIW at K-14 Korea, First Lieutenant Robert F. Niemann, was shot down over North Korea and officially listed as missing in action and later as killed in the crash of his jet fighter. Haunted by the loss of his close friend, John conducted extensive, well-documented research to close the book on his friend's fate. His research uncovered considerable evidence that Lt. Niemann and numerous US pilots and aircrew were held captive in Russia and China following both the Korean and Vietnamese wars—and that scores of these men were not repatriated with their comrades.

I personally have no evidence of American aircrew held captive by the Russian, Vietnamese, and Chinese governments. However, when I was interviewed for a clandestine assignment to Jungle Jim, forerunner of the current Air Force Special Operations Command, I was questioned by an air force brigadier general who remained in the shadows throughout the interview. While I could not see his face, the stars on his collar were in plain sight. I was told that if I answered any of the three questions unsatisfactorily, the interview was over:

Are you willing to fly old, obsolete aircraft?

Are you willing to fly combat missions?

If sent into combat and shot down, are you willing to be disowned by your government?

Evidently all questions were answered to the general's satisfaction, as I soon received classified orders transferring me to Hurlburt AFB, Florida. It was the last question of the interview that supports John's research on unaccounted-for airmen shot down over enemy territory.

This book is good reading and tells a story as yet untold.

General John L. Piotrowski, USAF (Ret.)

Acknowledgments

I WISH TO EXPRESS my sincerest gratitude to several people who contributed their time and effort to this book. First is Colonel Joe Shriber, USAFR (Ret.), whose computer knowledge and editorial help has been invaluable. Without his guidance, this book would not have been possible. Mr. Gil Hasler's excellent photographs from our early F-86 days were a godsend. Gil was my squadron-mate in the 334th Fighter Interceptor Squadron during the last months of the Korean War. I had the honor of flying his wing on his 105th and last mission of the war.

Thanks are also due to Professor (Emeritus) Ken Rowe, better known in military circles as Lt. No Kum-Sok—the North Korean MiG-15 pilot who escaped to freedom after the Korean War. Ken provided much useful information and allowed me to use major parts of his book, *A MiG-15 to Freedom*, describing his life under the brutal Communist government.

Lieutenant Colonel Ed Jones, USAF (Ret.), was a big help in writing about his ejection from an F-106. Due to faulty design, the hydraulic flight controls failed during an acceptance test flight of a new production airplane, forcing him to try out the airplane's new ejection system.

Colonel John Morrissey, USAF (Ret.), provided invaluable details concerning premature bomb detonations responsible for killing aircrew. Two problems were involved: the carriage of World War II bombs equipped with obsolete fuses, and the flawed design of a new type of proximity bomb fuse.

Special thanks also to Colonel Willard S. Gideon, USAF (Ret.), for his pictures and proofing of chapter 22. He was shot down and captured near Hanoi on August 7, 1966, and although seriously injured, he managed to survive seven years as a POW. This chapter also documents our airmen who were captured alive by North Vietnamese, Soviets, and Cubans in South Vietnam, Laos, and North Vietnam, and were never repatriated.

General John L. (Pete) Piotrowski, USAF (Ret.), was most gracious in sharing his family biography for use in his life's story in chapter 29. General Pete has been a valued friend since we were both lieutenants in 1958. His knowledge, drive, and upfront leadership in combat took him from airman basic radar technician to commander of US Space Command. His story will be inspirational for generations to come.

Preface

AS A TEENAGER IN the post–World War II era, the strains of the rousing air force song, "Off we go, into the wild blue yonder, climbing high into the sun…" invariably brought goose bumps to my skin and ignited a burning ambition to someday become an air force fighter pilot. Having had the good fortune to realize my dream, it seemed appropriate to document some of the events that occurred during my tours of duty. The stories begin in 1952, the year my life as an air force fighter pilot began. The Korean War saw the first use of jet fighters in combat by the USAF. Of special importance was the introduction of the new swept-wing North American Aviation (NAA) F-86 Sabre, the first operational fighter capable of breaking the sound barrier (achieving supersonic airspeed in a dive). Its design was based on original German studies and wind-tunnel tests, which were improved upon by engineers at NAA. The result was an aerodynamically flawless jet fighter. However, as you will see, it did have some problems along the way.

Writing chapter 22 was an emotional undertaking because it concerns my fellow airmen, who after being captured alive in North Korea, North and South Vietnam, and Laos were never repatriated. During the Korean War, thirty F-86 pilots are known to have been captured and turned over to the Russians. In fact, in the early 1990s, Russian President Boris Yeltsin confirmed that some were taken to Moscow for "intelligence exploitation." Yet none of these airmen were repatriated or accounted for in accordance with the armistice agreements or the Geneva Conventions.

Regarding our war with North Vietnam, recently declassified documents show that 705 captured US airmen *were not* repatriated. In fact, as you'll read, the Cubans took 17 of our airmen from Hanoi to Havana for "medical experimentation in torture techniques." None of these men were ever identified or accounted for. However, the remains of African-American navy F-4 pilot Lieutenant Clemmie McKinney, thought to have been one of the 17, were repatriated from Hanoi in 1985. He was shot down and captured near the demilitarized zone (DMZ) during a period when Fidel Castro was visiting the Cuban Engineers—called the Girón Brigade—who were maintaining the roads in the area. Recent information shows that following his capture McKinney was photographed standing with Castro.

It was in the area of the DMZ that the Cubans had a POW camp for captured Americans—none of whom was ever acknowledged or repatriated. The Russians also had a POW camp nearby but across the border in Laos. Yet to mention this brings vehement denials from official sources. I can only suggest that if you doubt what you read then check out the references with Google. You'll find it an emotional experience—I sure did.

The overall purpose of this book is to give you a realistic look at life in the USAF—the wild blue yonder—during the Cold War era. For those of us who survived to retirement it was an exciting, history-making, action-filled life—interspersed with numerous moments of great sadness.

Chapter 1

The Fighter Pilot Philosophy

Setting the stage for the jet-fighter-pilot mind-set.

IT WAS ABOUT THREE minutes after 11:00 p.m. on the night of October 12, 1952, when I pulled up to the main gate at Nellis AFB, Nevada—Fighter City, it was called. Despite the late hour, jet fighters were still in the traffic pattern. The lights of Las Vegas had been dazzling enough, but the base's variety of fighter aircraft and the fact it was home to many of the jet aces who were newly returned from the Korean War made it especially awesome to a new flying-school graduate.

I was reporting in to attend combat-crew training in the F-86 Sabre. My class would be the first to train solely in the F-86. Previous classes had been required to spend half their time in the now obsolete F-80 before getting just a taste of the F-86.

My training was preparatory to a combat tour in Korea, for which I had volunteered. In truth, I had mixed feelings about the assignment. It was in fact exactly what I had requested, but as a new father, rumors of the base's accident rate and the possibility of being shot down in combat gave me strong feelings of guilt. Still, I couldn't escape the inward excitement of becoming a pilot of the fastest airplane in the US Air Force.

When I got out of my automobile to sign the paperwork required for a temporary gate pass and to ask the location of the billeting office, the two gate guards were preoccupied with a telephone call. Finally, the sergeant in charge hung up the phone, turned to his companion and said, "The wing commander just pranged on the end of the runway."

With my pregnant wife and baby daughter now rousing from fitful sleep on the front seat of my automobile, I was almost overcome with guilt.

A few days later, with my family ensconced in a barracks apartment, I began life as a student jet-fighter pilot. It was heady stuff. We ate lunch at the Jet Pilots Mess. While it was designed to provide a low-gas-producing diet, in case of a decompression aloft that caused painful distension of the stomach and intestines, it immediately became a status symbol. If you didn't fly jets, you didn't dare enter the Jet Pilots Mess.

Most of the pilots were lieutenants and captains, with an occasional major or lieutenant colonel, all involved with the jet fighters. One day during lunch, a major from base operations—the pilot of the base C-54 (DC-4)—came in and sat down at a table with his food tray. Immediately two captains from an adjoining table jumped up and physically threw him out into the street. I was aghast at captains manhandling a major. But nothing more was said; nor did I see the major again in the Jet Pilots Mess.

There were other status symbols that fed the male ego. One was the anti-G suit. The garment was designed to provide protection from blackout during high-G maneuvers—wherein the blood is pulled from your head toward your abdomen and legs. (G refers to the pull of gravity and centrifugal force.) When maneuvering at high speed and pulling four to seven Gs, without the G-suits your vision would go black and you would momentarily lose consciousness. But with a G-suit the air bladders in the legs and abdomen inflated to help prevent your blood from pooling in your legs. This helped maintain your consciousness and vision.

After the flying was over, some of us students enjoyed walking down the street from the squadron to our apartments still clad in the tight fitting G-suit. It was the ultimate status symbol, clearly identifying us as jet-fighter pilots. Further adding to the luster of our role, we worked with the jet aces from Korea: Major Bill Whisner was my squadron commander, Captain Ivan Kincheloe was one of my instructors, and Major Boots Blesse was the squadron operation officer. This of course added to one's self-image.

I would proudly walk in the door of our barracks apartment and take off the G-suit. But before sitting down to dinner, I faced the chore of hand-washing a bucket full of dirty diapers. In those days there were no washing machines in base apartments. The alternative was a long drive into North Las Vegas to the coin-operated Washeteria. This aspect of the fighter pilot's life was very closely held information.

To understand the fighter-pilot philosophy during the 1950s and 1960s, you must understand the prevailing attitudes of the era. First, at Nellis AFB most of the instructors were P-51 and P-38 veterans of World War II—an era where flying safety took a back seat to combat proficiency. The AAF Statistical Digest shows that in the United States alone, from December 1941 until August 1945, the US Army Air Forces lost 14,903 aircrew members in 13,873 airplanes—1,170 aircraft per month or 40 per day.

In the 1950s and early 1960s, the overriding operational philosophy was that if you weren't having accidents, you weren't training realistically. This lack of concern for safety was exacerbated by the demand for seemingly mindless aggressiveness. In fighter squadrons you'd find a sign over the operations desk that read, "Every man a tiger!" This was the indelible fighter pilot's creed that some failed to temper with good judgment.

The base also had an unusual mix of aircraft. Throughout most of the 1950s the Nellis AFB fleet consisted of the newly re-designated F-51 Mustangs, F-80s and T-33s, F-84s, and of course the revered F-86 Sabres. Then, in the mid-1950s, the F-51s were withdrawn and the more advanced F-100A and two-seat F-100F models of the Super Sabres were added. When combined with the fighter-pilot philosophy, the mix of airplanes proved quite hazardous.

Colonel Clay Tice Jr., commander of the 3595 Flying Training Group, struck the philosophical keynote early. His speech to new students began, "Welcome to Nellis Air Force Base, men, the finest fighter-weapons school in the world. We're going to do one of three things to you here: wash you out, kill you, or make you one of the best fighter pilots in the world. The choice is yours" (Escalle 2013). Thanks to this foundation, throughout the 1950s there was at least one fatality each week—sometimes two if there was a midair collision. And mind you, these were just the *fatal* mishaps.

In his bestselling book, *The Right Stuff*, Tom Wolfe tells of the experience of astronaut Mike Collins during combat-crew training at Nellis AFB. In the eleven-week course, "twenty-two of his fellow trainees had died in accidents," an extraordinary rate of two fatalities per week (Wolfe 1979, 16). Test pilot Bill Bridgeman told of sixty-two air force pilots killed during thirty-six weeks of training in 1952, or 1.7 per week. (The loss of test pilots at Edwards AFB in California was a story unto itself.)

The proximity of the Las Vegas casinos combined with the World War II safety philosophy was yet another factor in the accident equation. To some it proved to be financially as well as physically devastating. The feeling was that real fighter pilots could stay out "partying" until shortly before briefing time for the first mission of the day. After all, the flight would last less than an hour. Thus during the preflight briefing it was common to have the instructor and a couple of students red-eyed and reeking of booze. The prevailing theory was that a cup of squadron coffee and a doughnut, combined with 100 percent oxygen in the airplane, would sober one up.

A typical example involved a new student fighter pilot who had partied with the guys on the Las Vegas strip on the first three nights of the week—getting to the bachelor officer's quarters (BOQ) for a couple hours sleep in the wee hours of the morning. After three nights of fun he was scheduled for an early morning flight in an F-80C to qualify in skip bombing, rockets, and strafing. Skip bombing was a low-level event that involved putting a practice twenty-five-pound bomb through a ten by twenty foot rectangular polyethylene target strung between two metal poles. The aiming point was a large black bull's eye in the center of the target.

In the F-80C the trick to putting the bomb directly through the target was to fly toward the target at four hundred knots at an altitude of about ten feet. Any extra altitude or excess airspeed meant a "skip over"—a missed target. In this case the student was flying the number-two position. Once established in the racetrack pattern and at four hundred knots, his first bomb was a skip-over. To help his student qualify, the instructor promptly transmitted, "Real tigers get low."

The pilot of the number-four aircraft described the crash: "I could tell from his radio transmissions Number Two was determined...I watched as he put his aircraft right through the middle of the target and into the ground...I figure he had about six hours total sleep all week."

In preflight briefings aggressiveness was emphasized. In some misguided souls it superseded good judgment, even rational thought. One former student tells of arriving mid-afternoon in Sin City: "I got into bed about 02:00 AM and was awakened at first light by all the activity on the Nellis flight line. I looked out of the BOQ window and watched a pair of F-86s just after takeoff. As the student pilot was attempting to join up with his flight leader he overshot the lead aircraft. In a determined attempt to salvage the join-up, he sucked it in tight, then flipped over and augured-in near the highway that passes the base."

The same graduate tells of being an escort officer for the body of a good friend who was in a class ahead of him. The deceased had played blackjack in one of the local clubs until the early morning hours. Then, during the first mission of the day, while engaged in a mock dogfight with his instructor, they both failed to disengage at the established minimum altitude. Unfortunately, the student crashed and burned (Escalle 2013).

Yet another instance involved an F-86 student who, like the F-80 pilot, pressed his luck on a skip-bombing run and got too low. The range officer reported over the radio, "Borax Two, you hit the right target stanchion!" The student replied, "Roger." His instructor said nothing. Then, despite a deep gash in the leading edge of his right wing—ever the tiger—he climbed to pattern altitude and rolled in for the dive bomb event. (Real tigers didn't quit.) Unfortunately, during the dive recovery, which typically required about five Gs, his wing failed. The range officer callously listed his score as "twelve o'clock unscorable," meaning he impacted well past the dive-bombing circle.

Frequently, instructors would lead their four-ship formation to the gunnery range but find that a previous flight had not yet cleared the area. Because it was now their assigned range time, they wouldn't orbit and wait for the shooters to get clear. Instead they would lead their flight into the middle of the active bombing or strafing pattern. And as you might guess, this frequently led to midair collisions.

Sometimes, once a flight's range mission was completed, if any fuel remained, an instructor would lead his flight to the Nellis AFB traffic pattern and bounce (mock attack) an airplane on the initial approach for landing—or better yet on takeoff. If you were the one landing, you simply ignored the attack, since typically your fuel pointer was reading close to zero.

It happened to me on my second flight in a Sabre—my first without an instructor chasing me. I had just lifted off on the early morning mission, my landing gear still retracting. Suddenly a flight of four Sabres made a mock attack on my aircraft from the shadow of Sunrise Mountain to the east. With my airspeed just above 220 knots, all I could do was gamely turn into them—despite departing fighters on the adjacent runway.

Some accidents resulted from failing to respect the mountainous terrain. For example, a student flying alone at six thousand feet and four hundred knots in the training area spots another Sabre just beginning a mock attack on his aircraft. When he sees that his attacker has the advantage—ever the tiger—he quickly rolls inverted and tries a "split-S" maneuver to escape. This involves rolling inverted and pulling through at high speed just above the ground. But alas, what this tiger failed to consider was that the terrain elevation underneath was 3,500 feet. As a result he scatters himself and his airplane over a half-mile of the red lava rock landscape.

Still, it was the landing traffic pattern that accounted for a great many fatal mishaps. In the 360-degree overhead procedure, you were judged by the snap of your pitchout and the tightness of your pattern. If it was tight enough, the perfect pattern could be completed with the throttle at idle-power—referred to as a power-off traffic pattern. As a result, it was common to walk out of a building and see a large column of black smoke boiling from the end of the runway. Some tiger had gotten his traffic pattern a wee bit too tight.

Whenever you saw that column of smoke, you hoped it wasn't someone you knew. But all too often it was. You would find out on your way home from work, when you spotted the blue staff cars of the wing commander and base chaplain parked in front of a neighbor's house. If the deceased had been a student, three weeks later only one or two close friends would remember his name. If he had been a longtime instructor, the base commander would sometimes name a street in the housing area after him.

Yet the accidents were not all in the air. Some involved the hardworking ground crews who kept the airplanes flying. Shortly before graduating in December, I was scheduled for an early morning bombing and strafing mission on the gunnery range's convoy of trucks and tanks. While walking from the squadron operations building to my assigned aircraft, there was suddenly a muffled explosion. People on the flight line were excitedly running around in circles. Then a small group of line crew began congregating behind the left wing of a Sabre. As I approached I could see a sergeant lying motionless, his otherwise white face now a strange blue-gray color. He was the crew chief of the mishap aircraft, and with two helpers they had been removing the empty left pylon tank from underneath the Sabre's wing. But as he held it by the tail cone against his chest, someone pressed the electrical pylon tank release button instead of pulling the manual release lanyard, and the fumes in the tank exploded—sending the pointed tank tail cone into his chest like a cannon shell. In short, he was dead.

A day or so later—once again by the dawn's early light—our four-ship flight of Sabres had the engines running, and we were awaiting taxi clearance from the Nellis control tower. Suddenly, the tower began frantically transmitting: ATTENTION ALL AIRCRAFT! ATTENTION ALL AIRCRAFT AT NELLIS AIR F ORCE BASE! HOLD YOUR POSITIONS! DO NOT MOVE! WE HAVE A FOX EIGHTY GOING ABLE SUGAR ON THE RAMP!

With that I looked up ahead and saw the tails of several airplanes moving at odd angles. Once we were cleared to taxi, the problem became obvious. A jet engine specialist had been working on an F-80 in the parking area rather than the designated engine run-up area. With the airplane's tail section removed, he was running the engine at full power and relying on the ship's brakes and wheel chocks to hold it in place. But they weren't good enough: the aircraft had jumped the chocks and ricocheted at full power through the closely parked jet fighters. The final score was five F-80s destroyed and one B-26 damaged. The sergeant had become a jet ace and airman third class all at the same time.

As the Christmas season approached, there were numerous parties scheduled for both the instructors and graduating students at the Officers Open Mess—the O-club. Built in 1941, when the base was first established as an aerial gunnery school, the wooden structure was the seat of all base social activity. Word among the instructors was that for the past three years the wing commander had applied for funds to replace it with a permanent modern building. But each year Air Training Command had refused to fund it.

It was December 23, and two of the physicians from the base hospital had just been promoted; so a promotion party was scheduled. Since one was a flight surgeon, many fighter pilots attended to help celebrate. By all reports the party was a huge success, but for some reason in the wee hours of the morning the darn place caught fire. The *Las Vegas Review Journal* said, "The flames spread through the building with such rapidity that the personnel in the club had to flee as fast as possible...None of the furniture or equipment in the structure could be saved." The destruction was so total that investigators were unable to determine the cause. The end result was a beautiful new state-of-the-art structure. Today it still serves as the center of all social activity, and every Friday night at happy hour, the building rings with heartfelt renditions of old fighter-pilot folksongs like "Mary Ann Burns, Queen of All the Acrobats," "Sammy Small" (who was sexually handicapped), and a host of rather naughty ditties.

Chapter 2

Becoming a Combat Veteran

Surviving the first year as a jet-fighter pilot.

IT WAS JUNE 19, 1953, and my twenty-sixth combat mission of the Korean War. Our flight of four F-86 Sabres was descending at high speed in a loose fingertip formation. Flight leader First Lieutenant Ivan Ely had us weaving between the towering cumulous buildups, with dark stratified cloud layers lurking below. As we descended, the moisture-laden air colored the high-speed shockwaves on our wings and oval

Plexiglas canopy. Having recently had my twenty-fourth birthday, and with three hundred hours of flight time, my baptism of fire by a Russian-flown MiG-15 had occurred ten missions earlier.

Thus far, as I had envisioned, fighter-versus-fighter combat had proven to be the most challenging endeavor I had ever experienced—a win-or-lose shooting competition. To borrow a phrase from English literature, "It was the most dangerous game." Having finished flight training at Bryan AFB, Texas, in September 1952—Class 52-Fox—I had now been a rated air force fighter pilot for nine months. Upon my graduation from flight school, my instructor had said, "Lieutenant, if you can survive your first year as a fighter pilot, you'll probably make it to retirement."

I soon learned what he meant. Surviving the following two months of F-86 combat crew training at Nellis AFB, Nevada, proved to be a major challenge. Fortunately, despite the base's record of a pilot killed every week, my class suffered only one major accident—a midair collision between Lieutenants Mike Flynn and Dan Felix during air combat maneuvering (dogfighting). Dan had been locked onto a "bandit," and when they hit, his Sabre sliced Mike's airplane in half. Fortunately, both pilots ejected successfully and landed uninjured.

Having survived training at Nellis, flying fighter-interceptors against MiG-15s in Korea was a cakewalk—although weather conditions could be foul. Our training had thoroughly prepared us for air-to-air combat with the Russian veterans of World War II. (As we learned later, the Chinese and North Korean pilots were simply students with very limited flying experience.)

At K-14 (the United Nations designation for Kimpo Air Base), the aggressiveness factor was reserved for the combat area. To stop landing accidents, the wing commander, Colonel James K. Johnson, had mandated a square traffic pattern. No more tight 360-degree power-off patterns with the inevitable smoking funeral pyre in the runway overrun.

Our assigned mission that day was a so-called fighter sweep—searching for enemy aircraft along the United Nations' established Yalu River boundary of North Korea and China: MiG Alley, it was called. But the miserable weather we were encountering made contact with the enemy seem unlikely.

Departing K-14, I noted the overcast began at around two thousand feet; but about twenty miles north, in the up-sloping foothills and mountains toward the bomb line (front lines), the clouds appeared to merge with the ground. Lieutenant Ely—call sign Rifle One—was an experienced World War II veteran. After takeoff, while awaiting join-up of the two-ship element—Rifle Three and Four—he was attempting to keep us clear of the clouds. But as we neared the bomb line, the sky was becoming increasingly dark and ominous. The second element had not yet joined up, and a misty rain was now splattering my windscreen, with long streaks of water running back over the canopy. From a slightly loose wing position, the total devastation of the countryside near the front lines was becoming visible.

To assist the second element, Rifle One had reduced engine power and was watching his flight instruments, vainly trying to avoid being swallowed by the descending cloud layer. As visibility continued to diminish, I was becoming increasingly uneasy. Then a casual comment by one of my instructors at Nellis came to mind. He had said, "We spend two months teaching you to obey and follow your leader blindly. Yet if you do that in combat you'll get killed."

Suddenly through the dark mist I saw artillery shells bursting on the hillside ahead. If our flight path continued through that deadly artillery barrage, catastrophe was inevitable. Quickly I transmitted, "Rifle Lead, PULL UP! PULL UP!" Then in a zoom-climb maneuver I was out of there.

Ironically, the second element had been very near, and we all broke out in a loose trail formation at eight thousand feet, sandwiched between layers of blue-gray alto-stratus clouds. We quickly joined up, and with the second element now in position, our flight of four Sabres climbed in a close fingertip formation through the stratified cloud layers all the way up to forty-five thousand feet.

Officially, our mission that dreary day was a combat air patrol along the Yalu River boundary with China, the area called MiG Alley. Chinese airspace had been designated as forbidden territory by the United Nations (UN) command. This unprecedented wartime restriction had been established by the UN in an effort to contain the hostilities. In effect it allowed our adversaries—Soviet MiG-15 fighter units and elements of the nascent Chinese and North Korean air forces—a safe haven in China. This gave them a distinct tactical advantage.

In the sanctuary of Chinese airspace, the MiGs regularly climbed above our F-86A and E-model Sabres to between fifty thousand and fifty-three thousand feet. After reaching high altitude, they would cross the border into North Korea, descend, and attack in elements of two aircraft. They disengaged simply by climbing back to altitude and heading back north for the border.

Still, their high-altitude capability was not without limitations. At and above fifty thousand feet they were riding very close to their so-called low-speed buffet boundary—the point where the wing's air-flow begins to burble (stall). Consequently, it was not uncommon to see some hapless MiG pilot suddenly begin spinning out of control. Sometimes in panic, while still at very high altitude, the pilot would eject. This meant he died of either hypoxia or hypothermia, or more likely a combination of both. The air in the stratosphere has very little oxygen, and the temperature is -56.4 degrees Celsius.

The rules at the time allowed the first pilot to see and call out a spinning MiG to claim credit for a kill. Of course this assumed someone saw the MiG pilot eject, or verified seeing a fireball on the ground when it crashed.

Fortunately, the new F-86Fs we were now flying had increased engine thrust. Thus in the spring of 1953 we were routinely at forty-nine thousand feet altitude chasing MiGs. We could actually go higher but only by exceeding the engine's exhaust gas temperature limit. But at that altitude our typical cruise-climb airspeed of Mach 0.8 was very close to the Sabre's low-speed buffet boundary. To maintain altitude in a level turn that exceeded fifteen degrees bank required a slight increase in pull on the control stick (G load). As a wingman you quickly learned that a little too much bank caused a prestall burble. This resulted in an instantaneous loss of ten knots indicated airspeed, and you began to lag behind your element leader. This not only made you look bad but also set you up as an easy target for the high-flying MiGs. Fortunately, the Sabre's near flawless aerodynamic characteristics made it free of bad habits—such as the MiG-15's unrecoverable spin. And, as we would learn later, the MiG's airspeed was limited to Mach 0.92 (92 percent of the speed of sound), whereas ours was unlimited.

Our previous engagements had occurred between forty-five thousand and forty-nine thousand feet. But on this dreary day the clouds seemed to go up forever. "Nuts," I mused. "Just another formation proficiency flight. The MiGs certainly wouldn't be flying."

Normally, after forty-five minutes of climbing we would be looking down at the Yalu River, and our two wing-pylon tanks would just be going empty. If our offshore ground radar station—call sign

Mongoose—reported enemy air activity, then at this point we dropped the pylon tanks to reduce aerodynamic drag and save fuel.

At what I presumed to be the Yalu River boundary, Lt. Ely turned our flight generally west-northwest and began descending—trying to stay clear of the blue-gray layers of clouds. Although the sky remained dark and ominous in this new direction, the clouds seemed more strati-fied, interspersed with towering white cumulous buildups. Soon we were in a clear corridor between two large cells and able to spread out into tactical formation and begin looking around.

Eventually we leveled at seventeen thousand feet, with the clear cor-ridor between the buildups providing good visibility and an occasional glimpse of the dark, featureless ground.

Shortly thereafter, feeling somewhat bored and disappointed, I saw that the fuel gauge showed fifteen hundred pounds. It was time to go home. Dutifully I transmitted, "Rifle Two has BINGO." This indicated minimum fuel for the trip to home base. Rifle Leader promptly replied, "Roger, Rifle Two." Suddenly, out of nowhere, there was a lone MiG-15 flying straight and level about two thousand feet ahead and slightly to our left.

Excitedly I transmitted, "Rifle Lead, you have a MiG at eleven o'clock level!"

"Roger, got him Rifle Two."

I watched fascinated as he closed on the beautiful sky-blue fighter—the bright red star of the Chinese Air Force clearly showing on its fuse-lage. The enemy pilot obviously had his engine powered back and flew leisurely, as if out sightseeing. By now I was essentially in a loose tactical formation with both Rifle Lead and the MiG—anxiously awaiting the first burst from my leader's six .50-caliber machine guns.

At a range of about one thousand feet Rifle Lead fired his ini-tial salvo—an easy task for the F-86F's A-4 radar-ranging gunsight. Unbelievably Rifle Lead's first burst went over the MiG. "Oh God!

He'll get away," I said into my oxygen mask. To save himself, all the MiG pilot had to do was make a hard turn left or right and disappear in the clouds.

The miss meant Rifle Lead's radar-ranging feature was inoperative; or perhaps, like an overeager deer hunter, he had "buck fever." Meanwhile, in disbelief, I watched as the enemy pilot continued straight and level at a reduced airspeed, making no attempt to escape certain death.

Lt. Ely's second burst was deadly. Pieces of the MiG's aluminum skin flew from the top of fuselage just aft of the cockpit and back toward the vertical stabilizer. This meant a hit in the engine and tailpipe. Normally this combination would cause the ship's engine to fail or the aircraft to begin burning. Yet the beautiful aircraft continued flying straight and level. Surely the pilot was dead—or more likely paralyzed with fear.

Because of my fuel state and Lt. Ely's knowledge of our actual location—across the border in China—he abruptly turned to leave. Excitedly I called, "Finish him, Rifle! Finish him!" I had remained in potential shooting position off the MiG's right side and about one thousand feet out. But, as a wingman, firing my guns without permission from my flight leader could get me reassigned to the motor pool or mess hall upon landing—and ignominiously sent home. But, following my call, Rifle Lead turned back and realigned to finish the job.

As Lt. Ely slid into trail position and prepared to shoot, another MiG suddenly popped out of the wall of clouds on our left. To my utter horror the aircraft was on a collision course with Rifle Lead. Worse yet, a quick burst from its thirty-seven-millimeter cannon would literally blow Lt. Ely out of the sky.

Fortunately, the cannon blast never came. In retrospect, because the MiG had just popped out of the clouds, it seems obvious the pilot was flying by reference to his flight instruments and, until the last second, had failed to see Ely's aircraft. "PULL UP! PULL UP, RIFLE!" I screamed. With his attention locked on the MiG, for a moment he failed to react. "Rifle Lead, PULL UP! MIG AT NINE O'CLOCK!"

The obvious urgency of my transmissions finally broke his concentration, and with that the Sabre zoomed-up sharply. The MiG pilot suddenly looked up too, and in frantic desperation, he pushed over abruptly. Miraculously, they avoided colliding, but by mere inches.

Quickly, Rifle One realigned and, with a short burst, again peppered the doomed fighter's fuselage, and the beautiful aircraft dropped off into a spiral dive to the right. Because the firing had been from the six o'clock (tail) position, I fully expected the MiG pilot to eject and save himself. After all, his aircraft had armor plate behind the seat to protect him. But he failed to eject.

Lt. Ely continued in firing position at about one thousand feet, with me on his right wing—but still fascinated with the enemy aircraft. We followed the doomed fighter down into the dark drizzling void beneath the clouds. No terrain features were visible, only the blue-black haze marking the ground. I began to take spacing on the doomed fighter and had just started my pull-up when a bright orange flash marked the airplane's demise.

Quickly, Rifle Lead transmitted, "Did you see him hit? Did you see him hit, Rifle Two?"

"Roger, Rifle! I saw him." He needed an eyewitness to get credit for this aerial victory.

Now back to reality, my head was moving rapidly; looking to the rear, overhead and side to side. Where was Rifle One? With apprehension swelling, I searched the cloudy sky for my leader. But he had been swallowed up by the clouds. I had become so mesmerized with the impending kill and proximity to an enemy aircraft that I had lost sight of my leader. This was a cardinal sin for a wingman, but I hoped the weather and the aerial victory would be mitigating. To this day I don't know when we parted company with Rifle Three and Four.

Dejectedly, I transmitted, "Rifle Lead, I've lost you!"

"Roger two," was all he said in reply.

Still, I was elated. On my sixteenth mission I had had my first swirling dogfight from high altitude with a copper-colored MiG-15. In that case I had been the hapless target but fortunately managed to shake my Russian attacker. Today marked my first participation in an actual aerial victory. And, while this was certainly not a swirling fight, to my mind it put me in the league of air force veterans I had grown up watching in the news releases of World War II. Self-satisfied, I climbed through the murky clouds toward Kimpo Air Base.

Now further enhancing my veteran status was the forthcoming instrument approach into K-14 (Kimpo Air Base)—solo. Heretofore I had been latched onto my leader's wing in close formation while he executed the approach. This was heady stuff for a newly minted fighter pilot. Suddenly all my training was coming together in one mission.

The trip home would be simple. Believing we were over the Yalu River near its confluence with the Yellow Sea, I turned the sleek fighter to a course of 165 degrees. Flight time for the two-hundred-nautical-mile flight back to K-14 should take not more than forty-five minutes. With my fuel gauge now showing nine hundred pounds (about 142 gallons), if I glided at idle power from altitude, it was enough to reach home plate. While I never got used to it, the World War II veterans in our midst took sadistic delight in landing their flights with less than a hundred pounds (16 gallons) of fuel. On several occasions at Nellis I had landed with less than fifty pounds (8 gallons) of fuel. Obviously this would be one of those days.

In a euphoric state I climbed through the clouds to cruise altitude. Upon leveling off, I thought back to my teenage days flying a Piper J-3 Cub out of Auburn-Opelika (Alabama) airport. By age nineteen, and with about two hundred hours of Cub experience, I was sick of light airplanes. If only I could fly jets. Now I was doing it—flying the air force's first fighter capable of exceeding the speed of sound.

In my years of flying Cubs, the only navigation instrument available was the magnetic compass. With the magnetic compass, a map, and a watch, I could go anywhere. Thus, continuously checking the magnetic compass had become an ingrained habit well before air force pilot training.

Now on a heading for home on my electrically powered directional gyro (DG) with nothing to do but maintain cruise altitude, I casually looked up at the top frame of the windscreen to check the magnetic compass.

I was instantly petrified. It simply couldn't be! The mag-compass read 345 degrees. If that reading was true I was climbing deep into China rather than headed for home plate. The potential for a 180-degree error in the DG had never been discussed in training. I knew that a power failure to the instrument caused the OFF flag to show. But our instructors had emphasized, "Always believe your instruments!" But this?

I resolved the problem with country-boy logic: God, I reasoned, provides the magnetic lines of flux that turn the magnetic compass. Man provides electrical power to the slave gyro. Thus, I'll go with God. In what was the most difficult decision in my life, I established a 25-degree bank and turned to 345 degrees on the DG. On rollout, the mag-compass finally settled on 165 degrees. Still, with 345 degrees showing on the DG, I remained filled with self-doubt. About ten minutes later the DG suddenly fast-slaved to 165 degrees. Now they both read the same. I had made the right choice, and it appeared I'd have just enough fuel.

After fifty-five minutes en route, the low-frequency automatic direction finder (ADF) needle was pointing steadily toward the K-14 radio beacon. Upon checking the identifier "JK," it was unusually loud. Mongoose, our Ch-o-do island radar site, was very busy helping both US and Republic of South Africa fighter-bombers recover from their strikes deep inside North Korea. In my now-confident state, I saw no reason to add to their continuous chatter. Then the ADF needle swung. With a little less than four hundred pounds of fuel (sixty-three gallons), I had made it.

Promptly I reduced the engine power to idle and deployed the speed brakes, then worked my way down in the minimum altitude published for the teardrop instrument approach into K-14. Unaccountably I didn't break out of the clouds as expected at two thousand feet. Still, I continued descending toward minimums. A light drizzle was again splattering the windscreen, and now the clouds were beginning to break. Occasionally I would glimpse the ground. At eight hundred feet I broke clear of the clouds. Something was wrong. The river didn't look right; it was running east-west instead of north-south. It wasn't the Han that ran by Kimpo. Everywhere was total devastation. Suddenly it hit me. PYONGYANG! OH GOD! The capital of North Korea. How could that be?

Quickly I slammed the throttle full forward and popped back into the clouds. Then, as the landing gear retracted, I resumed the heading of 165 degrees. A quick check of the fuel gauge showed three hundred pounds (forty-seven gallons). At this point I was thoroughly confused and, shall we say, somewhat apprehensive.

I had been fully aware of the radio beacon the North Koreans had activated in their capital city, using the identical frequency and station identifier "JK" as our own beacon at K-14. The obvious purpose was to entrap unsuspecting pilots and capture an airplane. But the fifty-five-minute flight home and my low fuel level had caused over-optimism. In short, I forgot.

Now with three hundred pounds of fuel remaining, I had two choices: Turn west toward the Yellow Sea and fly fifty nautical miles toward Ch-o-do Island where, following my ejection, Mongoose would provide a rescue helicopter. Or I could use the remaining fuel to climb the hundred nautical miles toward Kimpo Air Base and, with luck, glide over the bomb line, where I could either eject or make a flameout landing at my home base. I opted to try for home base—K-14.

Mongoose's frequency had been jammed with chatter from the fighter-bombers—that is, until they heard my Mayday call. Now while climbing back to altitude I interrupted the chatter and transmitted: "Mongoose, this is Rifle Two, squawking Mayday. I'm lost with three hundred pounds of fuel remaining." Immediately a calm voice replied, "Roger, Rifle Two. We have your squawk. Continue your 165-degree heading. You are now eighty nautical miles from K-14."

What a relief! My chest had been tight with apprehension. But now it seemed certain I could make the bomb line and avoid capture.

Then, very casually, a South African Air Force F-86F fighter-bomber pilot provided comic relief. In a calm English-accented voice he said, "I say, Mongoose, when you're through with the Yank, could you send the chopper over for me? I have a flameout, you know." I couldn't help but laugh. The effect was immediately calming. It reminded me of the saying, "I felt sorry for myself because I had no shoes, until I met a man who had no feet."

Now reassured, I quickly told Mongoose I was trying for K-14 and to send the rescue helicopter for the South African pilot. After all, he was over the cold waters of the Yellow Sea.

As I climbed through twenty-five thousand feet, a cool, calm voice came through: "Rifle Two, this is John Black. Over!" This was the call sign of Fourth Fighter Wing Commander Colonel James K. Johnson.

"Roger, John Black, Rifle Two here." He was sitting in his blue staff car near the end of the runway, awaiting the tardy return of members of Rifle Flight.

"Aaahhh, Rifle Two, why don't you shut down the engine and glide home. Then you can restart over Kimpo and land."

He was unaware that I was not at forty thousand feet and that I had just made an instrument approach into Pyongyang and was desperately trying to gain enough altitude to enable a glide across the bomb line and avoid capture. After considering "John Black's" advice, and not wanting to argue with the wing commander, I answered simply, "Roger, John Black; I'm shutting down." Then with the throttle still at full power and climbing through twenty-seven thousand feet the fuel gauge pointer touched zero. And, right on cue, the engine spooled down as if stop-cocked. Now I was a glider pilot—hopefully with enough altitude to make it across the bomb line and maybe even reach Kimpo Air base.

With better than a two-mile-per-thousand-feet glide ratio, I figured the Sabre would take me at least fifty miles. To eject behind enemy lines near the battlefront would be fatal. The North Korean army had just recently shot and killed a good friend, Lt. John Southerland. After his aircraft was hit by antiaircraft fire near the bomb-line, he had successfully ejected from his F-86 fighter-bomber. Then, as he descended under the white canopy of his parachute, his wingman, Lt. Oscar Brooks, saw the enemy's tracers and watched helplessly as John's lifeless body floated to earth.

With the recommended 185-knot glide speed established, my eyes were glued to the attitude indicator. While in the clouds, it was the primary instrument that kept you oriented as to which way was up. Meanwhile the ADF radio beacon needle was once again pointing straight ahead. And again the Morse code identifier read "JK." Meanwhile, Mongoose continued to provide range and magnetic heading information. But it was John Black's continuing calm reassurance that kept me thinking positive.

It soon became obvious that my instrument scan was a problem. I was constantly looking out of the canopy, hoping to see the ground and go visual. Since we were a day fighter-wing our entire operation shut down when the weather was questionable or at official sunset. In fact, at sunset even the twelve ships on alert were towed back to their squadron revetments. The guys were then trucked to the Officers Open Mess— unofficially called Swig Alley.

Part of my instrument scan problem was that, during training at Nellis, real fighter pilots didn't practice instrument approaches. Instead they took their T-Birds (T-33 instrument trainers) to the air combat maneuvering (ACM) area and engaged in dog-fighting with anyone they happened to encounter. Even though instrument flying had been my strong suit in pilot training, at the moment I regretted not having used the time to hone my weather-flying skills.

As the altimeter passed through twelve thousand feet, suddenly everything became eerily silent. I could no longer hear John Black talking. Quickly I leaned over to turn up the volume on the ADF radio, but there was no sound. A fine rain was again misting my windscreen. Then my airspeed began to decay below 160 knots. To regain glide speed I added some nose-down pitch. But both my airspeed and altitude continued to drop.

With the airspeed indicator needle pegged at 120 knots, the cockpit was eerily quiet, and I felt light in my seat. Yet the attitude indicator showed the aircraft was flying wings level. Then it hit me: The OFF flag was showing in the artificial horizon. The lead-acid battery was dead!

By now I was completely out of ideas. I sat there holding the control stick—waiting. My plan was to eject at two thousand feet. I only hoped to see something on the ground that would indicate I had passed the front lines. As the altimeter showed nine thousand feet, the rain on my canopy seemed to increase. My Sabre seemed to be falling in slow motion, and I continued to feel light in my seat. Still I resisted the urge to eject, as my position had to be very near the front lines.

Then, as the altimeter needles passed through sixty-five hundred feet, my right hand began nervously fingering the ejection seat handle—and quite frankly I began praying. Suddenly, as if God were answering my prayer, the world brightened—like someone had turned on the lights—but although the clouds were bright with sunlight I still couldn't find a horizon or see the ground to get oriented.

Then some overhead movement caught my attention. With the altimeter passing through six thousand feet, I looked straight up through the top of the canopy, and there was K-14—Kimpo Air Base. In the best fighter pilot tradition, I had fallen out of the clouds, flamed-out and inverted, directly over the airfield—thus completing my first solo instrument approach…in a manner of speaking.

Quickly I rolled the aircraft upright and turned downwind for runway fourteen. With the landing gear extended manually, I held the recommended gear-down glide speed of 155 knots. The turn-to-base leg of the flameout pattern was based on a touchdown at midfield. This would preclude landing short in the rice paddies as one of our sister squadron pilots had done two weeks earlier. The burn spot where he crashed was still visible in the rice paddy below.

By aiming somewhat long, once you were certain of making the runway, you could reduce the airspeed by extending the flaps and speed brakes and shorten the landing roll. Because I was just about in the right position for the final turn, down went the flap handle, with the throttle-mounted speed brake switch selected to *open*. But nothing happened. "Of course not, dummy," I said to myself. The battery was dead, and both systems were electrically activated. I was obviously too high for a no-flap, no-speed-brake landing.

Cross-controlling in a full-deflection side slip was another option. Yet I was somewhat reluctant since the flight controls of the Sabres were fully hydraulic, with the hydraulic pump operated by engine compressor revolutions per minute (rpm). With about 15 percent windmill rpm, I was uncertain as to how much side slip the Sabre could handle before the flight controls locked solid. Certainly the emergency electric pump was not available.

Now, another critical decision became necessary. I was turning onto the final landing approach with the aircraft still aimed at midfield. As I adjusted my aiming point to the end of the runway, the airspeed read an impossible 190 knots. And although I had the sixty-two-hundred-foot runway made, without flaps and speed brakes I was unable to dissipate airspeed or adjust the touchdown point.

Once again I had two choices. First, I could attempt a 360-degree turn to dissipate altitude and airspeed. But with limited training in flameout landings, and having never tried it without flaps and speed brakes, I was not certain I had enough altitude to reach the runway. My second choice seemed more feasible, but also risky. With K-14 having the shortest jet runway in South Korea, air force civil engineers had recently installed an overrun barrier. This consisted of a pair of US Navy anchor chains laid along either side of Kimpo's thousand-foot newly paved overrun. To catch a fighter's landing gear, a tennis-net-like assembly had been stretched directly across the end of the runway. An aircraft overshooting the runway would catch the web with its nose gear. This pulled up a heavy-duty cable that anchored the net, which was attached at each end to the giant anchor chains. The cable would then catch the airplane's main landing gear, and the excess energy of the overshooting aircraft would be dissipated as the landing gear dragged the two giant chains to a stop.

I decided to take a chance on this overrun barrier. Then, in a desperate effort to decelerate, I tried a hard side-slip. This helped. Still, I crossed the runway threshold at about 175 knots, and at 160 knots, spiked the aircraft onto the runway. I tried the brakes lightly, but it was immediately obvious I was flirting with blown tires. This would lead to loss of directional control, and at 150 knots I could roll up into a ball alongside the runway. Instead, I sat back and hoped that the newly installed barrier cable worked as advertised.

To get a symmetrical pull on the chains, we were instructed to hit the barrier net directly in the center. I stayed off the brakes and aimed directly for the center of the net. As I left the runway I took a quick look at the airspeed indicator; it read 150 knots. "Oh, God. This had better work!" I said to no one in particular.

Then, like a navy pilot hooking an aircraft carrier's number-three wire, the main landing gear caught the cable. As the aircraft came to a stop I was pulled forward firmly but smoothly against the shoulder straps. It tilted forward for a moment, as if about to flip inverted, then settled back on the main landing gear. For a moment all was quiet—until the fire trucks came roaring up.

The end of the story included both good news and bad news. The good news was I had made it and saved the airplane; and best of all I had avoided capture. The bad news was that the nosewheel strut was bent—and the newly received F-86F was assigned to our squadron commander.

Postscript

This mission was the culmination of all my training and youthful ambitions. Best of all, I had completed a combat tour and survived my first year as a fighter pilot. To my mind, I was now truly a combat veteran.

A few months later, on a long boring trip on an American Airlines DC-6B, I was en route home to join my wife and two children and see my parents. Sitting in an aisle seat and dressed in my air-force-blue Ike jacket, embossed with silver pilot's wings atop two rows of ribbons, including an Air Medal for the combat missions, I felt vaguely akin to Audie Murphy of World War II fame. In college I had been plagued with a round cherubic baby face. Now I felt certain I looked like the seasoned combat veteran I had become.

The main landing gear struts showed superficial damaged from the barrier cable

During the long flight from San Francisco to Dallas Love Field, I became friendly with Bonnie, the flight attendant in my area. We talked for some time about family and friends, and of course the Korean War. Then, as we approached Dallas Love Field, during a lull in her duties, she walked up to my seat and began staring at my wings. I tried to remain humble, what with the ribbons and all. Finally, with an earnest look on her face she said, "Gee, you don't look old enough to be a pilot!"

Once back in my hometown of Auburn, Alabama, I was anxious to visit the coffee shops where everyone knew each other. It was now the Christmas season 1953, and the university students had gone home for the holidays. I remembered the attention the returning World War II veterans received—with their flight jackets and flashy patches. Now I had my own. In addition I was one of the first jet pilots from the local area. I felt sure that everyone would want to hear about flying jet fighters and the air war I had just finished. Heck, it might even make the front page of our local newspaper, *The Lee County Bulletin*, or even the *Montgomery Advertiser*.

But after two days at home nobody had called. Maybe they didn't know I was back from the war. After all, it had been two years since I had departed for the air force.

With thinly veiled bravado, I donned my blue nylon flight jacket with all its patches, including a 334th Squadron patch that said *Lt. John Lowery*. In town I stopped by the Tiger Café, owned by local World War II veteran, Pierce Jackson.

Pierce was about five foot six and weighed at least 350 pounds. He was the source of all news in the area—next to the *Lee County Bulletin*. Behind his counter, the wall was covered with photos of Auburn Tigers—top football players from several generations. Auburn was a football town. I felt certain Pierce, of all people, would be eager to hear about the Korean War and my combat experiences.

Casually I walked in and took a seat at the counter. Pierce came over in his grease stained apron and asked, "What ya gonna have, Jon?"

"Coffee, Pierce," I said, anxiously waiting for my jacket to stimulate conversation. Even after adding cream to the coffee, taking a couple sips, and scalding my tongue, Pierce only stared out the front window and said nothing. Meanwhile I continued looking at the football heroes on the wall in front of me.

Finally, when my cup was half empty, Pierce came over and in a half-hearted effort to be friendly said, "How 'bout them Auburn Tigers? Did great this yeah, huh?"

"Yep, sure did," I replied—although I didn't have the foggiest idea of how the 1953 football season had been. Then, after a long pause he said, "Jon, you been outta town or somethin'? Ain't seen you round lately." With my ego now shot, and mustering my best southern accent, I responded, "Yeah, Pierce, I bin travlin' sum."

Chapter 3

The Jet-Age Gladiator

In only thirty missions, Captain Ralph S. Parr downed ten enemy aircraft, becoming the eleventh double jet ace on the last day of the Korean War.

WALKING CASUALLY FROM OUR SQUADRON'S sandbagged revetments toward the operations building, four of us had just landed from a combat mission and were headed to our mission intelligence debriefing when the deafening whine of engines from another returning flight of F-86 Sabres caught our attention. At the time, all fighter-interceptor pilots instinctively checked the gun ports of returning flights for the dark gray soot that indicated their guns had been fired. This would imply contact with MiGs. And sure enough, the .50-caliber blast shields of the number-four aircraft showed the unmistakable signs. But something else about it looked odd: the ship's entire fuselage was badly scorched from nose to tail, as if it had been burned by a giant blowtorch.

It was June 7, 1953, and the pilot of the scorched aircraft was Captain Ralph S. Parr. The flight had been his sixth combat mission flying the Sabre. His flight's mission, like ours, had been a fighter sweep—to intercept and destroy any and all enemy aircraft found over North Korea. His fouled gun ports and seared airplane represented visual confirmation of the first two of Captain Parr's soon-to-be ten aerial victories.

Despite having already completed a combat tour in F-80 fighter-bombers and having gained extensive stateside experience in the Sabre, Captain Parr was considered a "new sport" in the Fourth Fighter Interceptor Wing's 335th Fighter Interceptor Squadron. This required him first to fly in a support role as wingman before earning the right to initiate an attack and fire his guns as element or flight leader. In fact, he relates that his first five missions were nothing more than practice formation flights.

On this fateful mission, Shark Flight consisted of four F-86Fs flying a fluid-element tactical formation—euphemistically called the fluid four. This formation allowed the flight leader to search ahead for "bandits" while his wingman maintained a visual watch to the rear. In the search mode the second element would be stacked about fifteen hundred feet higher and weave back and forth as the flight turned or maneuvered, protecting the lead element and simultaneously searching for bandits.

For this mission Captain Parr was flying as Shark Four—wingman to element leader Lt. Al Cox—Shark Three. Normally, it was forbidden for a wingman to fire his guns unless he had specific permission from his element leader. But Cox knew of Parr's extensive jet-fighter background. Thus while walking to their aircraft, Cox had volunteered, "You have more Sabre experience than I've got total flying time. If you should see something, call it out. If I can't see it I'll clear you to take the bounce and cover you." This statement would prove prophetic.

Shark Flight departed Kimpo Air Base heading north toward MiG Alley—the Yalu River boundary with China. About thirty minutes later while climbing through forty-two thousand feet they reached the river and turned northeast to parallel the Chinese border.

According to Parr, "The weather was beautiful with unlimited visibility. With the two elements almost line abreast, I was looking north into China. Suddenly I saw a flight of four MiGs perpendicular to our flight path with a dive angle of about fifteen degrees and firing at us."

Quickly Parr called, "Shark Lead, we've got MiGs in close firing: BREAK LEFT!" He and Shark Three broke hard left into the attackers, but for some reason the lead element broke right. This separated the flight. With the attack thwarted, and because flight integrity was required, the two Sabres turned west toward the confluence of the Yalu River and Yellow Sea before reluctantly turning south toward home base.

Parr relates: "After that encounter I was trying my best to look in sixteen different directions at once to keep us from getting bounced again. Then I looked down very low and saw something flicker across some light-colored sand bars along the Yalu River shoreline, and I called them out.

"After my call, Al said, 'I don't have it. You take it!' So I rolled over in a split-S maneuver and, with one hundred percent power and clean as a whistle (no external pylon tanks), went straight down. To recover from my dive I had to pull nine Gs just to miss the ground. Then I leveled off at about three hundred feet—still going very fast.

"I looked up and spotted two MiGs quite a ways ahead. As I closed rapidly to about four thousand feet I noticed there weren't two, there were four...no, there were eight. Then off to my left I saw eight more. Immediately I decided to put a big notch in the MiG leader directly ahead.

"Based on the MiG's leadership position he was obviously the most experienced of the lot. So with a good closure rate I drove in on him. As I prepared to fire, the eight sitting off to the side must have seen me and

33

called out to their leader. Now the eight up ahead went into a break: like a soft banana being fed into a high-speed fan, they seemed to splatter in all directions.

"I stayed with the leader and fired at about as close to a tracking shot as I could get. But with a deflection angle of about seventy degrees, I had to use 9.5 Gs to do it. I could see about eight to twelve bullets strike his aircraft, but there was no way I could stay with him without making a square corner.

"Although my A-4 gun sight was in 'electric cage' when I pulled the trigger, the gun vibrations blew the sight's fuse, and my sight reticle disappeared. I discovered also that when pulling over 7.5 Gs, the motors lifting the ammunition to the six .50-caliber guns lacked the power to feed the cartridges. Thus my guns started to slow to a stop. To prevent them from jamming, I got off the trigger. Then the MiG and I continued with an old-fashioned dogfight, one on one, me and the leader rolling canopy to canopy, three hundred feet above the ground.

"In an effort to slow down, I had the throttle at idle and speed brakes out and was using as much uncoordinated flight control as possible to induce maximum drag. At times we were literally eyeball to eyeball. I could see both his feet on the rudder pedals. He could probably see mine too.

"What happened next I don't know, but I detected a faint movement that put him just slightly ahead. I thought to myself, 'Damn you: that's going to cost you, friend.' Then I got a little more spacing and slid in behind him. We were so close I was afraid the nose of my aircraft would take off the trailing edge of his horizontal stabilizer.

"Then my wing entered his jet wash, which helped push me back a few more feet. Now with his aircraft about ten feet ahead I didn't need a gun sight. I just leaned the guns against him and pulled the trigger.

"Each time the guns fired I would stall and have to work my way back into firing position. I suspected he was heavy on fuel because occasionally his wing caps would vent. About the fourth or fifth time I hit him it was like a bucket of water sloshed over my windshield. I had ruptured one of his fuel tanks—saddle tank probably, right up next to his engine.

"Still staying close, I worked my way back into firing position. This time when I fired, he burst into flames. And again, the gunfire and turning caused me to stall, and I dropped down through his jet wash. Good thing too, because when the flames came back, instead of going down my air intake they went over the canopy and the top half of my aircraft—all the way down the top of the fuselage and around the tail. The soot was still there when I landed at Kimpo Air Base.

"With its engine now burning, the MiG hit the ground and exploded. So I pulled up rapidly and looked rearward. I had company closing real fast and close. There were five MiGs lined up on me. Then I heard the first one open fire; then the others opened up too. Tracers from their cannons were arcing toward me, and I was working diligently to keep my Sabre out of the sheets of cannon fire. Apparently I was doing the right thing, because one at a time they overshot and slid past me.

"Then I looked back again and here came another one. But he wasn't set up quite right. In fact it looked like he was going to break off. In order to draw him in to where I didn't need a gun sight, I eased up on my turn a little. That allowed him to gain on me and encouraged him to come closer.

"I guess he thought he had me. And when he got close enough, I reefed in my turn. Suddenly he realized he couldn't make the turn and attempted to break off, whereupon I rolled up and over the top. Now behind him I pulled the trigger and walked the tracers through his aircraft. As the fight continued, I took two or three more quick shots back and forth and once or twice got some hits." Subsequently the MiG was seen to crash.

From his gun-camera film and Lt. Cox's statement, Captain Parr was credited with two confirmed kills and one damaged. Needless to say, it was the last time he flew as a wingman.

Three days later, June 10, at an altitude of twenty-five thousand feet, he downed a third MiG as it made a climbing turn toward the Yalu River sanctuary. Normally, Sabre pilots planned on shooting at a maximum range of two thousand feet. Now, with the enemy aircraft about four thousand feet ahead, Captain Parr put his radar-ranging A-4 gunsight on the MiG, and with about thirty-eight degrees of angle-off, he fired a short burst. Despite the long range, his bullets struck, and the MiG-15 burst into flames and the pilot ejected.

Five Down

On June 18, he scored another double that reads like a replay of his first two credits. Once again his flight was protecting the fighter-bombers striking targets deep in North Korea. As luck would have it, the weather was clear with patches of low stratus close to the ground.

Parr relates, "From altitude I looked down, and as my eyes focused on a patch of clouds I saw a couple of airplanes slide underneath headed back toward their home base in China. So I called 'padlocked,' and took the bounce. [The term *padlocked* indicated the pilot was totally concentrating on the enemy aircraft, and the wingman's sole duty was to keep his leader informed of any attacking aircraft.] This time I descended at an angle rather than straight down, sort of a curving dive, to give me a more dimensional idea of cloud bases and how much cloud-to-ground clearance I had to work with.

"Actually, when I got down low the clouds were mostly small scattered to broken stuff, seven hundred feet above the ground. I must have been doing almost .9 Mach number [600 knots], which caused wing roll to the right [shock-wave-induced aeroelastic wing twist].

"Once underneath the clouds I found we were much closer to the MiGs than anticipated and closing like gangbusters. There were three of them, and I came steaming up behind one and quickly squeezed off a short burst. My burst clipped his tail and put two or three strikes in the top of his fuselage between the cockpit and tail. Since I was much too fast I decided to pop up on top of the clouds where the others couldn't see me. But as I started up, the MiG skipped off the very top of a volcanic hill. He sort of splashed like an egg. The other two MiGs went into violent gyrations, trying to locate the source of the gunfire.

"Then I dropped below the clouds again and quickly latched onto the number-two MiG. He had started to turn and too late realized I was behind him. He pulled hard, but I was already tracking him. I held down the trigger for about two or three seconds and saw multiple hits in his fuselage and left wing. The wing was essentially sawed off about the midway point.

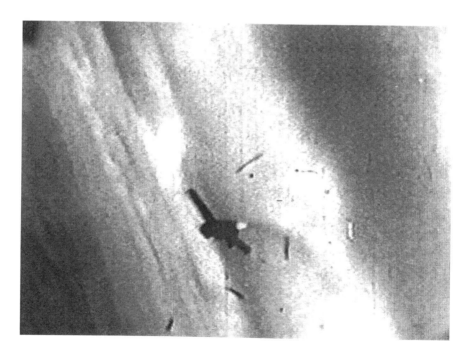

The six .50 calibers essentially sawed the MiG's wing off, making the score Parr four.

"I tried the same thing on the third MiG—popping above the clouds then dropping back down. I looked up ahead and spotted him still running for the Yalu River sanctuary. Suddenly he changed directions to get into clouds. But the cloud formation was small enough that I figured he would either go straight through or turn. In either case it would be too late, as I'd be right with him. But when I popped out I had guessed wrong. He just vanished and I never saw him again."

On that fateful day, June 18, 1953, both Captains Parr and Lonnie Moore achieved the magic five victories to become jet aces. In the post-flight debriefing Parr said, "I was halfway home before I realized I'd made ace. You get pretty focused when in enemy territory, because in this game, losing can be permanent."

With the armistice only a little over three weeks away, Parr scored his ninth kill. "I carved him from a four-ship formation of MiGs that were cruising toward their home base at around sixteen thousand feet. We were very near the Chinese border, hiding just inside a high thin solid cloud layer and looking down for returning MiGs. Suddenly there was a flight of four headed generally in our same direction but angling from right to left.

On June 18, 1953, Captain Parr gets number five to become a jet ace.

"As I dived to engage they saw us and immediately broke in all directions. I latched on to the number-four aircraft, which had turned hard to the right. Then I called to my wingman, Lt. Colonel Robert J. Dixon, 'Lead is padlocked.' Dixon immediately responded, 'Lead, you're clear.'"

In desperation, the MiG pilot pulled up and began frantically rolling. Parr relates, "I got dead astern and rolled in unison with him—firing two or three short bursts, each of which hit his aircraft. Then as his airspeed ran out he essentially stopped in midair. Then suddenly his aircraft exploded."

The MiG fell off to the right, and Parr saw the canopy come off. But apparently the ejection seat failed to fire because the pilot rolled out of the cockpit and down the right wing. "I saw his body bump as he hit the two wing fences. After he cleared the burning wreckage I circled to see if his parachute opened, but it never showed."

Double Ace

Captain Parr's tenth credit, a Soviet IL-12 transport, was the last aircraft to be downed during the Korean War. It occurred during the afternoon of July 27, 1953, just hours before the scheduled armistice. It would become the most politically contentious incident of the Korean War. On this mission, he was leading one of three flights of F-86Fs escorting a marine photoreconnaissance aircraft. The mission was to photograph a dirt airfield in the bed of the Yalu River. But North Korea was covered by an undercast, which stopped abruptly at the river.

Parr relates, "I looked down and saw an aircraft flying close to the river on the Manchurian side. From altitude it looked a little like an air force C-47, which we sometimes used with loud-speakers for psychological warfare. Yet on the last day of the war this seemed unusual—especially this far north. Meanwhile, our radar site Mongoose was reporting enemy aircraft just slightly west of us.

"I had been watching this aircraft for some time when it slowly crossed the Yalu River into North Korea. Simultaneously, we were approaching the designated target. I asked the recce pilot if he would be able to get his photographs. His response was, 'No! I'll have to abort because the target is socked in.'

"At that I asked permission of the mission commander to check out the bogie. With permission received, and my wingman, First Lieutenant Edwin J. (Ed) Scarff, covering me, I throttled back and descended to about five hundred feet above the aircraft. Then I moved slightly to the right side to check its marking. To my surprise it had the same markings as the MiGs—a big red star, but no civilian markings." This was verified by Lt. Scarff, who added, "We knew we were over North Korean territory due to the distinctive river boundary; and our mission was to check the aircraft inventory on their airfields."

Subsequently, Parr made two more identification passes. Then, after rechecking his map to ensure he was south of the Yalu River, Captain Parr shot it down.

The Soviets were outraged. Immediately they claimed it was a civilian airliner with the truce team aboard, and two hundred miles north in Manchuria. An investigation showed that if one draws a line from the aircraft's departure point of Port Arthur, China, to its destination, Vladivostok, Siberia, it crosses the Yalu River into North Korea exactly where Captain Parr saw it enter.

Captain Parr (R) poses with Major Kerstedder shortly after being appointed operations officer of the 334th FIS.

In retaliation, on July 29, 1953, two days after the armistice, a Soviet MiG-15 shot down an RB-50 over international waters off the coast of Siberia. The RB-50 was on a routine ferret mission to monitor Soviet air defenses. Seven members of the crew are thought to have survived and been picked up by one of the fifteen Soviet PT boats that had been positioned to recover survivors (Cole 1994, 10). The eighth survivor, copilot

41

Captain John Roche, avoided capture by hiding in the flotsam and sea fog.

The Soviets reported that no one survived. But two years later, a returning World War II Japanese POW reported sweeping the streets in Soviet INTA prison camp Number 1 with First Lt. Warren Sanderson, one of the RB-50's six Ravens (electronic warfare officers). Unfortunately, none of the bomber's crew was ever returned, nor did our government pursue the issue.

Chapter 4

Bedcheck Charlie

Navy Lt. Guy Bordelon becomes the war's only prop ace by scoring at night against North Korean fabric-covered training planes and piston-engine fighters, used to harass US Forces with air raids.

IT WAS MY FIRST NIGHT as a member of Easy Flight, one of five flights of the 334th Fighter Interceptor Squadron. Our unit was one of three squadrons of the 4th Fighter Interceptor (Day) Wing, based at K-14 (Kimpo Air Base), South Korea. It was late January 1953 and beastly cold outside. I was sleeping in the top bunk of a double-decker, with the other seven flight members aligned along the four walls of the ancient brick building.

It was just after midnight when the sound of antiaircraft fire from the gun batteries surrounding our base brought me upright and semi-terrified from a deep sleep. One set of quad-fifties (four-barreled .50-caliber anti-aircraft guns) was about fifty yards from our building and was shooting like the enemy was at the base's main gate. Through the windows the sky was alight with their tracers.

Instantly I jumped down from my bed and began dressing, quickly donning my parka, .45-caliber pistol, and steel helmet. I was aghast at the lack of response from my flight-mates. No one else had stirred. Surely they could hear all the gunfire! "AIR RAID! AIR RAID!" I yelled.

As I got to the door, expecting to run and jump into the sandbag rein-forced trench nearby (which I later learned was used as a urinal by the old heads, since only new sports ever used it), again I yelled excitedly to my flight-mates: "Air Raid! Air Raid! Get going! Get going!" Yet nobody stirred. Then from under his covers someone said sarcastically, "Forget it new-sport! It's just Bedcheck Charlie." Immediately I knew I'd been had, since I'd never heard the term and knew nothing about "Bedcheck Charlie."

Background

The pilots of the wood and fabric covered Polikarpov PO-2 training airplanes were flown by North Korean women. Of course this was insti-gated by the Russians who had used this harassment technique success-fully against the Germans in World War II. Because the small PO-2 biplanes were of wood and fabric construction, they were only mildly detectable with radar. In addition, their 110-horsepower engine generated little heat that could be detected by German planes equipped with infrared seekers.

The PO-2 biplanes were flown by North Korean women pilots.

The North Koreans had added the Yak-18A, a training airplane that was faster and had more metal parts, giving it a more positive radar image. The two-placed tandem-seat trainer with retractable landing gear was equipped with a 160-horsepower radial engine. With a speed comparable to our T-6 trainers, it was fitted with bomb racks on the wing center sections and a small-caliber aft-firing machine gun for the backseat crewmember.

The North Korean women pilots operated from a small field very near the Panmunjom truce village. At K-14 they were considered a nuisance, but on the night of June 29, 1953, they did cause significant damage at Inchon Harbor.

The Yak-18As were modified to carry bombs and were faster than the biplanes.

The action began at 0200 hours (2:00 a.m.) while I was the assistant combat-duty officer in the Fourth Fighter Group command center. The duty officer, a first lieutenant from a sister squadron, was asleep on a nearby cot. I was sitting half-awake at the illuminated control panel when the telephone rang and the Ground Controlled Approach (GCA) operator said, "Lieutenant, I have a blip on my radar screen that looks like some kind of airplane, but 'radar hill' doesn't see it." Radar hill was a large radar facility located about a mile north of Kimpo that served as both an approach control and air-defense early warning facility. The Fourth Fighter Group instruction book said that only radar hill could declare an air raid. The GCA radar was a more limited system, used specifically to guide airplanes to a safe landing in bad weather and at night—with no authority to declare an air raid.

Suddenly there was an explosion nearby. I awakened the duty officer and told him of the explosion and the GCA operator's call—and that radar hill had nothing showing on their scopes. I then asked if I should set off the air-raid siren. Still groggy and only half awake, he responded, "No, it was probably just someone booming the field!" Then he lay back down to resume sleeping.

I was puzzled. The expression "booming the field" referred to someone diving at supersonic speed with the shockwave hitting the ground. But the F-86 was the only supersonic airplane around, and we were a daylight, fair weather interceptor wing. No fighter pilot in his right mind would be flying at 0200 hours, never mind diving through the sound barrier.

Then it happened again—yet another explosion very nearby. With that, I ignored all the instructions and grabbed the siren's toggle and began sounding the alarm. Although radar hill still didn't show an aircraft, following a third explosion, the antiaircraft guns began firing into the air.

It was Bedcheck Charlie all right; and that night, using either hand grenades or mortar rounds, she heavily damaged the Armament Quonset of the 334th FIS and a personal equipment Quonset belonging to the 67th Tactical Reconnaissance Wing on the west side of the field—killing a sergeant who was asleep in the structure. Later that month another of the small trainers—in this case a Yak-18A—managed to hit the massive POL (jet fuel) storage tanks at nearby Inchon Harbor, igniting 5.5 million gallons of jet fuel. From nearby K-14, we watched the big tanks smoke and burn for three days. But Charlie's success that night was short-lived.

Air Base Defense

Several countermeasures had been attempted. An air force jet-powered F-94B Starfire had proved too fast, one colliding with the slower aircraft and killing the fighter's two crewmembers. At Kimpo Air Base, the base's two T-6 trainers were equipped with wing pods containing .30-caliber machine guns, with the base-operations officer sitting alert after sunset. Although scrambled a couple of times, he never made a successful contact.

47

Later we began seeing a US Navy F4U-5N Corsair with its wing pod containing a radar antenna sitting strip-alert after sunset. The Corsair was from a detachment based aboard the USS *Princeton* (CVA-37), but temporarily based at the marines' K-3 (Pohangdong) base in southern South Korea

In due course, at around 2300 hours (11:00 p.m.), the air-raid siren went off. Quickly we fighter pilots swarmed the nearby antiaircraft gun emplacement. But the Corsair was already airborne and searching for Charlie with its radar. Over the antiaircraft gunner's radio speaker we all heard the command, "All guns; HOLD YOUR FIRE! HOLD YOUR FIRE!"

Meanwhile, unbeknown to our assembled group, the radar hill operator was attempting to get the Corsair pilot to fly across Kimpo Air Base and intercept Bedcheck Charlie on the northeast side of the airfield. Reportedly, the pilot had been assured that the antiaircraft guns were on hold, and he finally consented to make a pass directly over the airfield.

Photo by T/Sgt James O. Helms

48

With the sky flooded with light from the searchlights, from the southwest and headed directly over Kimpo Air Base, a dark shape emerged. Unaware of the arrangements made with the Corsair pilot, the assembled group of fighter pilots immediately began yelling, KILL HIM! KILL HIM!" With that, the corporal manning the antiaircraft gun opened fire. He was quickly joined by one, then two, and finally the base's entire antiaircraft defense network. Like a Fourth of July celebration, the sky was ablaze with fireworks. But the Corsair pilot simply ignored the fireworks and continued his intercept mission.

It was US Navy Lieutenant Guy Bordelon who had been sitting alert at K-14 in his blue-black Corsair. Once scrambled, his aircraft was being controlled by a marine radar operator based at K-16, Pyongtaek. The controller quickly vectored him onto the intruder's tail, which Bordelon identified as a Yak-18A. As he closed, the Yak-18's rear-seat gunner fired his antiquated light-caliber machine gun. With that, Bordelon's four twenty-millimeter cannons promptly blew it out of the sky.

Almost as soon as he reported the kill, his controller vectored him to yet another Yak-18A. As he approached it, the Yak's rear gunner also opened fire. Again, Bordelon opened up with his four cannons and blew it to pieces, "watching as large burning pieces fell to the ground" (Sherman 2000).

The next night, June 30, Bordelon scored once again. This time he was flying patrol north of Inchon when the radar controller vectored him onto some unknown targets. The radar vectors placed him behind the intruders, which he identified as La-11, Lavochin fighters, in loose trail formation. Once cleared to fire, he pulled up on the rear aircraft and fired two short bursts, whereupon the aircraft began to burn then dived straight down into the ground. The lead fighter tried to follow the burning aircraft; Bordelon closed to point-blank range and fired on it too. The enemy leader tried evasive maneuvers then started to climb, whereupon Bordelon fired another short burst, and the aircraft exploded (Hammel 1997).

Lt. Guy Bordelon is shown telling his crew chiefs about one of his night intercept missions.

With credit for four kills, on the night of July16 he scored his fifth aerial victory. The radar controller had again vectored him onto a fast moving target. Once in range he could see the distinctive flame pattern of an La-11. Apparently the enemy was now monitoring the frequency, because when he received permission to fire, the La-11 immediately began violent evasive maneuvering. Bordelon followed him through antiaircraft fire from the ground and fired a long burst, with the La-11 then exploding like a bomb (Sherman 2000).

With an unprecedented four kills in two nights, and a fifth about two weeks later, Lt. Bordelon had become the first and only propeller and night ace of the Korean War.

Later, during a party at K-3, Bordelon became friends with an air force lieutenant who was assigned temporary duty to the marine base from the Fourth Fighter Group at K-14. The lieutenant, whose nickname was Dixie, was a recent Naval Academy graduate but had chosen an air force career. Over drinks at the officers' club, Dixie had talked Bordelon into letting him fly his Corsair, since Dixie had flown only jets and had never been in a World War II prop fighter.

Next morning Bordelon briefed him thoroughly on his aircraft, and emphasized the necessity for lots of right rudder on takeoff to counteract propeller and engine torque. Their unit had experienced several takeoff accidents due to pilots failing to counteract the strong left-hand torque produced by the large propeller turned by a powerful engine. Dixie then cranked up the engine, and with everyone watching, began takeoff-roll in Lt. Bordelon's Corsair. Unfortunately, he overcompensated for torque and ground-looped the aircraft to the right, destroying the historic aircraft. Later, at fighter-aces conventions, Bordelon enjoyed telling the story of the air force pilot who wrecked his historic airplane.

Sadly, on December 19, 2002, Commander Guy Bordelon, USN, Retired, the navy's first and only propeller and night ace of the Korean War, died of natural causes. But his spectacular record in combat in Korea remains forever in the history books.

Chapter 5

A Case of MiG Fever

Jet ace shoots down one of his favorite wingmen.

CRUISING AT FORTY-FIVE THOUSAND FEET, the formation of four Sabres had just started a gentle turn south, marking the clear azure sky with contrails—the long white ribbons of super-cooled moisture droplets that formed in their wake. Suddenly the VHF radio came alive: "Red Four has friendlies closing at five o'clock!" Quickly, Red Leader replied, "Roger, Red Four." The date was June 15, 1953, and their mission that day was a combat air patrol along the Yalu River—MiG Alley.

Red Flight consisted of four seasoned fighter pilots: the flight leader, Captain William (Champ) Champion, was nearing his one hundredth and final combat mission. Champ's wingman, Red Two, was First Lieutenant James H. (Buzz) Sawyers, a relatively new sport in the squadron but already a seasoned veteran. The element leader, Red Three, was First Lieutenant William (Mailbox) Mailloux, who, like Champ, was nearing the magic one hundred missions and a ticket home. Red Four was First Lieutenant Richard L. (Fearless) Frailey, a veteran of sixty-five missions and a favorite wingman of double jet ace Major James Jabara.

To members of Red Flight, this attack by friendlies was incomprehensible. The only other flight scheduled on combat air patrol was being led by their squadron's executive officer, Major James Jabara. As the air force's first jet ace, he was flying a second combat tour in an effort to increase his score of aerial victories.

During our training at Nellis AFB, we had been briefed, "Never let *anyone* track you at six o'clock—even friendlies—because you never can tell when someone has MiG fever." This referred to an overeager pilot having the illusionary perception that a swept-winged F-86 was a MiG-15. At the time, that briefing sounded farfetched to a newly rated second lieutenant. I remember saying to a fellow classmate "How could anyone make such a mistake?"

It happened on January 26, 1953, shortly after I arrived at the Fourth Fighter Interceptor Wing. It was a crystal clear, very cold winter's day, and the midmorning missions had just landed. I was standing in the corner of the Fourth Fighter Group Intelligence debriefing room, listening to the returning pilots describe the mission. Instead of the animation and joviality I had seen earlier, I saw serious faces all around.

The mission had been a combat air patrol along the Yalu River. When I quietly asked one of my Nellis classmates what was wrong, he replied that a senior pilot from the group operations staff had just shot down and killed Second Lieutenant Bill Stauffer. "MiG fever," he said softly. The subject was dropped and never mentioned again.

Now the fever was about to strike again, this time in my own squadron—the 334th Fighter Interceptor Squadron.

Although now famous as the air force's first jet ace, on this, his second combat tour, Major Jabara had trouble getting back in the game. After five months of trying, he had failed to score his first kill. Yet even some of our squadron's lieutenants were successfully finding MiGs. Rumor was he had vision problems. "Cousin Weak Eyes," some called him.

Finally on May 15, thanks to an eagle-eyed lieutenant, Major Jabara's luck had changed. His wingman that day was First Lieutenant Gilbert F. Hasler. During a fighter sweep along MiG Alley, the second element, Rifle Three and Four, had turned toward home base with Bingo fuel—just enough to get there safely. Because the lead element's fuel state was still above Bingo, Maj. Jabara (Rifle One) and Lt. Hasler (Rifle Two) were making one last sweep along MiG Alley

Lt. Hasler relates, "A short time later, on a generally northeasterly heading along the river boundary, I was straining my eyeballs looking toward our nine o'clock position [off the left wing] when I saw a sun flash, then four small dots that would be airplanes. I continued to stare because if I looked away I'd be unable to reacquire them. As I continued my gaze I was able to identify them as MiGs. Quickly I transmitted, 'Rifle Two has four MiGs at nine o'clock, far out, turning toward our six [tail]. Do you have them?'"

"Negative, Rifle Two," replied his leader.

Hasler then said, "Follow me!" and assumed leadership of the element.

Hasler continues, "I immediately turned us left, and almost simultaneously the MiGs also turned left. Now we were approaching each other head on. For some reason, as we closed the MiGs began to turn right. Apparently they didn't see us, because with a short left turn we were now in their six o'clock [tail] position. Major Jabara quickly resumed the lead position then slid in behind the MiG leader and began shooting. His armor-piercing incendiary (API) .50-caliber bullets lit up the aircraft's aft fuselage like sparklers. His second burst severed its vertical stabilizer. Suddenly the MiG's canopy came off and the pilot ejected."

Lt. Hasler said, "With the second element of MiGs sitting high at our seven o'clock position, they initiated an attack. As they closed, I called, 'Break left, break left! They're coming in firing!'" Hasler remembered: "Their twenty-three millimeter projectiles looked like white golf balls; the thirty-seven millimeter rounds looked like white tennis balls. I could hear their *whoosh, whoosh* as they went past my canopy."

With the now burning lead MiG tumbling end over end toward the earth—thanks to a sharp-eyed lieutenant—Major Jabara had now scored the first kill of his second combat tour. From then on, he was on a roll.

Major James Jabara debriefs his flight following his first kill of his second combat tour.

Triple Ace Competition

By March of 1953, the 334th squadron had three jet aces: Captain Leonard W. (Bill) Lilly was the operations officer; Captain Manuel J. (Pete) Fernandez was C-Flight commander, and Major James Jabara was the squadron executive officer. In late May of 1953, Captain Lilly completed his one hundred missions, and with credit for seven MiGs destroyed, he returned home to the United States.

With the war winding down, a fierce competition developed between the Fifty-first FIW and Fourth FIW to see who among the remaining aces would be the first credited with fifteen kills, thus becoming the USAF's first triple jet ace. In the Fourth FIW, the 334th Squadron had Major Jabara and Captain Fernandez. In their 39th Squadron the Fifty-first FIW had Captain Joe McConnell. By mid-May, Captains Fernandez and McConnell were leading with Major Jabara in third place.

With Fernandez notching 14.5 victories and McConnell's score at 13, the Fifth Air Force Commander Lieutenant General Glenn O. Barcus sent a message grounding both officers and ordering them to catch the next flight home. Fernandez, who was completing a twenty-five-mission combat tour extension, was immediately grounded. Thus he went home with 14.5 victories. Joe McConnell's commander *claimed* he hadn't seen the message. The next day Joe flew two additional missions, downing three more MiGs. With 16 confirmed kills, this made him the first triple jet ace of the Korean War.

Now it was up to Jabara to beat McConnell's score—and he was trying hard to do just that. Where Fernandez and McConnell had been skilled tacticians, Jabara was an excitable street fighter who would fearlessly wade into the fray. He was simply too impatient to get the MiGs in the rarified air of the stratosphere. Instead, he became adept at hunting around the Chinese airfields—a practice forbidden by the UN but tacitly condoned by the incumbent Fifth Air Force commander.

Once during this period, while returning from a fighter sweep I overheard Jabara and his flight on the squadron frequency engaged in a heavy-breathing, hard-maneuvering dogfight. Mongoose had said there was nothing flying, but the famous ace had stumbled into a bunch of MiGs—no doubt around one of their airfields.

As we continued listening, another flight commander, who had just arrived in the patrol area, overheard the ongoing air battle. "Where are you, Jabby?" he said. "We'll come and give you a hand!" Breathlessly Jabara replied, "Don't bother! There's just enough for us!"

Because of Major Jabara's poor vision, he showed a distinct preference for lieutenants with sharp eyesight who would literally vector him toward an enemy aircraft then hang onto his wing regardless the intensity of the ace's maneuvering. Because he had the requisite eyesight and had proven calm under fire on numerous missions, "Fearless" Frailey was one of Jabara's favorites, and he was regularly scheduled as Jabara's wingman.

Frailey's eyesight was not the only reason Jabara requested him as wingman. For some reason Frailey could always stay with him during his full-throttle cruise in the patrol area—colloquially known as *balls to the wall*, a phrase derived from the round ball atop the throttle lever of World War II fighters.

During the Korean War era, each squadron had its own integral maintenance capability. In consequence, before a mission, Jabara would order the maintenance officer to increase the thrust of his engine. This involved installing one or two small blocks—referred to as *rats* by the pilots—on the inside edge of the tailpipe lip. This caused a slight increase in the turbine discharge pressure, which in turn increased the engine's exhaust gas temperature (EGT) and hence the thrust output of the engine.

Normally the engine mechanics used rats to get an engine's substandard exhaust gas temperature up to the specified limit. But in Jabara's aircraft, the attachments allowed him to get an EGT well above the allowable limit. Up to a point, the hotter exhaust gas temperature increased the engine's thrust and made the aircraft faster than normal.

Unknown to others, Dick Frailey was a boyhood friend of the squadron maintenance officer, and each time he was scheduled to fly with Jabara, as if by magic, his aircraft too had extra rats in the tailpipe. Thus he could always stay on Jabara's wing, regardless of his leader's full-power setting.

On one mission as Jabara's wingman, Frailey was credited with an aerial victory. It was the only time Jabara was known to have allowed a wingman to fire his guns. As Jabara was finishing off his second score of the mission, a MiG-15 joined up on Dick's right wing. The MiG pilot's canopy and windscreen had frosted over, and he was busily trying to clear a spot on the Plexiglas. Frailey relates, "I called Jabara and told him I had a MiG on my right wing, and he said, 'Take him!' When I looked back the MiG pilot had cleared a spot and was looking at me. At that point he snapped right and down. I followed and was lining up my guns when he suddenly ejected." On that mission the four-ship flight received credit for four MiGs destroyed—Major Jabara with two, element leader Captain Bill Mailloux with one, and Lt. Frailey with one (Dick Frailey, e-mail to author, June 9, 2011).

Major Jabara shares the honors with his flight members Bill Mailloux and Dick Frailey, who together downed four MiGs in one mission.

Some of Jabara's credits were for "spinners." These were MiGs spotted spinning from high altitude. Because the MiG-15 was unrecoverable in a spin, the young and inexperienced Chinese and North Korean pilots would sometimes panic and eject at very high altitude. As mentioned earlier, an ejection in the stratosphere meant the pilot died of either hypoxia or hypothermia, or a combination of the two. The person who first spotted a spinner was usually credited with the score. But with Major Jabara leading a flight, all spinners went to the flight leader.

Lt. Bruno Giordano was another of Jabara's favorite wingmen. Like Lt. Frailey, Bruno too had the eyes of an eagle. On one particular mission I overheard him call Major Jabara, "Rifle Lead, I've got two spinners; one at nine o'clock and one at eleven o'clock." Immediately Jabara transmitted, "If I've got a good wingman, I've got two kills!" Without hesitating the West Point graduate replied, "If I've got a good leader, I've got one and you've got one." Alas, Jabara took credit for both spinners. (Lt. Giordano later scored a gun kill while flying as element leader with another flight.)

The Fever Strikes

On the morning of Frailey's mishap, I encountered him departing the personal equipment room dressed in the usual G-suit, life vest, and backpack parachute. However, on his chest, secured by parachute cord, was a new telephoto Canon camera. "What's the camera for Dick?" I asked. He responded, "I intend to be the first pilot in the air force to get a still photo of a MiG-15 in flight."

With the Korean War winding down and the MiG-15s becoming reluctant to fly, Red Flight Leader, Captain Champion, was nearing his hundredth mission without scoring a MiG kill. In an effort to find enemy aircraft flying, Champion had taken Red Flight to high altitude and was making a wide sweep into China near two of their training bases. Because of Red Flight's location and high altitude, the lure of their four white contrails proved conducive to an acute case of MiG fever, by the fiercely competitive (and visually challenged) Jabara.

60

Following Red Four's call of friendlies closing at five o'clock, Captain Champion began turning the flight into the pursuing Sabres, tightening the turn in an effort to make them overshoot, or at least recognize the F-86's distinctive silhouette. Still the friendlies continued to close the distance aggressively.

According to Lt. Frailey, "The attacking flight leader seemed to be tracking Red Leader. Then as the turn tightened he switched to Red Three, and, finally, because of the ever-increasing intercept angle, he locked onto me."

Tenaciously, the jet ace continued to press his attack on Red Four. A subsequent look at his gun-camera film showed that Jabara opened fire with his six .50-caliber machine guns at three thousand feet. This was considered long range for the Sabre's gun and sight combination—with fifteen hundred feet recommended as best. Ultimately, Jabara fired nine bursts, hitting Frailey's Sabre with at least three bursts.

Frailey remembers, "The first hits were on the left wing…It sounded like a heavy rain on a tin roof. The second burst punched holes in my canopy and shattered the instrument panel…The cockpit was filled with debris. Then the final burst hit the engine," whereupon the airplane entered a spiral dive. "The hydraulic controls became very sluggish and difficult to move." But with great effort and some limited engine power Frailey managed to regain control, and in a gradually descending flight-path he struggled south toward the Yellow Sea.

Meanwhile the VHF radio was alive with frantic shouts: "Cease fire! Cease fire! We've got friendlies firing at Sabres!" With Jabara monitoring the squadron frequency, the frantic calls broke his concentration, and he stopped firing.

Dick's engine had been badly damaged, and he was trailing blue-gray smoke. Fortunately, his VHF radio still functioned. Element leader Red Three was now flying beside his wingman's badly damaged Sabre and transmitted, "Red Four, you're smoking pretty badly. Looks like you'll have to leave it. Continue on heading one nine zero! We'll try to make the sea."

Major Jabara too had brought his flight into a protective position on the badly smoking Sabre.

When someone suggested he should eject soon, Frailey said he didn't want to eject, because he had his Canon camera with him. "Screw the camera!" Jabara said. "I'll buy you a new one!"

Frailey related, "It was very cold in the cockpit. I was wearing only my summer flight suit. At high altitude, with air circulating through the cockpit, I was freezing." Finally, over the Yellow Sea, and about fifteen thousand feet altitude, with heavy smoke now flooding the cockpit, Lt. Frailey transmitted, "Red Three, she's not going any further. I'll have to go!" And with that he ducked his head and pulled the right armrest to blow the aft-sliding canopy's damaged frame. Then he sat upright and ejected from the airplane.

Once out he began tumbling rapidly end over end in his seat. The wind caught his helmet and pulled it back on his head. This caused the oxygen mask to ride-up and cover his eyes. Frantically he fumbled around trying to find the seat belt release, then pulled the release, and kicked hard to get free of the seat. Quickly he jerked the parachute's D-ring, and the canopy snapped open—whereupon his feet hit the water of the Yellow Sea.

He relates, "I immediately became tangled in the parachute's risers. After what seemed like forever, I got free and pulled the lanyard on my Mae West [life preserver]." But it failed to inflate. Later he discovered that a .50-claiber bullet had passed between his arm and chest and ripped open the bladders.

"The sea was a dirty yellow. I had just inflated the one-man life raft and was struggling to climb aboard, when I looked up and saw an air force SA-16 Albatross flying boat taxiing toward me."

The incredibly brave crew of the rescue aircraft had landed within range of the shore guns, and bullets spouted the water all around them as the enemy attempted to find the amphibian's range. Hurriedly, the wallowing Albatross pulled alongside Frailey's small rubber boat, and someone threw him a donut life preserver. They frantically began hauling him in, and as he bumped the side of the heaving flying boat, two sets of arms quickly snatched him aboard. With his feet still dangling from the open hatch, one crewmember holding his arm tightly, and the other—"a very large man"—sitting atop him, Frailey heard a thunderous roar as the pilot applied full power and fired the JATO (jet-assist takeoff) bottles. Suddenly, they were airborne.

The SA-16 crew landed within range of the shore guns to rescue Lt. Frailey then used JATO to get airborne.

According to Frailey, the flight home was anticlimactic. While en route, the aircraft commander asked him for his .45-caliber pistol. At the time he didn't give this request much thought. Later he learned they were afraid that upon landing he might shoot Major Jabara. To prevent hypothermia he was stripped of his wet flight suit and wrapped in blankets. Upon arrival at Kimpo Air Base, a crewman requested that Frailey remain on the gurney for off-loading. After all, this would add drama to the moment.

A crowd of his fellow Fourth FIW friends had gathered to welcome Frailey home. But as they exited the airplane one of his benefactors slipped and dropped his end of the litter. This dumped the naked pilot onto the hot asphalt tarmac. As the irreverent crowd cheered wildly, Frailey stood up and indignantly snatched for his blanket. Wrapped Indian-style and with utmost dignity, he stood erect, and to the cheers of his fellow fighter pilots announced, "Screw it! I'll walk!"

The next day Frailey and Jabara reviewed the gun-camera film. Major Jabara was both apologetic and contrite for the rest of his combat tour. Following that unfortunate episode, Dick Frailey flew nine more combat missions. One day Jabara approached him and said that the war was about over and that he (Jabara) was going home. He then asked Frailey if he would like to accompany him. Being short of a hundred missions, Dick would otherwise have to wait out the twelve-month rotation cycle in late fall. The offer was accepted, and Dick went home to his family and a choice assignment flying new F-86D interceptors for Air Defense Command out of Hamilton Air Force Base near San Francisco (Dick Frailey, personal contact, June 8 and 11, 2011).

Major Jabara finished his second Korean combat tour as the number two top-scoring jet ace of the USAF, with fifteen confirmed enemy kills. (Frailey's downing didn't count.) This first-generation Lebanese-American had proved himself a dedicated warrior and fearless fighter pilot in two wars.

Postscript

Years later, Colonel James Jabara was en route to assume command of an air division, an assignment that undoubtedly would include his promotion to brigadier general. He was killed with his sixteen-year-old daughter when she lost control of her Volkswagen Beetle. They were buried together in Arlington National Cemetery. Lieutenant Colonel Frailey is now happily retired in Tumwater, Washington.

Chapter 6

Balls of Solid Brass

An H-19 helicopter crew attempts a daring rescue of an RAF-exchange Sabre pilot deep in North Korea.

WAR STORIES OVER THE YEARS have led many to believe that only fighter pilots display courage under fire. Perhaps it's the speed and storybook glamour of dog-fighting—man against man—that gets them top credit for skill and bravery. But as any combat veteran knows, successful war fighting requires close teamwork by all elements of our armed forces. It is perhaps the ultimate in group effort. You learn quickly too that courage under fire is not exclusive to fighter pilots. The guys—and now gals, too—flying air-sea rescue missions provide classic examples.

This saga began in the predawn hours of March 27, 1953. In an effort to rescue a downed F-86 Sabre pilot who was thought to be alive and evading capture, the crew of an air force H-19A flew their unarmed helicopter into the bowels of a buildup of North Korean and Communist Chinese armed forces. At the time, their mission set a helicopter record for time aloft. Their brazen flight at fifty to one hundred feet above the Yellow Sea and literally over the heads of the enemy set a record for intestinal fortitude.

F-86 Loss

The downed Sabre pilot was Squadron Leader Graham S. Hulse, a Royal Air Force exchange pilot assigned to the Fourth Fighter Interceptor Wing, based at K-14 (Kimpo Air base) Korea. Assigned to the 336th

Fighter Interceptor Squadron, the aggressive Brit had already been credited with two MiG kills.

On March 13, 1953, Hulse had been leading a flight of four Sabres on a high-altitude combat air patrol. While cruising along MiG Alley, Hulse spotted a formation of MiG-15s and turned quickly to engage them. Singling out a member of the enemy formation, he began firing—scoring hits on the airplane's right wing. Immediately, it began streaming a dense white vapor trail of jet fuel from its ruptured wing tank.

Realizing he had excessive overtake speed, Hulse zoomed up high and to the right of the damaged enemy aircraft (the perch position it was called). This set him up for another diving attack.

Meanwhile, his wingman, Major Eugene M. Sommerich, began firing at the damaged MiG. As Major Sommerich fired, scoring hits on the MiG's fuselage, Squadron Leader Hulse eagerly resumed his attack with a diving curve of pursuit. Unfortunately, in a moment of Buck Fever, Hulse misjudged his firing pass, and it took him in front of the enemy aircraft.

With his concentration glued to the now heavily damaged MiG, Major Sommerich suddenly saw his flight leader's aircraft and quickly released the trigger. Meanwhile his gun camera continued recording the events unfolding ahead.

Seeing that the attacking Sabre would pass in front of him, the enemy pilot gamely began firing his thirty-seven-millimeter cannon. As the F-86 passed in front of the MiG, one of the thirty-seven-millimeter rounds hit the Sabre's left wing at midspan, blowing it off. Squadron Leader Hulse ejected successfully and landed in northernmost North Korea—only twenty-six miles south of the Chinese-Russian MiG-15 base at Dandong Air Base, Antung, China, near the coast of the Yellow Sea.

Meanwhile Major Sommerich resumed firing and scored numerous hits on the MiG's fuselage. Shortly thereafter it began to burn, and then fell into a spin—crashing near Ch'olsan, North Korea (1953, *Fourth FIW History,*, 7).

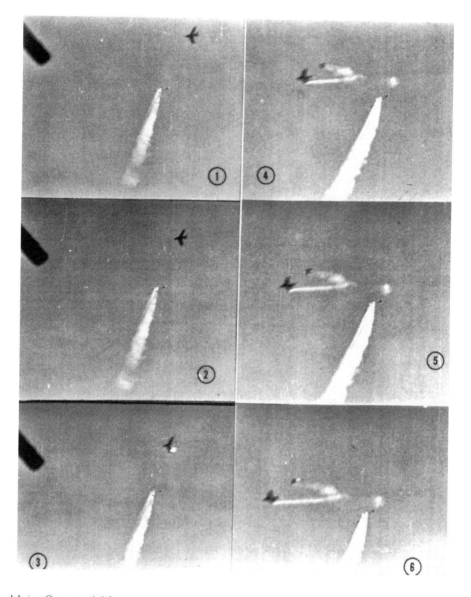

Major Sommerich's gun camera documents RAF Squadron Leader Hulse's fatal mistake.

After what was presumed to have been a successful parachute landing, Squadron Leader Hulse began a two-week odyssey, evading the enemy's ground forces and periodically communicating with other Sabre flights on his URC-4 VHF survival radio. Several pilots reported seeing the signal of the day spelled out with rocks on a nearby hillside.

For almost two weeks there were mixed reports of Sabre pilots hearing a carrier tone transmitted on the emergency frequency. Some pilots insisted they had voice contact. Intelligence sources speculated that Hulse was in the care of friendly guerrillas. Others believed the enemy had captured him and was forcing him to cooperate. Meanwhile, at Fifth Air Force headquarters, plans for a rescue attempt were afoot. The mission would require the deepest penetration into enemy territory ever attempted by a helicopter.

Spook Flight

The organization tasked with the rescue attempt was a secret group associated with Fifth AF Intelligence. Located at Seoul City Air Base (known as K-16 by the United Nations Command), the unit was publically identified as a detached helicopter flight of the 581st Air Resupply Squadron. In reality, the small unit was a part of the Far East Command's Liaison Detachment. This unique group of United Nations intelligence and guerilla organizations operated under the umbrella name Covert and Clandestine Reconnaissance Activities, Korea; it was later renamed Combined Command for Reconnaissance Activities, Korea (CCRAK).

This spook unit consisted of six pilots and four new Sikorsky H-19A helicopters, each powered by a single six-hundred-horsepower Pratt & Whitney R-1340-57 engine. The ground crew comprised a staff sergeant and twelve young and inexperienced airmen first and seconds, all of whom were recent tech-school graduates.

Most of their clandestine work was accomplished at night from Cho-do (*do* is the Korean word for island), a US-occupied island only ten miles west of the coast of North Korea but sixty miles behind enemy lines.

The ground crews acquired their only hands-on experience with the H-19 when they were temporarily assigned to the adjacent 2157th Air Rescue Squadron while awaiting arrival of their unit's helicopters and pilots. Yet despite their inexperience, as one pilot would remember, "We never had a problem these guys couldn't resolve, and we never missed a mission due to a mechanical.

An H-19 lifts off at Cho-do for another classified mission inside North Korea.

"This secret unit's secondary role was to back up the air rescue squadron, which they did with a vengeance. In fact, the unit's commander, Captain Frank J. Westerman, (later promoted to spot-major) and his administrative officer, Captain Lawrence A. Barrett, quickly established a reputation for intestinal fortitude. On January 14, 1953, they made a daring rescue under fire of air force Lieutenant Charles R. Cottrell of the Eighteenth Fighter Bomber group after his F-51 Mustang was shot down just east of Chinnampo—almost directly on the enemy's main supply route. On February 24, 1953, during the height of a major battle, Captain Joseph E. Barrett and First Lieutenant Frank M. Fabijan rescued US Marines Major David Cleeland of VMA-312. After being downed while strafing enemy troops, Cleeland was able to crash land his Corsair on the frozen surface of Annyong Reservoir, ten miles north of Haeju. As the helicopter approached the highly visible pilot, the North Koreans rushed out from their protected shoreline positions onto the ice in a determined effort to capture or kill Major Cleeland. Fortunately, more Corsairs and air force F-80s arrived overhead and began strafing the now clearly outlined enemy troops. The North Koreans fought back with an eruption of gunfire along the shoreline. In the midst of the battle, the H-19 crew braved the intense gunfire and successfully plucked Major Cleeland off the ice (Haas 1997, 88). For their heroic effort, both helicopter pilots and the crew chief, A2C Thomas Thornton, received the Silver Star.

Perhaps the unit's most notable rescue was accomplished by Lieutenants Donald G. Crabb and Robert F. Sullivan with medic A1C Art Gillespie. On April 12, 1953, they rescued jet-fighter ace Captain Joseph C. McConnell Jr. of the Fifty-first Fighter Interceptor Wing. McConnell had ejected from his damaged Sabre, landing in the cold waters of the Yellow Sea near Cho-do. Ironically, he landed practically in front of the waiting helicopter and was promptly rescued. McConnell subsequently downed eight more MiGs to become the top jet ace of the Korean War.

The Rescue Attempt

The helicopter crew for Hulse's attempted rescue was composed of Capt. Westerman and Lt. Sullivan. To save weight, no crew chief or medic was aboard. Their flight planning showed they would be pushing the range of the H-19 to the extreme. If they didn't prowl around inland too long, the mission was feasible—but just barely. In a worst-case scenario, they would land the helicopter on one of the numerous reefs off the coast west of Pyongyang, destroy it, then be picked up by an SA-16 Albatross amphibian. The Albatross was along to provide navigational assistance over the vast expanse of the featureless Yellow Sea—and to rescue the crew if the helicopter's single reciprocating engine failed or they ran short of fuel.

Lt. Sullivan explained, "We couldn't follow the [North Korean] shoreline because we'd run out of gas. And since the H-19 had no long-range navigation capability, a straight shot across the water would not be sufficiently accurate…The SA-16, with a navigator as part of the crew, was needed to get us in and out."

At Tan-do, the island where the helicopter was to cut inland toward Ch-olsan and effect the rescue, the Albatross was to remain west over the sea, flying a low, racetrack pattern. Then, following the rescue attempt, the amphibian would lead the H-19 crew back across the Yellow Sea to their forward base at Cho-do.

Their goal was to reach Hulse's last reported area at first light. But at the last minute, Fifth Air Force inexplicitly moved the pickup point twenty miles. Captain Westerman immediately balked: he reasoned that no Caucasian was going to move twenty miles in less than twenty-four hours in that environment. But Fifth Air Force reportedly had re-flown the reconnaissance mission, and the new location was believed valid.

The mission required staying below radar coverage. This meant flying in the predawn blackness at fifty to one hundred feet above the surface of the Yellow Sea for more than two hours. According to Lt. Sullivan, who had volunteered for the hazardous mission, "All of us had experiences where during cruise at low altitude we lost depth perception over the featureless, becalmed sea, and flew the nose wheels into the water: Or, at low tide, we sometimes bounced off the mud flats." Obviously, the potential for enemy ground fire was only a part of the hazard they faced (Robert Sullivan, e-mail, August 24, 1999).

Captain Barrett and Lt. Sullivan enjoy a lighter moment on Cho-do.

On March 27, 1953, at 0300 hours, the H-19 departed from Cho-do. Shortly thereafter, the Fourth Fighter Interceptor Wing at K-14 (Kimpo Air Base) launched an armada of F-86s. They were to fly top cover and prevent interference by the MiG-15s based just across the Yalu River.

A few miles north of Cho-do, Mongoose told the H-19 crew that the Albatross was en route. Almost immediately, the voice of the Albatross's navigator directed the helicopter to make a course correction of two degrees right. The SA-16 crew had been following the helicopter on radar and now passed it on the left—"probably because they could see our exhaust on the left," said Sullivan.

The Albatross, commanded by air force First Lieutenant Augusto Muzio, continued several miles north then circled left and established a racetrack pattern to keep the slower helicopter located with its radar.

Lt. Sullivan explained the H-19's cruise-control dilemma regarding speed and fuel consumption: "First, heading north toward the pickup area, we cruised with a full rich mixture. Helicopter people didn't muck about leaning mixtures at fifty feet off the water on a black night—at least not those who wanted to survive...We flew at normal cruise—sixty to seventy knots—all the way up, so as not to get too slow for the SA-16, which was three times faster. The search too was done with a full rich mixture. The return trip was much slower—using the endurance power setting at forty-six knots, and in manual lean on the fuel-air mixture control. In an attempt to get more range, we had the cylinder head temperatures really hot" (Robert Sullivan, e-mail, May 23, 2004).

Their ingress point was Tan-do, an island off the tip of the peninsula leading toward Ch-olsan—the area in which both the MiG and Sabre had crashed. According to Lt. Sullivan, "We were going to pass Tan-do, then hook northeast in a valley on the east side of a ridgeline that ran up toward Ch-olsan. We were assured by the intel folks that we would encounter nothing but farmers in the valley.

"We reached Tan-do a bit early and set up an east-west racetrack pattern west of the island—maybe five miles away, awaiting first light.

We flew four or five four-minute laps in this pattern until we got the first streaks of dawn.

"Finally we told the SA-16 crew we were going in and held to the east side of the ridge as planned. First thing we did was almost run the wheels through the top of a radar screen that no one knew was there. So much for secrecy...As we flew along, maybe fifty feet above the trees, we were looking down through camouflage netting at hundreds of boxes of all shapes and sizes. That netting is great for spoofing high-altitude reconnaissance aircraft, but at fifty feet it is worthless... We continued up the valley, still clinging to the side of the ridge, when all hell broke loose. There were an awful lot of people running about in the valley, all of them armed and firing...I would guess there was probably a regiment of troops. Some of the stuff they were shooting at us was exploding on the side of the ridge among their supplies." Sullivan told of a large fireball that came at them from the right— "probably an anti-tank rocket...It seemed to pass between the radio aerial and the tail boom" (Robert Sullivan, e-mail, August 24, 1999).

The determined crew continued north along the ridge, until a few miles south of Ch-olsan the terrain began to flatten out. Sullivan continued, "It was pretty obvious the helicopter wasn't going to survive in this environment. We had neither call signs nor frequencies for our top cover [fighters]. What we really needed was someone to suppress the ground reaction." Still, they reached the general area where Hulse was last heard from, but received no reply to their emergency frequency transmissions.

Captain Westerman then turned left and, using the northwest side of the ridgeline for cover, headed for the sea. To their surprise, there was nothing ahead but salt flats. For now they were out in the open and completely exposed. "I think we both said, *Oh, heavens* [or something similar]!" But apparently no one on that side of the ridge was upset, since there was no longer any ground fire. With the H-19's wheels straddling the rooftops, they went down to the tops of the drying sheds along the salt flats. "At that point," Sullivan said, "we got out of Dodge."

They continued due west until reaching the sea then turned south. "We looked up ahead and there was the SA-16, maybe five miles away and on the southbound leg of its race track pattern. We called and told the crew we had kicked up a hornet's nest...Frank and I figured that if the bad guys showed up [MiGs] we would get down in the weeds and hopefully work our way out of there." But the SA-16 crew would be in big trouble. After all, they were just minutes away from the MiG base at Dandong (Antung). Then the Albatross crew wisely radioed they would meet them farther south.

While continuing toward their rendezvous with the Albatross, the helicopter crew had a long discussion of their unsuccessful rescue. Essentially it was an intelligence failure. First there had been unanticipated hostile radar coverage of their entire ingress route. Then they had encountered unreported troop concentrations—not benign farmers—in the area of the Sabre's crash. These factors had made their flight incredibly hazardous. Still, despite their determined effort, both pilots were upset that they had failed to find Squadron Leader Hulse

In the end, they made it to the beach at Cho-do and refueled. Sullivan relates, "Our fuel was so low we were not certain we could reach the landing area safely. The twenty-minute fuel-low level light had been on for a week—or so it seemed.

"The Korean marines came down to guard the helicopter until we got it refueled. With those guys on guard duty that helicopter was perfectly safe. Then we returned the H-19 to our unit's helipad" (Robert Sullivan, e-mail, August 25, 1999).

At a highly animated intelligence debriefing, the returning Fourth Wing fighter pilots reported hearing *Go back! Go back!* on the emergency frequency, supposedly from Squadron leader Hulse. But the helicopter crew had heard nothing. Fifth Air Force intelligence would later report that the contacts with Hulse had been solely via a continuous tone, not voice. This left doubt as to Hulse's survival and evasion, which, based on what the helicopter crew discovered, seemed unlikely.

The historical record shows no further effort by the British government to determine the fate of their modern-day gladiator. Graham

Hulse was a true warrior, having known nothing but war throughout his lifetime. He had become a rated Royal Air Force pilot at age sixteen. He had flown as a teenager in the Battle of Britain and throughout World War II. In the late 1940s, he participated in the RAF's fight in the Greek civil war during their Communist insurgency.

In the end, Squadron Leader Graham Hulse was written off and the file closed with typical British stoicism: "Missing, Death Presumed" (Royal Air Force Museum 1999, 9).

Captain Frank Westerman received a spot-promotion to major and was awarded a second Silver Star. Alas, Lt. Sullivan lacked the time in grade for spot-captain but was awarded the Distinguished Flying Cross. The citation reads in part, "Lieutenant Robert F. Sullivan distinguished himself by displaying extraordinary heroism and gallantry in action above and beyond the call of duty on 27 March 1953, when he flew as copilot in an unarmed helicopter, on a rescue mission deep in enemy territory. Lt. Sullivan, well aware of the risks involved, volunteered for this hazardous mission, which would be the deepest penetration by helicopter into enemy territory during the entire Korean operations... Immediately upon reaching the enemy coastline the helicopter was subjected to intense enemy ground fire. Sullivan, also acting as an observer, remained in the area under intense enemy ground fire for a period of one hour and fifteen minutes searching looking for the downed pilot. During the search, which covered sixty-four square miles of terrain, Sullivan plotted three positive and one probable radar sites and two camouflaged supply areas. This exhaustive search was conducted to a point within 26 miles of the Chinese city of Antung.

"Following their return to K-16, because of all the intense fire they had somehow survived, the helicopter was examined closely. "Despite all the gun smoke, noise, and cordite smells, we didn't have a single bullet hole," said Sullivan. Later our mechanics did find a couple of burnished spots where bullets had ricocheted off a couple parts. One of those parts was a pitch change rod on the rotor head. "That would have been a beauty," Sullivan said.

RAF Squadron Leader Graham Hulse enjoys a pheasant hunt in the rice fields near Kimpo Air Base.

During the Korean War there were only two unsuccessful rescue attempts. One was the abortive effort to recover Squadron Leader Hulse. The other involved First Lieutenant Charles R. Spath, an F-86A pilot from the 334th FIS. Already credited with sharing a MiG kill, Lt. Spath was himself downed by a MiG on February 3, 1952. Following a successful ejection and parachute landing, he spoke to the rescue helicopter pilot on his URC-4 survival radio. As the H-19 approached, the helicopter pilot, Captain Gail Poulton, asked certain questions that Spath failed to answer correctly. Finally Lt. Spath transmitted, "You can write me off for saying this, but get the hell out of here. It's a trap." Lt. Spath was one of thirty Sabre pilots—not including two RAF pilots (which included Hulse)—known to have been captured

Finale

Despite the hazards involved with their super-secret intelligence missions and flying at very low level, often at night and behind enemy lines, CCRAK finished the Korean War with no combat losses. Although they did sustain their share of battle damage, they were accident free, and recorded no personnel injuries. This in itself was a record (Haas 1997, 51). But the valiant effort of Capt. Westerman and Lt. Sullivan in their attempt to find and rescue Squadron Leader Hulse merits the highest accolades a fighter pilot can bestow. They truly had "balls of solid brass." We salute them for their exceptional courage and dedication to duty.

Chapter 7

Last Mission of the Korean War

Only five hours before the armistice the RF-80 photo-reconnaissance pilot is shot down and dies in his burning aircraft.

IT WAS MID-AFTERNOON ON JULY 27, 1953, the last day of the Korean War. Because of clouds covering his target along the North Korean border with China, the RF-80 photo-reconnaissance pilot, Captain John K. Rhoads was alternately snatching his aircraft hard left, then hard right, apparently trying to find a hole in the clouds so he could bring home usable photo-intelligence. But his aggressive maneuvering was giving those of us in his escorting flight of four F-86 Sabrejets a very hard time. Just keeping him in sight was a major effort rather than watching for attacking Russian, Chinese, or North Korean MiG-15s.

As a newly christened first lieutenant, I was flying the number four position in the escorting flight of Sabrejets. Unfortunately, I had been saddled with one of the two remaining early model F-86A aircraft assigned to the 334th Fighter Interceptor Squadron. Because it had less engine thrust than the newer F-86E and F models, it had been used primarily for proficiency flying and training of newly arrived pilots. But on this last day of the war, a shortage of operationally ready aircraft and the midlevel altitudes typical of RF-80 reconnaissance missions resulted in the A-model being placed on the afternoon mission schedule.

Because of the aircraft's lower engine thrust, I was continually at full throttle trying to keep up with my element leader, First Lieutenant

Edwin Scarff. Adding to the problem was that the G-forces produced by our continuous hard maneuvering were causing the anti-G-suit we all wore (to prevent blacking-out due the pull of gravity and centrifugal force) to be constantly inflated; its tight squeezing of my legs and abdomen was getting downright uncomfortable.

The armistice agreement specified that the North Korean air force would be limited to the number of aircraft within their country on last day of the war. Because of our constant bombing of their airfields, they had transferred their entire air force to Chinese bases that were politically protected. Thus, to ensure their compliance, the United Nations Command needed to document the exact number of jet fighters they possessed in-country when the armistice took effect at the end of the day.

It was the last combat mission of the Korean War for all of us. Captain Rhoads and the RF-80 belonged to the 45th Photo Reconnaissance Squadron of the 67th Photo Reconnaissance Wing. The escorting Sabrejets were from the 334th Fighter Interceptor Squadron, 4th Fighter Interceptor Wing. Both fighter wings were based at Kimpo Air Base.

Captain Rhoads in his RF-80 with an F-86 escort lines up for takeoff at K-14 air base.

The 45th Photo Recon Squadron had been tasked with photograph-ing the North Korean airfields located near the Yalu River boundary with China, where their MiG-15s were likely to be based. This made our mission especially important. But in the 4th Fighter Interceptor Group's mission briefing, the weather officer had reported the entire target area would be covered in a solid undercast. In fact most of North Korea was covered in clouds.

Captain Rhoads had already established a reputation for aggressive flying. While most of their aerial photographs were programmed at fif-teen thousand to twenty-one thousand feet to avoid deadly antiaircraft fire, he was known to regularly get his photos at six thousand to nine thousand feet. And if he couldn't see his target well enough he would often go down to as low as three hundred feet and slow down to 250 knots to improve the photographic detail.

At the conclusion of the Fighter Group's briefing I overheard Rhoads telling a cohort from his squadron that he intended to get a Silver Star for the mission, "or die trying." Although the weather made today's last mission of the war look questionable, Captain Rhoads was obviously determined.

We arrived in the target area, and as predicted, it was obscured by clouds. In addition, our island radar station, Mongoose, located in the Yellow Sea off the North Korean coast, assured us the MiGs were not flying. With Captain Rhoads continuing his aggressive maneuvering, we turned south from the Yalu River, and in a vigorous zigzag fash-ion headed back toward home base. Then, about halfway home Rhoads finally found a hole in the undercast. Problem was it was over the North Korean capital of Pyongyang.

He immediately dived down over the city and began running his cameras. This also brought his escorting fighters into the lethal range of the enemy's antiaircraft guns. Then, despite a warning from Major Davidson, our flight leader, he inexplicably did the unthinkable and lined up for a second pass down Pyongyang's main street. I was so busy just trying to stay with my element leader I couldn't see all the fireworks. But I suddenly saw the RF-80 streaming a long sheet of flame from the tailpipe. The radio was eerily quiet. Then, very calmly, Major Davidson said, "You better get out of that thing." But Rhoads persisted and said, "I've stop-cocked her—think I'll try to make it to the water," as the Yellow Sea was very close in the west.

But shortly thereafter the aircraft exploded, and unfortunately Rhoads's RF-80 had not yet been equipped with an ejection seat. Major Davidson then transmitted, "Someone better stay to see if he gets out, and give him a fighter cap." We were now very low on fuel and had to head for home base immediately.

Back at K-14, with the sun setting in the west, and in the best fighter pilot tradition, we entered the initial approach for landing in right echelon and by now, *very low* on fuel. Then with five-second-interval spacing, we pitched out for the downwind, and in turn began turning to base leg. But I had a problem. The landing gear warning horn was blaring and the left main gear indicator light was showing red—unsafe. Quickly I checked my fuel gauge and it read 50 pounds (roughly eight gallons) remaining. Landing with an unsafe gear was a sure ticket to a major accident. To go around and try to pump it down with the emergency hydraulic hand pump in the F-86A-model was a big roll of the dice. Maybe 50 pounds of fuel was enough and maybe not. Still, I decided to take the chance.

With the Sabrejet's J-47 engine at full power, I retracted the landing gear and pulled up steeply to the downwind leg of the traffic pattern, then put the gear handle down—hoping that by recycling, the offending gear would lock down. But it was not to be. Then, with my right hand pumping the hand pump like my life depended on it—and half expecting the engine to quit at any moment—I turned a rather short base leg. My left hand was rather busy modulating engine power, extending the flaps, and flying the airplane.

Upon turning onto a short final approach, the gear-warning horn continued to blare loudly, with the left main landing gear "unsafe" warning light still showing brightly. My right hand was still pumping like mad as the fuel gauge pointer began touching the big *E*—as in Empty. Sweat was now running into my eyes, and I was especially thankful the engine was still running. Now, with no fuel aboard, if the landing gear should collapse, at least there would be no explosion and fire.

As the Sabrejet rounded-out in the landing flare and the airspeed diminished to 120 knots—and my right hand still pumping vigorously—the landing-gear warning horn suddenly stopped blaring; then the tires touched the pavement. Quickly I glanced down to see three green landing gear indicator lights burning brightly. Breathing a sigh of relief I rolled to the end of the runway, and as I turned onto the taxiway, the engine flamed out. Feeling greatly relieved, I sat back and relaxed as our squadron maintenance guys towed the aircraft to our sandbagged revetments.

It was the end of the war for all of us. And just five hours before the armistice, Captain Rhoads died trying to fulfill his mission and simultaneously earn a Silver Star. But instead of that award, on September 10, 1953, he was awarded the Distinguished Service Cross, the nation's second highest military honor. Because of his record of achievement in the squadron, for months thereafter the 45th Photo Reconnaissance Squadron operations scheduling board continued to list his takeoff time: "Rhoads-1530"—with the landing time missing.

Chapter 8

Escape to Freedom

North Korean MiG-15 pilot lands at Kimpo Air Base, South Korea, and realizes his boyhood dream to become an American.

IT WAS MIDMORNING, SEPTEMBER 21, 1953, when North Korean air force senior lieutenant No Kum-Sok braked his MiG-15bis to a stop in an open spot on the K-14 (Kimpo Air Base) alert pad. Having found a space vacated just minutes before by two Sabres from the 334th Fighter Interceptor Squadron, he parked among the Fourth Fighter Interceptor Wing's F-86 Sabres that were standing air defense alert.

The two fighters had been scrambled for a practice radar intercept mission. Yet, until that moment, our air defense network had been unaware of the North Korean MiG's presence.

Lt. No's escape had been a dangerous but carefully calculated undertaking. Throughout his flight to K-14, he had been vulnerable to attack by his own comrades, as well as American antiaircraft guns and the numerous fighters that were swarming around Kimpo Air Base like bees from a hive. He was especially fortunate too that the entire Korean peninsula was graced with clear, early fall weather.

At his newly assigned home airfield, Sunan Air Base, Lt. No had been scheduled to fly the first of sixteen recently delivered MiG-15bis jet fighters parked openly on the still-pockmarked concrete ramp. The aircraft had been smuggled in by rail and hastily reassembled in violation of the armistice agreement with the United States and United Nations. Unlike during his wartime flights out of Antung Air Base (now called Dandong), China, these late model MiGs were not fitted with external fuel tanks. This meant their range was quite limited. But having studied his map carefully in the preceding months, Lt. No knew that the aircraft's internal fuel supply was adequate to reach Kimpo Air Base, just north of the South Korean capital city of Seoul.

The North Korean's newly reactivated Sunan Air Base was located about 8 kilometers (five miles) northwest of their capital city, Pyongyang. This placed him about 153 kilometers (ninety-five miles) north of the thirty-eighth parallel, with Kimpo Air Base about 16 kilometers (ten miles) farther south. It was the closest he had been to the dividing line between North Korean and United Nations forces.

Lt. No's flight was scheduled to be the first takeoff from the Sunan runway, which was still badly scarred. The young lieutenant's assigned mission that day was a proficiency flight—his first since arriving from China at war's end. Ironically, as he walked across the ramp toward his assigned fighter, he encountered General Whal Lee, vice commander of the North Korean air force. General Whal was one of the few senior officers in their air force with any significant education—even some university training. Because of his cultured ways, the general was well respected by all who knew him. Upon seeing Lt. No, the general greeted him by name then patted him on the shoulder and advised him to take care when taxiing around the craters and ruts on the runway. Then with a grin he added, "Oh, yes, and don't get lost!"

Because he was scheduled as the first aircraft to depart, Lt. No reasoned he would also be expected to land first. This meant he'd be missed too quickly. To buy himself more time, he asked the number-two pilot to exchange slots with him and depart first. "I'll be up a little longer today," No told him. "Don't land too soon, for as soon as you do they'll tell me to land" (No 1996, 12).

As if by providence, about the time of Lt. No's takeoff, the US air defense radar on radar hill, just north of K-14, was shut down temporarily for routine maintenance. With this unique stroke of luck, despite his justifiably serious concerns, Lt. No was able to reach Kimpo Air Base unchallenged.

As he approached the American fighter base he could see F-86s in the traffic pattern, departing and landing to the north, into the prevailing wind, in order to minimize the landing ground speed and hence the ground roll. While all aircraft normally were landed into the wind, in this case, to avoid being recognized on downwind by the base antiaircraft unit, he opted to land downwind—into the landing and departing traffic. This had been routine procedure at Antung Air Base, where F-86s had been attacking their landing aircraft.

At first, observers and pilots in the traffic pattern didn't recognize the swept-winged fighter as an enemy MiG-15. Still, despite the hazardous approach and landing, he pulled to a stop in the strip alert area with an undamaged and fully operational airplane.

Background

Lt. No's resistance to communism had actually begun at age thirteen, when he began voicing his contrary opinions in school. He had been influenced by his English studies and the Voice of America broadcasts to which he listened regularly. His English teacher and sports coach, Chang See-Young, had been educated in a Japanese university and, as an army officer, had fought the Chinese Communist army. (He later moved south and died in combat as a member of the South Korean army.) But it was No's father who played the largest role in discouraging him from any pro-Communist views.

Then, despite his youth, he began to sense the danger of his rebellious attitude. He adopted the most sensible possible attitude behind the Iron Curtain: "I decided to keep my mouth shut" (No 1996, 38).

Upon graduating with honors from high school, he was accepted to Hungnam Chemical College, where for two years he studied basic technical courses. Then in July 1949 he was accepted into the North Korean Naval Academy. He had recognized the need for a college-level education, even from a Communist military academy. But he also reasoned that a naval career could offer the chance of escape.

Discipline at the academy was severe. Cadets had no days or weekends off, no chance to leave the base, no vacations, and no visitors until graduation, which was some three years hence. Questioning orders was not permitted. Beards and mustaches were likewise forbidden, and cadets were required to shave daily. However, they were provided with no razors; instead they pulled out the whiskers with their fingernails. Classes in calculus, physics, chemistry, meteorology, navigation, Communist history, gymnastics, calisthenics, even infantry training and marching for military parades, were held for seven hours a day and seven days a week. The cadets were allowed only two hours each day for study and about eight hours per night to sleep.

Living conditions were barbaric. During the Siberian-cold winter, both the barracks and classrooms were poorly heated. As for water, there were only three faucets in each barracks and no hot water. "The food was insufficient, and everyone was always hungry." Each meal consisted of one aluminum bowl of rice and one of thin soup. Both were "nutritionally deficient, and insufficient in quantity." Meals of course *never* included meat (No 1996, 50).

Twice each month the cadets were taken downtown for a bath with warm water then issued a set of poorly fitting but clean underwear. The dirty underwear, which they had worn for fifteen days, was washed and later reissued randomly. Toiletries, notebooks, pens, and ink were always in short supply. No described the academy as being "like a penitentiary, much more so in practice than in appearance."

One of Cadet No's classmates submitted his resignation, but it was flatly rejected—with a warning that he would be imprisoned if he submitted it again. Academy officials wanted no one leaving and spreading rumors about the extreme hardships the cadets were forced to endure (No 1996, 48–50).

Once the war started, their day-to-day life became even tougher. The 150 cadets in No's class were moved sixty miles north and housed in a newly constructed railroad tunnel not yet equipped with rails. The floor was muddy and the air dank. Here No and his classmates lived, taking infantry training and enduring endless political meetings that denounced American aggression.

Then one day a dozen doctors arrived at their tunnel and randomly selected a hundred cadets for extensive physical exams. While the project's mission was secret, Cadet No suspected it involved flight training. He recognized immediately the possibility of escaping to the south by air. Also, flight training would last a year, by which time he reasoned the war would be over.

Although not among those selected for the physical, he noted that his Communist Party history instructor was recording student scores on spin-tests being conducted in a swivel chair. Brazenly, Cadet No approached him and asked if he could take the test. The professor recognized him as having made an A in his history class three months earlier. After considering No's request for a moment, the professor nodded his head and said, "Yes, go ahead and take it" (No 1996, 69).

Ironically, out of the cadets who took the spin test and subsequent physical, only fifty were selected, with Cadet No being the only volunteer "for a special, unnamed assignment." It was not until after they had been transported at night by train to a Chinese airfield that the base's vice commander informed the group they were to be trained as fighter pilots. Subsequently they "worked from 0430 hrs.until bedtime, seven days a week, without a moment off" (No 1996, 72).

Lt. No and his fellow North Korean classmates completed their MiG-15 training in September 1951. Concurrently, their Communist

High Command decided to deploy their newly constituted fighter regiment to Uiju Air Base—the only surviving airfield in North Korea, located just south of the Yalu River, and completely outside of Chinese sanctuary. On November 7, his unit—the Second Air Regiment of the North Korean First Air Division—landed at Uiju Air Base.

The next day, along with twenty-three other MiG-15 pilots, the nineteen-year-old fighter pilot, with less than two hundred hours flying experience and only fifty hours in jet fighters, flew his first combat mission. Their procedure was to take off and immediately cross the border into the sanctuary of Chinese airspace, then re-cross into North Korea at an altitude higher than the early F-86As could reach. Fortunately, on his first few missions, he encountered no F-86s. But he did become aware of some of the MiG-15's limitations.

Amazingly, this new and supposedly combat-ready fighter pilot had never fired the aircraft's guns. Upon firing them he was instantly alarmed by the heavy vibration from the slow-firing thirty-seven-millimeter and twenty-three-millimeter cannons. He noted too that at three hundred meters (one thousand feet) "the tracer rounds dropped." Thus he realized that to hit a target he had to be closer than three hundred meters. Conversely he noted the Sabre had six fast-firing guns, "whose trajectory seemed to stay straight up to 1000 meters (3300 feet)." He relates, "The accurate trajectory of the guns in the Sabre was nearly three times farther than the MiG cannon."

Lt. No next learned that fighter pilots were expected to shoot their guns on every mission; yet due to lack of any training he had no concept of distances. As a result, he adds, "Like most MiG pilots I never hit anything."

Frosting of the canopy was another major problem. MiGs typically frosted up in the rear quadrants, preventing pilots from seeing enemy aircraft attacking from behind. The space between the double layers of Plexiglas, if properly maintained, was supposed to contain dry air, but this often was not the case. Adding to the problem was the lack of a rearview mirror in the cockpit. This simple item would have allowed the pilot to see an aircraft attacking from its vulnerable rear quadrants.

Worse still were the problems created by the MiG-15's T-tail configuration. Mounted halfway up the rudder, the horizontal stabilizer not only blocked visibility to the rear but also posed a major hazard to a desperate pilot forced to dive out when his ejection seat failed to fire.

The MiG's limited fuel supply was a *major* limitation. Without external wing pylon fuel tanks it could stay airborne for only about forty minutes. The engine too was limited to ten minutes at full power "to avoid an engine fire." However, Lt. No reported that to maintain a high airspeed, he and his fellow pilots typically flew at full throttle from take-off to landing; yet he had never heard of an engine fire. Still, in combat, even with the additional fuel provided by wing-pylon tanks, the MiG's maximum mission time was usually limited to less than thirty-five minutes (No 1996, 101,102, 117).

North Korean pilots also had learned from experience that the F-86s were supersonic in a dive, whereas their aircraft were not. Because the MiG-15 was equipped with cable-pulley flight controls, once reaching Mach 0.93 it experienced severe control surface vibrations and the control forces became extremely heavy and unresponsive. The North Korean pilots' commanders ultimately did confirm the Sabre's supersonic capability—information the Soviets had withheld, since it was further evidence that their MiGs were inferior to the Sabre.

Six weeks after arriving at Uiju Air Base, North Korean commanders decided the North Korean air division should abandon the airfield. B-29 raids had made life unbearable and pocked their runway with twenty-foot bomb craters that kept their aircraft grounded most of time. The Chinese corps of engineers repaired the runway with baskets of stones and earth, and once these repairs were deemed adequate, the division deployed back to the sanctuary of Antung Air Base in China.

At Antung AB, the North Koreans were one of three air divisions (fighter wings) based there: the Chinese Second Interceptor Division, the elite Russian 324th Fighter Air Division from the Moscow Air Defense District, and now the North Korean First Air Division. Soon after they landed, Lt. No learned that the Russians were flying the more advanced

MiG-15bis (*bis* being Russian for *revised*). The VK-1 engine of the MiG-15bis had a thousand pounds more thrust; to improve its slow rate of roll, the ailerons were hydraulically boosted. In addition, the Russian aircraft had an armor-plated seatback to protect the pilot. Mercifully, a month after their arrival at Antung, antiballistic steel plates were installed in all the aircraft. Then, in November 1952, Lt. No's squadron finally received the improved MiG-15bis.

Political Factors

Their loss rate due to accidents and combat was horrendous. Worse yet, there was political attrition as well. One pilot in Lt. No's outfit, with about fifty combat missions, was suddenly discharged in disgrace, after the security officer learned that his brother had gone with South Korean forces in late 1950. During the same period, the popular commander of the North Korean Eleventh Air Division, consisting of mostly Yak-18s and IL-10 propeller airplanes, was accused of planning to defect to the West. Lt. No relates, "He was executed by firing squad without a trial." Another young pilot who had been No's classmate at the naval academy was upset by being forced to fly propeller planes rather than jets. He was overheard saying he would defect to South Korea if ordered to fight American jets. He too was promptly executed. The executions were conducted in private and kept very secret. Still, word usually leaked out—possibly, No believes, with official blessing.

The political heat affected Lt. No, too. His Uncle You Ki-Un, a major in the supply corps and a dedicated Communist, visited him in the spring of 1953. He told No that his mother had been killed in a bombing raid: but Uncle You knew she was safe in South Korea. When the Chinese army began retaking North Korea, she had been evacuated with a broken leg by the US Navy, from Hungnam to South Korea. Major You apparently told the First Air Force Division commander that Lt. No's mother was alive in South Korea. Then during April, American leaflets had been distributed offering $100,000 to a defecting MiG-15 pilot. These factors combined to trigger a security investigation of the young pilot. Fortunately, his battalion vice commander and the commander of their First Air Force had given high praise to Lt. No as both a fighter pilot and dedicated Communist. Thus he continued flying combat missions.

Aftermath

When word of Lt. No's landing spread around Kimpo Air Base there was pandemonium in the squadron areas: "A MiG just landed! A MiG just landed!" somebody yelled. Those of us standing around in operations ran for the squadron truck and drove to a spot near the end of the runway. And there it sat on the alert pad—a beautiful silver MiG-15bis.

Shortly thereafter, as a hedge against a North Korean attempt to bomb and strafe the airfield and destroy this valuable intelligence catch, the remaining alert aircraft were scrambled. Lt. No Kum-Sok was then driven to Fourth FIW headquarters to meet the wing commander and, of course, intelligence personnel.

The maintenance troops attempt to hook-up a tow-bar to the beautiful enemy airplane.

In 1952, the North Korean government had decreed that family members of any defector would be executed. Fortunately, Lt. No's mother was safely settled in South Korea. It was not until a 1970 visit to Seoul that he learned of the retribution resulting from his escape. In discussing his case with a pilot who had defected in 1955, he learned that several of his associates had been executed. His best friend, who in fact did know of his plan, was the first to die. His execution was followed by those of the battalion commander, with whom he had spent his last day at Sunan; his vice battalion commander, who had vouched for his loyalty during the earlier security investigation; the battalion's political officer; the air division's chief weapons officer, who had sponsored No's Communist Party membership; his regimental commander; and the commander of the North Korean First Air Division. In addition, No suspects that his uncle, Major You, was executed, too (No 1996, 147).

Senior Lieutenant No, in USAF fatigues, enjoys his first day of freedom in the West.

MiG-15 Evaluation

Three USAF test pilots were chosen to evaluate the MiG: Brigadier General Albert Boyd, Captain Tom Collins, and world-famous test pilot Major Chuck Yeager. Captain Collins flew it first, followed by Major Yeager, then General Boyd. They found the Sabre superior in every respect. While the MiG-15 had a better thrust-to-weight ratio that allowed it to climb to fifty-five thousand feet, much higher than that of the early model Sabres, the F-86F could also reach that altitude—albeit not without exceeding the engine's exhaust gas temperature (EGT) limit. In the F-model, because of the engine's EGT limitation, missions were flown routinely at forty-nine thousand feet with a cruise speed of Mach 0.9.

General Boyd prepares to test fly the newly acquired MiG-15bis.

Among the predominant flight test findings were that the airplane had a strong nose-up pitch at Mach 0.83. As suspected, it was incapable of going supersonic. In fact its official speed limitation was Mach 0.92, at which point a red warning light illuminated. Above that speed the airplane encountered very strong control surface vibrations and control force stiffening. In one test Major Yeager made a vertical dive at full power, to establish once and for all the airplane's maximum speed. Yet the airplane never exceeded Mach 0.98—with the shockwave (created by the so-called sound barrier) causing the control surfaces to become unresponsive.

Major Yeager said later, "Flying the MiG-15 is the most demanding situation I have ever faced. It's a quirky airplane that's killed a lot of its pilots." In addition, their tests found problems with oscillating, unrecoverable spins, lack of any stall warning, a poor pressurization system, and a particularly dangerous emergency fuel pump (No 1996, 162).

Finale

Lt. No reported that by mid-1952, "four regular Soviet air divisions and two regiments—more than four hundred Russian pilots—were flying combat missions daily from bases in Manchuria." In March 1952, after almost a year in the war, the Russian 324th Fighter Air Division was ready to return home. Commanded by Colonel Ivan Kozhedub, the top Soviet ace of World War II, the elite unit had lost only 20 percent of its pilots. It returned to Moscow, and Colonel Kozhedub was promoted to Major General.

The Russian replacement division arrived at Antung Air Base along with another unit that was sent to Tatungho—an airfield located about twenty miles west of Antung. Alas, these replacement units were not as fortunate as the 324th had been.

While Colonel Kozhedub's division was engaged, our fighters had strictly observed the Manchurian sanctuary policy. In addition, the Russian MiGs held a significant altitude advantage against the early F-86A models. Then in April of 1952, things changed drastically when the Fifth Air Force Commander Lieutenant General Glenn O. Barcus, discontinued the Chinese airspace sanctuary policy. At Antung Air Base during the first week of April, Lt. No tells of watching as an armada of Russian MiG-15s attempted to recover from a high-altitude mission. He first heard the high-pitched whine of the F-86s' axial flow engines, then watched as five MiGs were downed while attempting to land—killing the five Russian pilots.

With the loss of Chinese sanctuary, over the next four months the two new Soviet divisions were almost entirely wiped out. As a result the Russian commander at Antung was sent back to Moscow in disgrace.

Lt. No reported that 80 percent of the MiG losses occurred after the elimination of the Chinese airspace sanctuary policy—a scenario made more deadly by the arrival of the improved high-altitude performance of the new F-86Es and Fs. By war's end, No relates, "the Reds lost more than 800 MiGs—400 Russian, 300 Chinese, and 100 North Korean—almost a hundred percent turnover."

The policy of ignoring the UN's Chinese airspace sanctuary continued until May 1953, when General Barcus completed his year as commander. On June 1, his replacement, Lieutenant General Samuel E. Anderson, quickly let it be known that he would make an example out of the first pilot caught crossing the Yalu River boundary with China. Unfortunately, that first miscreant happened to be one of the Fourth FIW Aces, who after an early June MiG kill, was promptly sent home in lieu of courts-martial. Rumor was that his gun-camera film showed clearly the runway of a major Chinese air base. This made his incursion difficult to defend before the United Nations, where it had been challenged. Later the general appeared to have mellowed, as the incursions into China by a few daring individuals continued until war's end—unchallenged by higher authority.

Meanwhile, the very intelligent North Korean fighter pilot immigrated to the United States and learned English. He then earned degrees in mechanical and electrical engineering from the University of Delaware. Subsequently, he married a lovely lady from Kaesong, Korea. They raised two sons and a daughter—the two sons graduated from college as engineers, and the daughter graduated as a lawyer. After working with several defense-related industries, Ken Rowe—his adopted

American name—ultimately retired as professor of engineering from Embry Riddle Aeronautical University in Daytona Beach, Florida. In retirement—and despite advancing age—Ken Rowe is a much sought-after speaker. His story, told in his book, *A MiG-15 to Freedom*, is a riveting account of his life under a brutal Stalinist-Communist government and his very brave escape to freedom.

Professor (Emeritus) Ken Rowe is shown enjoying retirement in Florida.

Chapter 9

Sabrejet Secrets

Although the F-86 Sabrejet proved a masterpiece of aeronautical engineering it had some growing pains along the way.

IT WAS MIDMORNING IN MARCH 1954 when my student and I—call sign Panther Flight—lined up for takeoff on the two-mile-long runway 21L at Nellis AFB, Nevada. It was a perfect day for flying—clear and cool with the area's usual unlimited visibility. My student, a second lieutenant just out of flight school, was making his first flight in the single-seat F-86E Sabre.

Because the aircraft was a single-seat fighter on a student pilot's first flight, he was chased by his instructor flying a separate aircraft. With the student in the lead position, at his signal we spooled up our engines to 100 percent power and checked the instruments. He looked over at me, and I nodded my head in affirmation that Panther leader was ready to roll. As pre-briefed, he tilted his head back then dropped it forward smartly. We released brakes together and began accelerating down the long runway.

He had shown no obvious signs of nervousness during our two-hour preflight briefing. But as we gained momentum I became concerned. He had long since passed rotation and takeoff airspeed but showed no signs of trying to get airborne. As the airspeed passed 150 knots I transmitted, "Rotate Panther! Let's fly!" But he startled me by suddenly snatching the throttle to idle and aborting the flight. Reflexively I followed suit. The runway was long, so there was no problem making the last turnoff.

"Panther Two: Why did you abort?" I asked.

Nervously he replied, "My elevator trim was miss-set." The fear factor, I mused; yet I fully understood. The fatal accident rate at Nellis AFB was horrendous.

My motive for hanging tough and getting him into the air was to prevent yet another "fear of flying" resignation. One recent class in the Combat Crew Training program had five resignations in one week. Even one of the instructors—a Korean War ace—decided he too had had enough.

Subsequently, my student finished the three-month course with no further problems. But when his assignment arrived to a stateside fighter squadron, he declined to continue. After all, he told me; he had a wife and two children, and they came first.

Fighter pilot resignations had become problematic air force–wide. Highly experienced Sabre pilots were having an inordinate number of accidents. In fact, during most of the 1950s at Nellis AFB alone there were an average of 52 *fatal accidents* annually—a pilot lost each week. Although not all were in the traffic pattern, it was common to walk out of a building and see a large column of black smoke billowing from the runway overrun. And with a knot in your gut, you knew that another pilot had "gone west." Yet in reality, many of these accidents were avoidable.

Hydraulic Flight Controls: It was early October 1952 when we graduates of Air Force Flying School Class 52-Fox began training for combat at Nellis AFB. Our initial flights in the already renowned Sabrejet were in the early F-86A models. Although capable of supersonic speed in a dive, the first hundred F-86As built had conventional flight controls, with cables and pulleys moving both the ailerons and tail surfaces. At high airspeeds the increasing air pressure caused the control forces to become very heavy. When approaching Mach-1—the speed of sound—other problems arose.

Flight tests of the Bell X-1 by then-captain Chuck Yeager had demonstrated that when approaching near-sonic speeds, a shockwave formed that prevented smooth airflow over both the wing and tail control surfaces. The resulting turbulent boundary-layer air caused severe flight control vibrations and loss of control surface effectiveness. To dampen these vibrations and keep the aircraft maneuverable, on February 9, 1951, the Sabre's manufacturer, North American Aviation Inc. (NAA), proposed to the air force a new and revolutionary flight-control system. The ailerons and tailplane of the new F-86E would be hydraulically operated—moved by the pilot's control stick via hydraulic actuators rather than the traditional cable-pulley arrangement. In addition, these actuators made the control surfaces irreversible, which prevented the high-speed vibrations caused by the shockwave-induced turbulent airflow—known as control surface buzz. Rather than a traditional trim tab to trim elevators or ailerons, the pilot electrically repositioned the control stick, which reset the control surface position (Wagner 1963, 54).

Captain Yeager's tests in the X-1 showed that to maintain pitch control in supersonic flight, some movable portion of the horizontal stabilizer had to be *in front* of the shockwave. Thus the proposed F-86E would have an "all-flying tailplane"; wherein the horizontal stabilizers and elevators functioned together. (In later aircraft such as the F-86D and F-100 series, the elevators were eliminated and the horizontal stabilizers, known as the slabs, became primary for pitch control.) Because the hydraulic actuators masked the pilot's feel for the aircraft, an artificial-feel bungee system was incorporated, which provided the pilot with the necessary control feel. This new design ensured that the forward portion of the stabilizer would always be in front of the shockwave (Wagner 1963, 54).

Tests of the new hydraulic flight controls showed that most of the undesirable compressibility effects were eliminated. Gone was the control surface buzz, and best of all, the pilot now had good pitch control at all airspeeds.

The revolutionary flight-control system was accepted by the air force, and the F-86E soon began replacing the A-models in combat and stateside fighter units. (Some of the A-models remained at Nellis to be used by students, and a few remained in Far East units.)

For the remainder of our training at Nellis, we found the F-86E a thing of beauty. Gone was the dangerously heavy pitch force required during pull-up from ground strafing or practice air-combat maneuvering. The E-model also put an end to the so-called "Jay Cee" maneuver—a high-speed porpoise during level flight wherein the startled pilot invariably uttered *Jeeeesus Chriiiist!* over the VHF radio. Eliminated too was the wing leading-edge "slat-lock," a feature adapted from the German ME-262. Upon climbing above five thousand feet, the pilot physically moved a lever that locked the slats. Upon descending below five thousand feet, they were unlocked, thus lowering the landing airspeed. Unfortunately, during high-speed and high-G maneuvers, one of the locked slats would break loose, allowing a single slat to extend. The resulting asymmetric lift immediately precipitated a very thrilling high-energy spin.

The E-model's flight controls were operated by two separate three-thousand-psi hydraulic systems, an engine-driven normal system, and an alternate system. If the normal system pressure dropped below two-thousand-psi during maneuvers, or if it failed, the alternate system would automatically take over. If the automatic feature failed, the pilot could pull the emergency override handle. This used the ship's battery to power the alternate system pump for about three minutes—just long enough to get you out of the combat area. In case of an engine flameout, the compressor's windmill-rpm provided enough normal system hydraulic pressure to continue operating the flight controls.

Yet despite the Sabre's sterling design and safety features, lingering in the back of every pilot's mind was the possibility of total hydraulic failure. This would cause a lockup of the flight controls. As if to validate our subconscious fear, and despite all the carefully designed safeguards, flight control failures began to occur.

The first known incident happened on July 8, 1955, at Nellis AFB. "Impulse Paris" flight had started engines at 0650 hours PST. Their mission was to be air-to-air gunnery—shooting at a target towed by a T-33 at twenty thousand feet. The flight leader and instructor was First Lieutenant Herschel D. Spitzer of the 3525th Aircraft Gunnery Squadron (later renamed the Fighter Weapons School). Impulse Paris Two was Captain Richard D. Stark, also of the 3525th squadron.

During takeoff roll, Paris Two, on Lt. Spitzer's left wing, dropped back slightly out of position. As they lifted off and climbed through three hundred feet, Paris Two suddenly banked right and passed beneath his leader's tail. After about forty degrees of turn, Paris Two transmitted, "Spitz, I've had it." Stark's Sabre continued in a right bank with the nose finally dropping below the horizon. Upon hitting the ground, the aircraft exploded and Captain Stark was killed (USAF Accident Report, July 8, 1955).

Later that month on July 18, it happened again, this time to an F-86F-30, the most advanced model of the Sabre. The student pilot, First Lieutenant David F. Kennedy, was flying the number-two position in a four-ship flight of Sabres. Their assigned mission was a simulated attack on a convoy of World War II trucks and tanks located on the base's gunnery range near Lathrop Wells, Nevada. On the first diving pass, the number-four pilot saw Lt. Kennedy hit the target with his five-inch high-velocity rockets and then recover from the dive. Number Four had just turned his attention to his own target when he saw a bright orange flash ahead and to his right. The number-two aircraft had flown into the ground and exploded, killing Lt. Kennedy.

It happened again on August 22, 1956, this time in the Williams AFB (Arizona) F-86 Combat Crew Training program. While this mission too was air-to-air gunnery, fortunately, the problem occurred at twenty thousand feet, on the last leg of the aerial gunnery pattern. I was the flight instructor (Panther One) and the student pilot (Panther Three) was Second Lieutenant Robert K. Dornan—later a successful radio talk-show host and a highly respected member of Congress (USAF Accident Report, August 22 1956).

Panther Three had climbed to the "perch" position, awaiting his turn to dive and fire on the banner being towed behind a T-33. Just after level-off, his aircraft abruptly began rolling rapidly to the left and continued with increasing violence. Dornan later reported, "The control stick felt frozen."

With the aircraft in a near-vertical nose-down spin, I followed him down, transmitting continuously, "Control stick forward, right rudder! Control stick forward!" As he passed through ten thousand feet I then began transmitting, "PANTHER THREE, EJECT! EJECT!" And out he came. I followed the beautiful white parachute canopy down and watched as he landed in the jagged lava rock outcroppings of Arizona's Kofa Gunnery Range.

Following Dornan's ejection, I transmitted on the emergency frequency for everyone to hear: "Cease fire! Cease fire on the Kofa Range. Panther Three has ejected." But alas, a flight leader and his three students following us had failed to monitor the emergency frequency. Consequently, the four-ship flight of F-86s continued firing at the banner, each with their six .50-caliber machine guns.

After hitting the ground, Lt. Dornan could hear their gunfire and quickly took cover underneath the overhang of the lava rock formations. He later told of hearing the spent .50-caliber bullets hitting in the rocks all around him "with a sound like metallic raindrops."

Meanwhile I instructed the number-two student to lead number four back to home base, while I landed on the gravel-surfaced runway at nearby Gila Bend Air Force Station. I then boarded the rescue helicopter and directed the pilot to my student's location. With the overhead gunfire now stopped, the helicopter landed in a small clearing in the desolate lava-rock moonscape terrain. At first Lt. Dornan was nowhere to be seen. Then suddenly he walked out from behind the protective rock overhang. With a bloodied forehead from being struck by the departing canopy during the ejection sequence, his parachute in his arms, and a very serious look on his face, his first breathless words to me were, "Just like *The Bridges at Toko-Ri!*"

Cause of the Failures

Determining the cause of these flight-control failures was critical to pilot confidence in the famed aircraft, not to mention the national defense effort. Incidents of hydraulic flight-control failure were occurring in F-86-equipped units throughout the air force. In fact, after accepting a newly manufactured Sabre at NAA's Los Angeles factory, Korean combat veteran Captain Fred Hughes, an instructor from Nellis AFB, crashed into the ocean just after takeoff, when the flight controls froze.

The problem was finally resolved in the summer of 1956, when Captain Charles White, a senior instructor at Williams AFB, managed to land an F-86 with locked ailerons. Examination of Captain White's aircraft and re-inspection of the wreckage of others finally led investigators to the source of the problem. The control seizures were being caused by a piece of a Teflon backup ring used in the aileron actuators. The Teflon rings would occasionally be sheared when the actuators' components were being assembled during manufacture. In flight, the sheared fragment would eventually find its way into a fluid passageway where it blocked the flow of hydraulic fluid, thus locking the ailerons—or the entire flight-control system, as with Captain Stark and Lt. Dornan.

Implementing a routine check for this condition was considered impractical since inspecting an installed backup ring required disassembling the actuator. Thus a more detailed and careful assembly of the aileron actuators by the manufacturer was deemed the only remedy. Fortunately for all of us, this solution worked.

Tailpipe Rats

As the Sabre's operational history progressed, experienced pilots began having an alarming number of takeoff and landing accidents. Ultimately they were found to be caused by two basic problems: improperly positioned tailpipe segments used to increase engine thrust, and inadequate information concerning the takeoff and landing characteristics of new airplanes equipped with fixed leading-edge wings rather than the traditional aerodynamically operated leading-edge wing slats.

Because the Sabre's GE-J-47 engine was equipped with a fixed-area tailpipe, the combination of rpm and exhaust gas temperature provided a direct indication of thrust output. At 100 percent rpm, if the tailpipe temperature was less than 690 degrees Celsius, the engine was underpowered. In order to obtain maximum (rated) thrust, the diameter of the tailpipe had to be slightly reduced. To do this, an engine technician would install one or more metal segments on the inside lip of the tail pipe—universally referred to as "rats." The segments effectively increased the turbine discharge pressure a finite amount, which in turn increased the EGT to the required figure. Still, what the technicians and pilots often didn't know was that *where* the segments were located on the tailpipe lip was critical to a successful takeoff.

Compounding the problem was that during the Korean War some of the senior squadron pilots would have the maintenance officer install an extra rat in the tailpipe of the aircraft they were scheduled to fly. This produced an EGT hotter than the 690 degree limit and, up to a point, provided additional thrust and hence potentially greater airspeed. One of the first mishaps occurred in the Fourth Fighter Interceptor Wing, at K-14 (Kimpo Air base) South Korea. Crash of the aircraft, which belonged to the 336th Fighter Interceptor Squadron, occurred on June 24, 1953—about a month before the Korean War hostilities ended.

It was to be a routine test flight following an engine change. The badly injured pilot, First Lieutenant Sam Jackson, later told investigators that during his takeoff roll there were no abnormalities in either the EGT or aircraft acceleration. "At one hundred knots I exerted a slight back pressure on the [control] stick, which normally was sufficient to raise the nose to takeoff attitude. Yet there was no change in the relative position of the nose of the aircraft." It simply wouldn't rotate to a takeoff attitude.

After several attempts to lift off, and by then with plenty of airspeed, Jackson aborted the takeoff and elected to catch the newly installed "runway overrun barrier."

At the time, the runway length at K-14 was only six thousand feet—the shortest jet fighter airstrip in South Korea. A longer runway had been needed for some time. Now, because of the increased takeoff and landing requirements of the new fixed-wing leading-edge Sabres, US Army engineers were in process of constructing an extension at both ends. (Note: The "runway overrun barrier" was later improved and designated the "BAK-12 Arresting System.")

The badly burned Sabre pilot told the Accident Board that he "slowed somewhat and made a good cable-pickup near the centerline of the runway. I saw the nylon tapes fly as I engaged the cable and started off the paved end of the runway. I was unaware that earth-moving equipment had been preparing the overrun for resurfacing. In addition, there had been heavy rains creating mud and potholes."

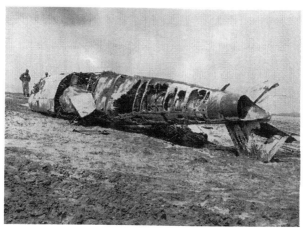

The Sabre entered the overrun and made a good cable pickup; but once in the overrun, the nose wheel immediately hit a pothole and snapped off. Simultaneously the barrier cable broke loose from the anchor chain on the right side. This caused the aircraft to cartwheel and shed its wings, leaving the burning fuselage rolled almost upside down in the muddy overrun. Lt. Jackson told investigators, "Burning fuel poured down on me and I was burned everywhere except my hands and feet."

Fortunately, a field grade officer and a sergeant were just passing the end of runway. Using an axe and a knife, they were able to break away the canopy and cut the pilot loose, then pull him to safety.

The Accident Board at first found the cause to be "pilot error:" But armed with later information provided by North American Aviation Inc. regarding the effect of improperly placed tailpipe segments, the reason for the accident was changed to "cause unknown."

Then, in November 1953, once again at K-14, another Sabre—this time from the 334th Fighter Interceptor Squadron—was forced to abort takeoff and take the overrun barrier. The pilot's story was familiar: "I was leading a flight of four. Upon brake release my wingman and I accelerated normally to rotation speed. I then eased back on the [control] stick, but the nose wheel seemed stuck to the runway...Then I eased to the middle of the runway and took the barrier in textbook fashion. The barrier cable caught my main landing gear; and, except for some bent landing gear door fairings, there was no damage—other than my ego."

Thanks to the newly paved overrun, his abort was a textbook example of the exceptional safety benefits of the runway overrun barrier in preventing rejected-takeoff accidents. Still, the failure of the aircraft to rotate to a takeoff attitude could not be explained. Consequently, the newly appointed squadron flight commander was demoted to line pilot.

Much later the secret to these unexplainable incidents was exposed when North American Aviation Inc. explained the phenomenon and added an explanation to the Pilot's Dash One (operator's handbook). It stated that the tailpipe segments were needed to "adjust the exhaust outlet area to produce as near as possible a stabilized exhaust gas temperature of 690 degrees C at 100% rpm during ground run-up...The initial segments are installed *at the bottom* of the tailpipe. As additional segments are needed, they are installed as symmetrically as possible, starting *from the bottom of the tailpipe* [editorial emphasis]. Initial segment installation beginning at the top of the tailpipe *is not recommended*, because it will reduce the tail down-load."

The NAA technical representatives explained that down-tail loading aids nosewheel liftoff and is a reaction caused by the tendency of the jet-exhaust stream to cling to the upper fairing shelf aft of the tailpipe. "*Whenever down-tail loading is reduced or lost, nose wheel liftoff speed will increase substantially*" (editorial emphasis). Of course this was a gross understatement, since numerous experienced pilots had been unable to get their aircraft to rotate at any speed. Nevertheless this information resolved the problem.

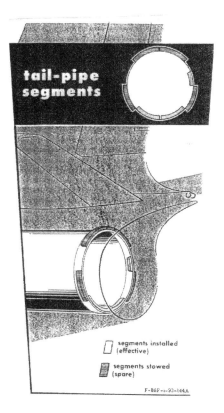

Figure 9-1 tailpipe segments

The Hard-Wing Sabre

Yet another carefully kept "secret" that was causing major accidents involved the changed takeoff and landing speeds of Sabres equipped with the "extended leading edge wing"—euphemistically called the "hard-wing." The aerodynamically operated wing leading-edge slats had been adapted from the German ME-262. This greatly improved the swept-wing airplane's low-speed handling and stall characteristics; but in combat maneuvering at high altitude the slats had proved detrimental.

To enhance the airplane's capability against the lighter and higher-flying MiG-15s, NAA test pilots suggested replacement of the wing leading-edge slats with fixed extensions. This, they theorized would lower the prestall buffet boundary at high altitude and concurrently decrease the airplane's turning radius. Thus in August 1952, NAA project engineers removed the leading-edge slats from three Sabres and perfected the "extended leading edge" modification. Wing area was increased from 287.9 to 302.3 square feet. The aerodynamic slats were replaced with a six-inch extension at the wing root, tapering to three inches at the wing-tip; hence the term "six-three leading edge."

Flight tests showed that the combination of an enlarged wing area and the addition of the newly developed J-47-GE-27 engine with 5,910 pounds thrust—later improved to 6,090—increased the Sabre's top speed at all altitudes. Best of all, the airplane could now climb above fifty thousand feet and turn at high altitude with the lighter MiG-15.

The bad news was that stall speed increased from 109 KIAS (knots indicated airspeed) to 122 KIAS, which increased both the takeoff and landing distances. Nosewheel liftoff speed on takeoff (rotation) increased from 95 KIAS in the slatted-wing aircraft to 110 KIAS with the hard wing. Liftoff occurred at 125 KIAS with the slatted-wing aircraft and 140 K with the fixed leading-edge model. Landing approach speeds increased from 130 KIAS to almost 150 KIAS. Concurrently, touchdown speed increased from 100 KIAS with leading-edge slats to 117 KIAS in the hard-wing model.

Power Curve Problems

When fighter units began receiving the hard-wing Sabres, the accidents began. The scenario was always the same: on takeoff, with normal readings on the engine instruments, the brakes were released and the aircraft accelerated to takeoff speed. But using the airspeeds provided by the then-current Dash One, the pilots would often rotate the nose for takeoff at the published speed and the aircraft would lift off in a nose-high attitude, then gain five or ten feet and refuse to climb out of ground effect. This was referred to as "getting behind the power curve" wherein aerodynamic drag created by the premature rotation exceeded the available engine thrust. The cause, of course, was lifting off too close to the airplane's stall speed. One of the first and most tragic of these mishaps occurred on June 3, 1953, at K-14 in Korea.

When the Fourth Fighter Interceptor Wing received its first extended-wing F-86F-30s, we pilots were verbally advised of the increased takeoff and landing speeds by our embedded NAA technical representatives. Meanwhile, across the field, the RF-80-equipped Sixty-seventh Tactical Reconnaissance Wing had received a few RF-86Fs, some having wing slats and others the fixed six-three wing leading edge. Because the Sixty-seventh TRW operated primarily RF-80s, their leadership was out of the NAA information loop and had no knowledge of the characteristics of the new "hard wing" (reconnaissance) version of the Sabre. Their only source of information was the Pilots' Dash One, which had not been upgraded to include the new modified wing data. Instead, it described only the speeds and procedures for aircraft having aerodynamic slats. Compounding the problem was that Sixty-seventh pilots had trained in the slatted-wing version and had not been briefed on the changed takeoff and landing speeds in the hard-wing aircraft.

This lack of information resulted in the death of Lt. Elliott B. (Jack) Sartain from the Kimpo-based Wing's Fifteenth Tactical Reconnaissance Squadron. He had been scheduled to fly as wingman—the number-two position—of a two-ship photo reconnaissance combat mission in a hard-wing RF-86F-30. His flight leader, Captain James H. Howell Jr. was flying an RF-86F equipped with wing leading-edge slats. Compounding the problem was that Captain Howell's aircraft had 120-gallon pylon tanks, while Lt. Sartain's airplane was fitted with 200-gallon tanks. To keep the fuel load equal, Lt. Sartain's airplane was serviced with a partial fuel load of 120 gallons.

At 1555 hours PST, Captain Howell and Lt. Sartain taxied for take-off. Both aircraft lined up on the runway and increased power to 100 percent rpm. Lt. Sartain nodded that he was ready to go, and they simultaneously released brakes and began their takeoff roll. At approximately 100 KIAS, Captain Howell rotated the nose of his aircraft for liftoff and shortly thereafter became airborne. He looked back and noted that Lt. Sartain was lagging. After Captain Howell retracted his landing gear, his wingman was no longer in sight.

Witnesses said that Lt. Sartain became airborne approximately half-way down the runway "in an extremely nose high attitude." The accident report states, "The aircraft climbed to approximately five feet in the air and continued down the runway without gaining altitude or [without] an appreciable increase in airspeed."

At the far end of the runway, a unit of the US Army Corps of Engineers was busily adding the needed runway extension to a more usable twelve thousand feet. Consequently, there were numerous army and some air force civil-engineering personnel pouring concrete into the framed outline of the runway extension. In addition, the area was congested with large and heavy earth-moving equipment.

Upon reaching the end of the runway, the struggling aircraft clipped the right runway overrun barrier stanchion then continued for another thousand feet. Still in an extreme nose high attitude, it then hit the blade of a 13.5-ton "Tourneaudozer" and exploded like a giant napalm bomb.

Lt. Sartain and four army engineers were incinerated, with several other soldiers severely burned. One soldier told investigators, "After it hit I saw this one man come running away from a fifty-ton roller. He was completely on fire and fell down. The [Sabre's] ammunition began going off before I could reach the burning man, so I took cover behind a Cat. There was another man behind the Cat and when we saw [that] the ammunition was going up in the air we ran over to the burning man and smothered the flames on his body."

Meanwhile on the east side of the field, in the Fourth FIW combat operations, a pilots meeting was in progress, wherein NAA chief test pilot R. A. (Bob) Hoover was explaining "the abnormal takeoff characteristics" of the extended leading-edge wing aircraft. At 15:40—just fifteen minutes prior to Lt. Sartain's conflagration—the Sixty-seventh TRW received notification of this important meeting.

In the ensuing accident investigation, the Board was blunt in their findings and recommendations. The cause was placed squarely on Air Material Command. The Board noted that the Pilot's Dash One was published with insufficient information on the characteristics of the extended wing airplanes. This misinformation had led the Fifteenth Tactical Reconnaissance Squadron to schedule an extended-wing aircraft to fly the wing of a slat-equipped aircraft.

Worse yet, when the two-hundred-gallon pylon tanks were only half filled, during takeoff roll the fuel pooled in the aft section of the tank. The weight of this fuel put the airplane aft of its center-of-gravity limitation. This exacerbated the abnormally nose-high attitude and contributed to Lt. Sartain's inability to recover. Consequently, the Board recommended an investigation as to why and how this dereliction transpired. Meanwhile, the same type of accidents continued to occur air force–wide.

Yet despite these problems, the F-86 Sabre ultimately was adopted by twenty-five nations, five of which—Canada, Japan, Spain, Italy, and Australia—manufactured their own aircraft. During the height of the Cold War it was the most widely used fighter in the world.

Perhaps the most amazing aspect of the Sabre's success is that in 1944, German engineers had laid out the basic design of a swept-winged supersonic fighter. They had even conducted successful wind-tunnel studies of a model. But the progress of World War II prevented their building a prototype.

After World War II, NAA's engineers used the German data to complete the job. The result was an aerodynamically flawless design. The F-86 Sabrejet was one of the few jet fighters with no bad habits. It was revered by everyone who flew it.

Chapter 10

Uncertain Hero

Killed in a late-night accident in an airplane loaded with illegal drugs, details of the death of Major Manuel J. Fernandez, USAFR (Ret.), the USAF's third top-scoring Korean War jet ace, remain classified. Yet his DEA handler verifies that he died fighting the drug war.

AFTER A RELATIVELY LETHARGIC JANUARY, the air war over North Korea's Yalu River border with China—MiG Alley—had become quite active. It was February 18, 1953, and Able Flight, a four-ship formation of F-86 Sabrejets from the 334th Fighter Interceptor Squadron, was escorting an RF-80 on a routine photoreconnaissance of airfields near the North Korean border with China.

Leading the flight was 334th squadron commander, Lieutenant Colonel Richard L. Ayersman. His wingman, Able Two, was First Lieutenant Ivan J. Ely. The element leader, Able Three, was Captain Manuel J. (Pete) Fernandez, with wingman, Able Four, First Lieutenant Don Hooten. They were flying the standard "fluid element" tactical formation—popularly called the "fluid four." The second element was riding high to support the flight leader, with the wingmen spread out so they could look around and protect their respective leaders.

Nearing the Yalu River boundary, Able Leader suddenly spotted an armada of thirty-two MiG-15s. Comprising two squadrons of twelve fighters each, and a separate formation of eight, they appeared intent on intercepting the RF-80.

As the Sabres engaged the enemy armada, Lieutenant Colonel Ayersman attacked a MiG in the lead flight of twelve aircraft, while Captain Fernandez selected a member of the second squadron of "bandits." Like an aroused hornet's nest, the sky immediately became a swirling mass of airplanes (Unit History, USAF, The 334th FIS History, January 53–June 1953).

As Ayersman began firing, members of the eight-aircraft formation, riding high and behind, counterattacked. While he continued to concentrate on his target, his wingman, Able Two, frantically began calling, "Break left! Break left!" One especially tenacious MiG was locked onto his tail and firing.

Able One broke hard into the attack while Able Two slid in behind the attacking MiG and opened fire. The enemy pilot immediately broke off his attack, but Lt. Ely had hit him hard. Trailing heavy black smoke, the badly damaged aircraft then entered a spin and crashed.

Meanwhile, Captain Fernandez had closed rapidly on his targeted MiG and opened fire. It immediately began smoking profusely, and the enemy pilot ejected.

Yet Able Flight was still in the milieu. Able Four suddenly called out two MiGs coming in fast from five o'clock low—their right rear quadrant. Frantically he called to Fernandez: "Break right! Break right!" As the two fighters turned hard into the attack, the MiGs opened fire and attempted to match the Sabres' sharp turn. But their angle-off was too great. Because of their determined high-G effort, both enemy aircraft were seen to snap out of control and begin spinning. Because the MiG-15 was unrecoverable from a spin, both aircraft continued spinning and subsequently crashed into the frozen ground. The final score for Able Flight was four MiGs destroyed and one damaged. Lt. Colonel Ayersman received credit for the damaged MiG, Captain Fernandez was credited with two kills, and Lts. Ely and Hooten were credited one each. Perhaps the most significant aspect of the engagement was that on that mission, Captain Manuel J. Fernandez became the twenty-sixth jet ace of the Korean War (Unit History, USAF, The 334th FIS History, January 1953 –June 1953).

Yet air force history shows that Captain Fernandez's first five kills were just the beginning. He proved to be not only a skilled fighter pilot but also a talented tactician in the high-altitude environment in which they were fighting.

In 1952–53, despite China's open participation in the war, United Nations political constraints continued to restrict the F-86 interceptors to North Korea's Yalu River border with China. Thus, while in Chinese airspace the MiGs enjoyed unprecedented political sanctuary. With UN forces exercising absolute air superiority on the Korean peninsula, the constant bombing of targets all over North Korea kept enemy airfields unserviceable. Therefore, except for a brief period in 1952, there were no enemy aircraft based in North Korea. Instead they were stationed across the Yalu River in China.

The UN's sanctuary policy allowed the enemy pilots to use the superior thrust-to-weight ratio of their lighter-weight fighters to climb above fifty thousand feet while still in protected Chinese airspace. Then, with our heavier F-86As and Es limited to forty-five thousand to forty-eight thousand feet, the MiGs would cross into North Korea and engage the Sabres at will. Occasionally, from their unreachable cruise altitude, they would dive down singly or in pairs and shoot at the Sabres. And unless someone happened to get a few lucky rounds into a MiG's engine, they would climb back to altitude and return to Chinese airspace (No 1996, 115).

President Eisenhower, the Joint Chiefs of Staff, and the State Department all reportedly disapproved of the sanctuary policy. In cases of "hot pursuit," they wanted the Sabres to be able to cross the border and complete an attack. But fear of enlarging the war caused other UN member countries to disapprove (Werrell 2005, 128).

Although the Chinese border policy was strictly observed in the early days of the Korean War, during April 1952, "hot pursuit" was unofficially condoned. In effect this gave Sabres carte blanche to go after MiGs where they lived—in and around their airfield traffic patterns. The Chinese had been expecting this and had briefed their pilots to watch for F-86s in their airspace. In mid-April, five MiGs were downed while attempting to land at Antung (renamed Dandong) Air Base, China (No 1996, 87).

Major Jabara congratulates Captain Fernandez upon scoring his fifth MiG kill to become the twenty-sixth jet ace of the Korean War.

Meanwhile, Captain Fernandez had been astutely observant: after struggling to reach the MiG's high altitude, most flight leaders were cruising between Mach 0.8 and 0.83 number. Yet Fernandez briefed the new 334th FIS Commander Lieutenant Colonel William L. Cosby Jr., that when leading a flight at high altitude he always cruised in a clean configuration (no pylon tanks) and at Mach 0.9 (90 percent the speed of sound). At this speed, he said, a MiG had never closed or attacked from the six o'clock (tail) position. This was an important observation because, as we learned later, it identified a significant limitation in the enemy aircraft's performance.

Captain Fernandez debriefs Major Jabara after having just scored his ninth and tenth kills, to become a double jet ace.

The Sabrejet was supersonic in a dive and remained controllable at its top airspeed of Mach 1.02. Conversely, above Mach 0.92, the building shockwave ("sound barrier") on the MiG-15 caused it to vibrate heavily and make it uncontrollable. In fact, the aircraft had a unique safety feature whereupon reaching its airspeed limitation of Mach 0.92, a red annunciator light illuminated, and its speed brakes deployed automatically (No 1996, 161).

Captain Fernandez explained that by dropping his pylon tanks when they first emptied (usually upon reaching the Yalu River boundary), with his IFF (Identification Friend or Foe—today called a transponder) turned off, he would cruise-climb to forty-nine thousand feet on a northward heading and cruise deep into Chinese airspace.

Once at altitude, using a delicate fifteen-degree bank to avoid the pre-stall buffet boundary, he would gently turn south. (With aircraft that had leading-edge slats, turns at high altitude were like balancing on a tightrope above the Grand Canyon; the slightest control roughness, or a bank angle exceeding fifteen degrees, required an elevator back-pressure that exceeded 1.25 Gs; this resulted in pre-stall buffet and an instant loss of ten knots of indicated airspeed, which was very difficult to regain.)

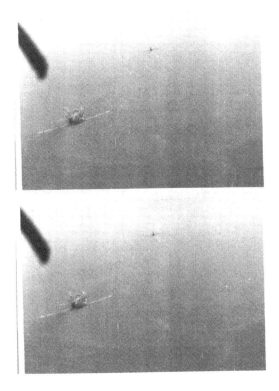

Capt. Fernandez zooms in front of Maj. Foster Smith to score another kill. Because Maj. Smith had already damaged the MiG, Fernandez received only half credit for the aircraft's destruction.

Using reports of "bandit" activity from Mongoose (the air force's island radar site at Cho-do), Fernandez would attempt to play his high-altitude turn to literally join up with one of the Soviets' stair-stepped, two-ship elements of MiG formations. Normally these ascending elements provided very effective mutual support against Sabres attempting to attack. However, with a Mach 0.9 cruise speed, it became irrelevant whether Fernandez joined on the lead (bottom) element, middle, or last (top) element of their formation since no MiG could close on a Sabre at that speed. If one did happen to get uncomfortably close, Fernandez simply lowered the aircraft's nose and accelerated, and the enemy aircraft couldn't follow. Subsequently this procedure would become the Fourth Tactical Fighter Wing Doctrine ("4th FIG Operations in MiG Alley –Tactical Doctrine," Colonel Thomas De Jarnette Commanding, 17 June 1953)

Although Captain Fernandez had completed his required 100 missions, he signed up for an additional 25. On May 17, 1953, however, with 124 missions to his credit, he was grounded from further combat. At the time he was the USAF's top jet ace with 14.5 kills. Meanwhile, his closest rival, Captain Joe McConnell, of the Fifty-First FIW, was in second place with 13 victories. But the Fifth Air Force Commander Lieutenant General Glenn O. Barcus, wanted to protect both pilots for posterity. Thus he notified the commanders of the Fourth FIW and Fifty-First FIW that both Fernandez and McConnell were to be grounded immediately and sent home. Somehow, however, only Captain Fernandez got the word, and the next day Captain McConnell flew two more missions and downed three more MiGs, becoming the air force's top jet ace.

Postwar Activities

On May 19, both Fernandez and McConnell returned stateside to a hero's welcome—including a meeting on May 27 with President Eisenhower. Subsequently, both aces were assigned to fighter squadrons at George AFB, California.

Captains Joe McConnell (L) and Pete Fernandez (R) are congratulated by President Eisenhower.

Shortly thereafter the F-86 Sabres were replaced by the new F-100 Super Sabres. With this new state-of-the-art aircraft, Fernandez again showed he was addicted to speed and high risks. In 1956 he won the Bendix Trophy with the new Super Sabre—averaging 666.66 mph in a near-sonic dash from George AFB to Oklahoma City—landing with only two minutes of fuel remaining (Davis 1978).

Fernandez later entered the air force's prestigious Test Pilot School at Edwards Air Force Base, California. But his high-school education hadn't prepared him for the graduate-level engineering and math. He spent the next two years in recruiting duty in South Florida getting reacquainted with friends. Then in 1960 his Spanish-language skills facilitated an assignment as advisor to the Argentine Air Force. In Argentina, Fernandez trained pilots in their newly acquired F-86F Sabres. During this tour of duty he also acquired the personal contacts that later became useful in his clandestine work for the US government.

Captain Fernandez is shown receiving the 1956 Bendix Trophy

Black Operations

Despite his stellar combat record and fame, Fernandez was a reserve officer, and in 1963 his active air force service timed out. Like any other reservist, upon reaching twenty years active duty, and despite fighting in two wars, Major Manuel John Fernandez was forced to retire.

123

However, upon retirement, Fernandez was flying again almost immediately. Instead of jet fighters, he now was operating transports carrying passengers or cargo. In 1965, while employed by Argonaut Airways and attending a DC-3 refresher course at Flight Safety International in Miami, he met fellow student Gerald Patrick (Gerry) Hemming. Gerry was a CIA operative who had been deeply involved with Operation Mongoose, the code name for the secret war conducted out of South Florida against Cuba during the 1960s. While that operation was now closed, Hemming was marking time and preparing for yet another secret assignment. His new mission was to capture Commandante Ernesto "Che" Guevara, who was known to be operating in the Congo with the Simba rebels.

Hemming later told an interviewer, "I was Pete's case officer after I recruited him at the officers club at the then-active Homestead Air Force Base...During this period we also flew on the Argonaut run from Miami to Key West. Pete's name had appeared on the back side of a 'Bigot List' of intelligence operatives approved to participate in the overthrow of Papa Doc Duvalier's Haitian dictatorship." (Bigot lists showed agents cleared for specific classified work.)

Fernandez was eager to join Hemming's Congo project, and his name soon appeared on the Congo operation bigot list. Then, without explanation, his involvement was disapproved. If by chance the ex-air force jet-fighter ace was captured it would cause great embarrassment to the US government. Thus his direct participation with Gerry Hemming's world of intrigue would have to wait (Robert Blurton, pers.comm, June 11, 2005). Sometime in 1964 the CIA began looking for a Spanish-speaking civilian pilot with a background in jet fighters. The mission (reportedly) was to steal a Soviet-made jet fighter from a Spanish-speaking country. Pete Fernandez was their man, and while no official details of the operation are available, he accomplished the mission and delivered a MiG-17 to Patrick AFB, Florida. Then in 1968, the Peruvian government was overthrown by a coup involving "left-wing" generals. As a result, the Soviet Union began increasing their military assistance to Peru. Among the airplanes they provided were turboprop Antonov 26 cargo-transport planes. They were reportedly equipped with a new secret guidance system that allowed extremely accurate cargo drops. US intelligence wanted a firsthand look at this new technology for possible use in its own covert operations. In 1972, Hemming tapped Fernandez to steal one of the aircraft. Both Hemming and Fernandez had connections in Lima. Pete's dated back to his assignment as an advisor to the Argentine Air Force and allowed him access to the military ramp at Lima International Airport, where he crawled into the cockpit of this multi-crew aircraft and (reportedly) flew it to Howard AFB in Panama.

If aircraft theft like this could be traced back to the US government, the resulting diplomatic flap could have seriously damaged US foreign relations. To insulate the government, Hemming was the so-called cutout liaison between the Feds and Fernandez. "This in essence is why black operations exist," Hemming said, "to be plausibly denied if exposed...Given the blatant violations of international law that these aircraft heists constituted, one can understand why the CIA would use a 'deniable' asset like Fernandez for the job" (Robert Blurton, personal correspondence, November 28, 2005). However, this rationale seems questionable: as with the Congo project, Fernandez's fame in military circles would naturally have made the US government suspect.

Succession

On July 1, 1973, the newly activated Drug Enforcement Agency replaced the CIA as the "action agency tasked to manipulate international drug dealing for strategic advantage." Concurrently, the US government formed a series of task forces to control and prosecute the criminal activity. The FBI and DEA quickly recruited Hemming into their South Florida Interdiction Task Force. The Task Force's primary mission was "to gather intelligence by flying loads [of drugs] to the Bahamas [and United States] in order to get intelligence on the Colombian-Bahamian drug cartels."

Hemming told the author, "Pete was one of my many assets for these operations...but one of the few that knew for whom and for what he was working. Many of my other assets, to this day, don't know that they were working for the Task Force. This protected the government from leaks and outright selling of identities and intelligence by corrupt federal agents to the criminal bosses."

When the Task Force was first formed, Hemming had explained to Fernandez that if arrested, they would never have to testify before a grand jury. After all, the Task Force's role was to gather intelligence, not enforce the law. Hemming noted, "That's a common operation for the company [DEA]." As an additional guarantee, the DEA's honcho for intelligence gathering and operations, Lucien Conein, had made an arrangement whereby his agency would claim that any "asset detained for drug smuggling was on a deep-cover DEA assignment...anybody involved can be busted but not convicted, because we weren't law enforcement, we were intelligence" (Robert Blurton, personal correspondence, November 28, 2005).

In the late 1970s, cocaine began to displace marijuana as the Colombian cargo of choice. While involving the same operational risks, the profit margin with cocaine was much greater. South Florida's already fast-growing economy suddenly went off the financial charts.

Mike McDonald, a twenty-seven-year veteran of the Internal Revenue Service and a part of the IRS Criminal Investigation Division, had worked with the FBI/DEA task force in Miami. In a 2000 PBS interview he explained, "In 1978 and 1979, the entire currency surplus of the United States was attributed to South Florida. Billions and billions of dollars... And where there is money there's a role for the IRS...Treasury came in and said that we need to participate in this war on drugs."

In 1978, Hemming and Fernandez linked up with the IRS criminal investigation teams. Hemming related, "I was approached by the chiefs of this special IRS intel group...[but] I did not accept the collaboration contract with these IRS folks unless and until I traveled to Washington DC and spoke personally with the top bosses of both the Treasury Department and the IRS. I wasn't about to take the word of some lower-echelon 'Miami cowboys,' regardless of the fact that they were in accord with my schemes and were experienced in recent covert operations" (Robert Blurton, personal correspondence, November 28, 2005; G. Hemming, e-mail, June 22, 2006).

At the time, corruption within law enforcement was epidemic. Both local law enforcement and members of federal agencies were untrustworthy.

Corrupted employees who handled intelligence reports were selling copies to the drug dealers. Even classified law-enforcement communications frequencies were regularly compromised. Hemming continued, "One of our infrequent contacts was Joe Norman in Key Biscayne, Miami, Florida—who had been intentionally exposed to the press by corrupt government officials" (G. Hemming, pers.com, June 28, 2006).

Meanwhile, a 1992 Government Accounting Office study of management within DEA found "a great laxity within national headquarters and two large field divisions…The doors to DEA's most critical secrets were literally left wide open." This directly compromised undercover operatives. A follow-up study showed that the DEA did nothing to correct the glaring deficiencies (GAO Report, 1992).

To protect the identity of his task-force operatives in this environment, Hemming kept them *undocumented*. Fernandez was one of his undocumented assets. In addition, if a federal agency was using someone in illegal activities or only wanted to be extra safe in case of a future problem, then the asset would be kept off the books. Of course, the drug smuggling conducted by the task force to gain credibility with the drug cartels was itself illegal activity.

Given the criminal penetration of the DEA, which in turn exposed the South Florida Task Force it coordinated, Hemming and Fernandez's participation in major drug crimes *without proof of their deep cover status* is understandable. With commendable tenacity in trying to win the drug war, they were relying on their government handlers to vouch for their status. While their dedication is highly commendable, it ultimately worked to their detriment.

Controlled Delivery

Drug shipments flown north with the South Florida Drug Interdiction Task Force's knowledge were allowed to land in the United States—a practice called "controlled delivery." Everybody got paid along the way until the very end, whereupon the midlevel wholesaler got nailed (Robert Blurton, personal correspondence, November 28, 2005).

Meanwhile, there were some big busts. In December 1977, using information from undercover assets, federal agents mounted Operation Snowbird. Their efforts netted two small planes, numerous boats, and a thirty-two-foot yacht—all packed with marijuana. The operation continued into 1978, with federal agents ultimately seizing $15 million worth of cocaine, $1 million worth of marijuana, five airplanes, four major vessels, and eighteen cars and trucks, while making fifty arrests.

Then in 1979, using intelligence provided directly by Hemming and Fernandez, a joint FBI/DEA task force in Miami brought down a Colombian organization called the Black Tuna Gang. They were a major marijuana smuggling ring responsible for bringing five hundred tons of the drug into the United States over a sixteen-month period.

Contract Termination

Left unsaid was that when a US government agency decided to terminate a relationship, the contact agent or "asset" would simply be set up for police to bury alive in the penitentiary. Federal officials would tip off local police, and the asset would be caught with a load of drugs and arrested. He would be prosecuted for the very activity that he had been conducting under the aegis of a federal government agency (Robert Blurton, personal correspondence, November 28, 2005).

In the mid-1970s Hemming did the unthinkable: he began speaking publicly about some of the CIA's most secret operations—political assassinations. In addition to testifying before the Senate Church Committee, he gave an interview in 1976 to *Argosy* magazine in which he outlined how the agency had used a front company—Bell Mortgage—to finance murder operations against President Salvador Allende of Chile and Panamanian leader Omar Torrijos. When asked by *Argosy* interviewer Dick Russell why, after all these years, he had decided to talk, Hemming stated: "I can still see the need for covert operations. But I can't see the FBI, CIA, or other government employees breaking the law. That's right around the corner from the Gestapo" (G. Hemming, e-mail to author, June 22, 2006; Russell 2006).

On August 23, 1976, while working directly with government agents, Gerry Hemming was arrested for drug smuggling and illegal transfer of a silencer. Subsequently, he was convicted of conspiracy to smuggle marijuana and sentenced to six months in prison. However, he remained free on appeal bond, and the conviction was later overturned (G. Hemming, telephone call, June 29, 2006).

In April, 1980, Hemming was arrested again for smuggling Quaaludes (methaqualone) into Florida. During his trial, Hemming named names; a 1982 issue of the *Miami Herald* reported Hemming was "trying unsuccessfully to convince a jury he had been working for the US government, infiltrating smuggling organizations." No one from any agency came forward to vouch for him.

The jury convicted Hemming, and he was given the maximum thirty-five-year sentence for smuggling drugs. He was released after serving eight years in the state penitentiary "on a chain-gang," he told the author with obvious bitterness ; G. Hemming, personal communication, June 29, 2006).

The tenuousness of the government's promises affected Fernandez, too. Although he had not been talking publicly, in April 1980, , he and two other crewmembers had flown a DC-6 loaded with new refrigerators and stoves to Barranquilla, Colombia. After offloading their cargo they departed for Florida. Shortly after takeoff they had a runaway propeller and couldn't maintain altitude. Fernandez declared an emergency, and they returned to Barranquilla Airport. Upon landing, the airplane was searched, and they were taken into custody by Colombian soldiers. No drugs or cargo were found. Still, despite their emergency, because they had not filed a flight plan for the emergency return, they were arrested and jailed for "violating Colombian airspace."

DEA agents visited Fernandez's wife and assured her that they would get Pete out of jail. Still, nothing happened. Only when she flew to Colombia and paid $19,000 to various people was Fernandez released. Once back in the United States, Fernandez arranged the release of his two crewmembers (Robert Blurton, e-mail correspondence, June 11, 2006; Jill Fernandez, personal communication, June 22, 2006).

On October 17, 1980, Pete Fernandez was killed in a predawn airplane crash on Grand Bahama Island. His cargo was high-grade marijuana that he was attempting to smuggle into the United States from Colombia. To the world press, this national hero had become a common criminal. His friends reserved judgment. After all, he had been a prime tactician in fighting the Soviet MiG-15s in the Korean air war. And it was a poorly kept secret that Fernandez had stolen a couple of Soviet-made airplanes for the CIA. Both his widow and Hemming verified that Fernandez was vehemently against the drug trade, which had directly touched his family.

But no one came forward to vouch for Fernandez's deep-cover status. Realistically, had any US government agency done so it could have jeopardized other "assets" in the field—as well as linked the incumbent Carter administration to active drug smuggling into the country (Robert Blurton, e-mail, June 11, 2006).

Interestingly, after Fernandez's fatal mishap, a nephew who was a Maryland police officer contacted the DEA to check on the rumors. He was told that an informant file for his uncle *did exist*, but that it was classified and therefore not releasable. Yet in a recent Freedom of Information Act request, a Fernandez relative was told by the CIA, FBI, and DEA that no files existed. While the files could have timed out and been purged, the author has found that many government agencies ignore, prevaricate, or obfuscate FOIA requests. In a 1980 *Miami Herald* article, Fernandez's widow reportedly was petrified with fear and told writer Fitz McAden, "I don't think I should talk about it." But much later in 2005 she told a close relative, "Pete was working for the CIA." When McAden questioned Broward County narcotics detective Nick Navarro, who was working on the case, he quoted Navarro as saying that Fernandez had been "helpful" in past drug investigations. Later, Detective Navarro refused (understandably) to elaborate (Robert Blurton, personal correspondence, November 28, 2005). In addition, an ex-DEA agent also confirmed Fernandez's deep-cover role in the drug-running airlift. But he is still active and cannot get involved.

Finale

As this case shows, working for the government "outside the law" with a complete lack of records was and remains a very hazardous undertaking. If arrested or killed while violating the law, friends or relatives have no way to prove you are bona fide. On October 27, 1980, high-scoring air-force jet ace, Major Manuel John Fernandez, age fifty-five, was buried in Arlington National cemetery—Section 60, grave site 1423. Yet after more than a quarter century, no agency files have been provided and no government official will verify that Fernandez was helping fight the war on drugs. Only his "cutout" Gerry Hemming and a few now-retired government agents have—guardedly—verified Pete's deep-cover status. To those of us who knew and respected this mild-mannered, fun-loving, dedicated Latino-American, he lived and died a true American warrior. Officially, he remains an uncertain hero.

Chapter 11

The Two-Place Sabre

A crash while demonstrating the new aircraft killed North American Aviation Inc. test pilot Joe Lynch and ultimately the badly needed Transonic Trainer.

THERE WAS NOTICEABLE EXCITEMENT ON the Nellis AFB flight line that late winter's day. It was March 17, 1954, and virtually the entire population of the air base had turned out to watch an aerial demonstration of two new North American Aviation (NAA) airplanes. Drawing only mild interest was the T-28B, a training aircraft with added potential, and a much more powerful engine than the A-model we had all flown in pilot training. The focus of the crowd's enthusiasm was centered on the newly minted two-place TF-86F Sabre, designated by its builder as the Transonic Trainer.

At "Fighter City," the Korean air war was still the principal topic of conversation. Hostilities had ended less than seven months earlier, and several of the jet aces were instructors at the renowned fighter-training center. Enhancing the Sabre's aura was that its pilots were still downing an occasional errant North Korean MiG-15. Thus the airplane's fame and our operational need for a two-place training version of this supersonic fighter generated significant interest.

A strong and cold thirty-knot northwest wind was blowing directly across the air base's two long runways. With gusts exceeding thirty-fiveknots, the wind made it too hazardous for student training and all flights had been cancelled. Instead we instructors brought our students to the flight line to watch these new aircraft perform. Because of the popularity of previous NAA F-86 flight demonstrations, flown by NAA test pilot R. A. (Bob) Hoover, many of the instructors' and students' wives had come too.

To ensure a clear view of the flying demonstration I brought my students to an area near the base operations building, where the two new airplanes were parked. A small crowd had gathered around the two-place Sabre, and pilot Joe Lynch was explaining the new aircraft's features. Captain Curtis Utterback, operations officer for the Ninety-sixth Fighter Training Squadron, asked Lynch if he could go along on the demonstration flight. But Lynch was heard to say, "No, can't do that on a demo, cause I might bust my ass."

The T-28B started the show, but the classic barrel roll after liftoff seemed unlikely in the high winds. Because the winds did not favor either runway, the demo pilot had chosen to depart from runway 03L. This would put his takeoff performance in front of the midfield crowd.

After liftoff he delayed maneuvering for a moment. Then with the landing gear retracting he rolled smartly into the crosswind. He dished out of the roll badly, and we all gasped as the aircraft barely missed smacking the runway. Still the pilot went on to perform a spectacular display of the airplane's capabilities.

As the T-28B landed, Lynch taxied the TF-86F for departure. With the Sabre requiring more takeoff distance, this would put his midfield liftoff almost in front of the main body of spectators. After lining up on the runway, Lynch held the brakes at full power for a moment, then released them and began his takeoff roll down the 10,123-foot runway.

He delayed nosewheel liftoff—a ploy to gain airspeed for the expected aileron roll—and, once airborne, hesitated for a moment, as if unsure because of the wind conditions. Finally, as the landing gear retracted, he began rolling left into the gusting wind and toward the assembled crowd. As he passed vertical his roll seemed to slow. It continued until the aircraft was almost inverted then stopped. Apparently changing his mind, Lynch began reversing the roll. But as the aircraft neared a vertical position again, the airframe visibly shuddered. The aircraft had stalled. Then in a steep left bank, as if in slow motion, the ship's nose dropped slowly, and the airplane arched downward and crashed in a giant fireball on the adjoining tarmac—almost directly in front of the base operations building.

The accident cast a pall on the badly needed transonic trainer program, and most of us felt the concept was dead. But six days later, on March 23, 1954, the air force authorized a second prototype. While the first aircraft had no guns or wing stations for practice bombs, this aircraft would have two .50-caliber machine guns with one hundred rounds of ammunition per gun. And, since the Sabre had already assumed a fighter-bomber role in Korea, there would be underwing racks for practice bombs. This news renewed our enthusiasm: it appeared there was still a chance for the badly needed two-place Sabre.

Background

By the end of hostilities in Korea, the Sabre models A, E, and F had compiled an outstanding record as both a fighter interceptor and fighter-bomber. In the interceptor role the three Sabre fighter wings had scored 792 MiG-15 kills, while losing only seventy-eight Sabres to MiGs. Because of the war, certain training and proficiency requirements had been waived. But now, in a peacetime environment, there was a distinct need for a two-place version: not only for the checkout phase in initial pilot training but also for the monthly and annual instrument flying practice that was becoming more important as the service became a truly all-weather air force.

Checking out a new pilot in the single-seat airplane had proved to be risky business. In fighter squadrons worldwide, semiannual instrument proficiency checks were performed by an instructor pilot who followed in a separate aircraft and evaluated the individual's instrument procedures while watching for other air traffic at the same time.

At Nellis AFB and later Williams AFB, Arizona, where F-86 crew training was conducted, both students and instructors were forced to practice instrument flying in a two-place Lockheed T-33 "T-Bird." The only similarity between the T-Bird and the Sabre was a jet engine. For an instructor who had been teaching the F-86 all year to be suddenly forced to fly this unfamiliar aircraft was impractical. Many times the instrument training was only halfheartedly accomplished.

Yet the importance of proficiency in instrument flying would become evident when the new Sabre pilot was transferred to Germany, South Korea, or Japan, where the weather could be quite challenging.

Sabre students and instructors had to fly the obsolete T-33 for instrument flying practice.

Transonic Trainer History

During its brief tenure, the TF-86F proved to be an exceptional airplane. The concept of training in type—later called "lead-in training" in fighters or bombers—had been established in undergraduate pilot training, with the use of the two-place Lockheed T-33A and single-cockpit F-80.

The two-place Sabre had been formally conceptualized on February 3, 1953. Then on April 8, 1953, North American Aviation issued the construction order as project NA 204. On July 9, this proposal went to Air Material Command with the suggestion that an F-86F-30 be modified by splicing an identical cockpit behind the pilot's seat and moving the wing forward eight inches. Length of the aircraft would be extended from thirty-seven feet six inches to forty-two feet nine inches, with an elongated clamshell canopy added. All standard F-86 features were to be retained, including the aerodynamically operated leading-edge slats. However, this first prototype aircraft would not have the six .50-caliber machine guns. Utilizing the same J-47-GE-27 engine, the trainer version was to be essentially identical to the F-86F.

On September 9, 1953, Air Material Command authorized the conversion of F-86F-30, serial number 52-5016. NAA engineers were ready, and on December 14 the airplane made its first flight. The rear cockpit gave the instructor all he would need to fly the aircraft. The only item missing was the emergency landing gear extension handle.

Performance of the new trainer proved superior to the single-seat model. The single-place Sabre was rated at 595 knots (688 mph), with a sea-level rate of climb of 9,300 feet per minute and a service ceiling of 48,000 feet. The trainer version had a top speed of 600 knots (692 mph), a sea-level rate of climb of 10,300 feet per minute, and a service ceiling of 50,500 feet. And it too was supersonic in a dive.

The TF-86F's rear cockpit was identical to the front, lacking only the emergency landing gear extension lanyard.

The Accident Aftermath

Officially, the explanation of the crash was that the airplane needed more vertical tail to improve controllability. In fact the need for a larger tail had been documented in the initial tests, and the dorsal fin had been enlarged. Concurrently, at Nellis AFB, after nearly the entire base witnessed the fatal accident, five combat crew students, already spooked by the base's unreal accident history, turned in their wings.

When the second TF-86F prototype was authorized, the production number chosen was serial number 53-1228, the last of the F-86F-35 models. This aircraft too was to be the same as the first, except for an enlarged tail and dorsal fin and two .50-caliber machine guns. It flew for the first time on August 5, 1954. A month later it began a series of demonstrations at various air force training bases.

Finale

On January 31, 1955, the TF-86F was assigned to the 3595th Combat Crew Training Wing for testing and evaluation. During this period, the author was tasked with evaluating the aircraft for use as a jet instrument trainer. It proved to be excellent in all respects. The elongated fuselage improved the airplane's already good longitudinal stability. Best of all it was equipped with the new high frequency visual omni-range (VOR) navigation system that was badly needed to supplement the unreliable and dated low-frequency automatic direction finder (ADF) "coffee grinder."

While the two-place Sabre concept was very popular, the Transonic Trainer was not to be. By the time this second prototype TF-86F was flying, the much faster afterburner-equipped F-100A Super Sabre was being delivered to Nellis AFB. The F-100 had a reputation for dangerous handling qualities. In fact on October 12, 1954, NAA test pilot George Welch had been killed during routine controllability flight tests. On February 7, 1955, the air force committed to buy the two-place TF-100F—later re-designated the F-100F. The lone TF-86F was then transferred to the 6515th Maintenance Group, Air Research and Development Command, at Edwards AFB, California. There, for the next six years, it was used as a chase plane by both the air force and NASA.

In March 1961, the TF-86F was declared surplus by the Air Force Sacramento Air Material Area. It was then disposed of and dropped from the inventory of air force airplanes. Rumor is that it was acquired by an aircraft manufacturer and used as a chase plane until being lost in an accident some years later.

At the time, the two-place TF-86F Transonic Trainer was the most advanced jet trainer available. It would have been an excellent replacement for the obsolete T-33A, used for many years in air force undergraduate pilot training. Best of all, it offered the potential for lead-in training for fighter-type aircraft to student pilots destined to fly jet fighters. But for those who needed its capabilities, the Transonic Trainer quickly became a fond memory.

Chapter 12

Midair Collision

On April 21, 1958, an F-100F on a local instrument-training mission out of Nellis AFB, Nevada, collided with Denver-bound United Airlines Flight 736.

THE EARLY MORNING INSTRUMENT-TRAINING FLIGHT was the student's first time "under the hood." With an instructor manning the front seat of the new two-place F-100F Super Sabre, the mission was designed to accustom the student fighter-pilot to the aircraft's sensitive flight-control feel while flying solely by reference to the flight instruments. This was to prepare him for bad weather and night flying in more changeable climates.

An instructor and student prepare for an instrument-training flight in an F-100F.

The mission profile called for some basic practice maneuvers followed by an instrument approach procedure into Nellis AFB. The approach involved an automatic direction finder (ADF) teardrop penetration from high altitude, utilizing local commercial radio station KRAM for the approach.

Weather that day was typical for arid Nevada—clear with thirty-five miles visibility. They were airborne as scheduled at 0745, with the student assuming control once the landing gear retracted and the afterburner of the J-57 engine was shut down.

The airplane's high indicated airspeeds, combined with the pitch sensitivity of its hydraulically operated flight controls, took practice to master. To help a pilot get the feel of the aircraft, the climb to altitude involved pegging the airspeed at Mach 0.67 at five thousand feet, Mach 0.7 at ten thousand feet, then leveling at thirty thousand feet holding Mach 0.82. For the following half hour he was to practice maintaining 280 knots indicated airspeed while maneuvering with basic flight instruments. Other maneuvers involved normal thirty-degree banked turns and steep forty-five-degree banked turns, along with maintaining altitude while changing airspeeds from a slow 220 knots to Mach 0.9. (Note: altitudes are specified since flight levels beginning at eighteen thousand feet had not yet been established.)

Once basic instrument practice was completed, the instructor selected the appropriate UHF frequency for Nellis VFR Approach Control (visual flight rules, otherwise known as "see or be seen") and requested an altitude assignment from which their practice KRAM jet penetration and low approach would begin. (Note: Nellis VFR Approach Control *was not* part of the Nellis control tower's air traffic control operation. The VFR controller was simply a jet-instrument instructor acting as an unofficial approach controller.)

The commercial station was used for practice instrument approaches into Nellis because KRAM's stronger signal offered greater accuracy than the obsolescing low-frequency radio range. An ADF procedure was necessary because trying to fly the published legs of the LAS radio using dots and dashes to signal an off-course position was impractical in the fast-moving jet fighters. The commercial radio station was located very near the Las Vegas radio range (LAS), which was used in bad weather for low-frequency instrument approaches into McCarran Field—the municipal airport (now classed as an international airport). LAS radio was also an important navigation point along the low-altitude AMBER-2 airway. In addition, the high-altitude Victor 8 Airway passed almost overtop LAS and Nellis AFB.

F-100 turns inbound to track the final ADF approach course to Nellis AFB.

The penetration descent involved departing from the initial approach fix—KRAM—on an outbound heading that was offset to the southeast of the inbound course. After losing roughly half the altitude, the pilot turned back through the airways to intercept the inbound track to the airbase. All this was well within established air traffic control's (ATC) airspace. The entire procedure was to be done under VFR.—

At their call, Nellis VFR Control promptly directed Sabre 755 to descend to and maintain twenty-eight thousand feet. This would be the altitude from which their letdown procedure would begin. At 0828 hours Sabre 755 reported over KRAM at twenty-eight thousand feet whereupon the VFR controller cleared them for an immediate jet penetration; with a request that they report completing the penetration turn.

Three minutes later, at 0831, Nellis VFR Control heard a weak but clear call, "Mayday, Mayday, this is 755, we've had a flameout." (The last word could have been *bailout* but the investigator wasn't certain.)

United Flight 736/21

United Flight 736—a Douglas DC-7—had departed Los Angeles with a crew of five and forty-two passengers. The ultimate destination of the transcontinental flight was New York City, with intermediate stops in Denver, Kansas City, and Washington National. For the Denver leg they were assigned twenty-one thousand feet along the Victor-8 airway, which as noted previously, ranged overhead both Las Vegas and Nellis AFB.

After reporting over Daggett at 0811 hours, they advised Los Angeles Center they were estimating LAS at 0831. Their next message was, "United 736, MAYDAY, midair collision over Las Vegas." No other transmissions were heard, nor did the crew respond to repeated calls.

The Collision

Approaching each other on a near-head-on collision course, the two aircraft had an estimated closing airspeed of 665 knots (765 mph). Just prior to impact, the F-100F instructor pilot apparently saw the DC-7, and in a desperate effort to avoid the collision, while pitching down about seventeen degrees, he made a frantic last second ninety-degree bank to the left. Nevertheless the right wing of the descending jet fighter clipped off eight feet of the DC-7's right wing, causing both aircraft to go out of control.

144

Trailing black smoke and flames, the DC-7 spiraled earthward in a near vertical descent, crashing just south of McCarran Field—almost exactly on course for the Victor-8 Airway. The F-100F, with its right wing and right horizontal stabilizer torn off, corkscrewed down violently and impacted in the desert south-southwest of McCarran Field. Despite having ejection seats, neither of the military pilots survived. Investigators felt the two fighter pilots failed to eject due to either injury in the collision or disorientation caused by the erratic tumbling of the aircraft.

Accident Board Findings

The Civil Aeronautics Board (CAB)—the predecessor organization to the National Transportation Safety Board (NTSB)—stated the probable cause was the human limitations caused by restricted cockpit visibility in both aircraft and the very high rate of closure in the near-head-on collision.

The military accident board had one primary finding, along with two factors that contributed to the mishap. The primary cause of the accident was listed as "inadequacy of the present control system which allows two or more aircraft to occupy the same airspace at the same time and relies solely on the ability of the individual pilots to see and avoid one another."

The two contributing factors included the high rate of closure of present day aircraft, "which exceeds the limits of human visual clearance while flying under VFR (visual) conditions." They felt too that "the pilots of both aircraft could have been preoccupied with normal crew duties which diverted their attention." The second contributing factor was the limitations to visibility "caused by the cockpit enclosures which restrict the pilot's visibility at certain angles" (USAF Accident Report, April 21, 1958).

The ATC Factor

In the spring of 1954, the author, then assigned to the Nellis AFB jet instrument school, was tasked with establishing Nellis VFR Approach

Control. It was not to be associated with the Nellis ATC system but had the sole mission of segregating military T-33 instrument-training flights to avoid midair collisions. (The F-100F did not become a factor until 1957.) In due time, VFR control of the jet-instrument-training flights was established at the base; however, it was immediately obvious that because of the civil airway traffic over Nellis, something was missing in the safety of our operation.

Because three airways intersected almost overhead of the airbase, and actual instrument approaches into both McCarran Field and Nellis AFB were accomplished using LAS radio range or VOR procedures, I went to the control tower at McCarran Field to discuss coordinating our VFR (visual) jet-instrument-training flights with the ATC tower chief. Because we were all using established federal airspace and the published ATC instrument approach procedures, it seemed important to have some means of coordinating our numerous training flights with the civilian air traffic flow.

The tower chief took me to his office on the floor beneath the tower cab and closed the door. When I briefly explained my mission, he exploded like a class six thunderstorm. "I won't have anything to do with a harebrained VFR approach control," he screamed. I was flabbergasted. While I was only a first lieutenant, I had never been screamed at by another adult in such a hostile manner. When I attempted to further explain the safety aspects, he went into a red-faced rage. Stabbing his finger toward his office door, he screamed, "Get out of my office with your stupid proposal!" With that, I departed, more or less with my tail between my legs. I was aghast at both his attitude and unconscionable behavior.

Legal Aftermath

A total of thirty-one lawsuits were filed seeking damages from either or both the US government and United Airlines. On September 24, 1958, based on the Federal Tort Claims Act, United Airlines filed for damages in the US District Court for the District of Delaware. The airline claimed the United States, through its agents in the US Air Force, was negligent in the operation of the F-100F and sought $3,576,698 in damages. The court found neither crew was negligent for a failure to see and avoid each other, but found the United States was liable "because of other negligence." Ultimately, on December 17, 1962, the United States settled with United Airlines for $1.45 million.

On January 8, 1964, the surviving relatives of two of the United Airlines crew were each awarded $343,200 from the government, with US District Court Judge Hatfield Chilson finding the "Air Force pilots did not use 'ordinary care' in operation of the jet fighter, and should have yielded right of way to the DC-7 airliner. *Judge Chilson also criticized the Air Force for not coordinating instrument training flights with civilian instrument flight rules traffic, and for failing to schedule flights to minimize traffic congestion*" (Wikipedia, July 14, 2011, emphasis added).

The accident of course resulted in an agreement requiring close coordination of air traffic between Nellis AFB and the ATC system. But forty-seven innocent people had to die to make it happen. Meanwhile, the Nellis AFB flying-safety officer—a captain who had flown combat in Korea—resigned his commission and went home to Wyoming to teach school. He told me later, "John, I just got tired of picking up body parts."

Chapter 13

The Ultimate Test

A night dead-stick landing with weather at minimums challenged the AT-28B pilot with the ultimate test of humanitarianism, flying skill, and courage.

IT WAS A DARK, FOGGY evening when air force Captain John L. Piotrowski departed on a short flight to reposition an AT-28B from the First Air Commando Wing based at Hurlburt Field, to nearby Eglin Air Force Base, Florida. The date was March 6, 1964, and the aircraft was needed the following day for new weapons tests. As a founding member and by now a thoroughly vetted combat veteran of the air force's new Air Commando Wing, Captain Piotrowski had been busy testing new weapons in the B-26 that were needed for use in the insurgency in South Vietnam. Because it had been eighty-nine days since he'd last flown the AT-28B, his qualifications in the single-engine aircraft would expire the next day. Going "noncurrent" necessitated a time-consuming flight manual review, along with a recheck with an instructor pilot—not to mention causing unnecessary use of their limited inventory of aircraft. Because he was involved in testing weapons in both aircraft, combined with periodic classified operational assignments in Vietnam, despite the foggy weather, he was strongly motivated to complete the flight to Eglin so that work could begin the next day.

The original North American Aviation Inc. T-28A was designed as an air force advanced-pilot-training aircraft and equipped with an 800 horsepower, R-1300 engine. The later T-28B was a navy pilot-training aircraft, but with a larger 1,425 horsepower, Wright R-1820 engine. The AT-28B assigned to the Air Commando's was a modified version of the navy trainer, which included two wing-mounted .50-caliber machine guns, two bomb racks on each wing, along with external fuel tank connections for use when island hopping to classified foreign destinations. It was intended for use by South Vietnamese pilots as both a trainer for their air force pilots, and, when loaded with weapons, as a fighter-bomber against infiltrating North Vietnamese forces. In reality, the AT-28B's capabilities made it a trainer on steroids.

Weather Check

Dutifully, Captain Piotrowski checked the weather and found both Hurlburt and Eglin plagued by an extensive overcast limiting the ceiling to two hundred feet, with fog restricting forward visibility to half a mile. This kind of weather was perfect for a ground-controlled approach and landing for a two-engine transport, but absolute anathema to a single-engine fighter pilot. Despite delaying his departure for the weatherman's optimistic prediction of some improvement later, after a two-hour wait, the ceiling was holding firm at two hundred feet. Meanwhile, a new official forecast showed no improvement for the next few hours.

At the time, all fighter pilots resisted flying in either weather or at night; but by now that was all Piotrowski had left. With the closest alternate in east Texas, he had the fuel tanks filled and dutifully taxied to the departure runway. Instead of a clearance direct to Eglin AFB, Air Traffic Control (ATC) cleared him to hold (orbit) nine thousand feet on a fix near Crestview, Florida—there to await his turn, as higher priority traffic made their approaches into Eglin AFB.

In-Flight Emergency

He departed to the south over the Gulf of Mexico; but as he turned toward the assigned holding fix, the red "ENGINE FAILURE" light blinked, then came on steady. While the light was designed to indicate the engine was about to fail, experience had shown that enough metal particles had accumulated in the ship's oil supply to activate the light and necessitate an immediate landing. Thus he declared an emergency and requested a priority approach and landing at Eglin AFB.

"They vectored me from a position on the west-side of Fort Walton Beach to just north of Eglin for a tight turn to final onto the North/South runway—just what I was hoping for. Shortly thereafter the engine quit—as in stopped running altogether," explained the hapless pilot. "I figured I was over the center of the urban area and bailing out of the aircraft at this point would result in significant damage in the city below and undoubtedly kill several people...The plane and I were going down as I attempted several air-starts."

He quickly declared a couple of Maydays and asked for a vector to the center of Eglin's north/south runway, hoping to find a clear area around the runway upon breaking out of the overcast. "They gave me a vector and cleared me down to five hundred feet: whereupon I reminded them 'the engine's not running. I'm coming all the way to the ground.

Advise the tower to get the fire trucks ready: I'm carrying a full load of fuel.'

"The weather forecast had been right, as I broke out of the overcast at two hundred feet, right over the top of a B-52's vertical tail fin at the north end of the [Eglin AFB] runway—the SAC (Strategic Air Command) Victor Alert area—where the bombers were sitting loaded with nuclear weapons in case of war. With the landing gear now extended and a quick right descending turn, I landed on the parallel taxiway—and the engine sputtered to life. So I taxied in to base operations."

The next morning, maintenance personnel replaced the contaminated oil and accomplished several engine runs to full power. Still, they could find nothing wrong. On the maintenance form 781, the engine technician wrote the dreaded words, "could not duplicate."

Convinced that Captain Piotrowski had simply faked the red light and engine failure as an excuse to get priority handling, the maintenance officer called and asked him numerous questions. Although the maintenance staff remained unconvinced that the engine failure emergency was legitimate, just to be cautious, the aircraft was scheduled for a functional test flight.

The test pilot called and again asked Captain Piotrowski for all the details of his supposed engine failure. Yet despite the pilot's continued skepticism, instead of the usual midfield departure with an AT-28 that required only a small portion of the runway, he lined up for takeoff at the very end of the base's fifteen-thousand-foot long runway. Then he pushed the throttle forward to its full fifty-two inches of manifold pressure and began gathering speed. Suddenly, the ship's engine blew apart, scattering parts and debris on the runway as it rolled to a stop.

Finale

Realistically, during that era, a fighter pilot flying an instrument approach to minimums in a single-engine aircraft was considered a major accomplishment. And to accomplish it at night, most fighter pilots would have been classed as deserving a Distinguished Flying Cross. But to lose the engine at night, with weather at published minimums, and not bail out to save yourself, was truly the ultimate test of skill, intestinal fortitude and concern for his fellow man. Still, there would be no DFC, no Flight Safety "Well Done" Award; not even an *attaboy* from his wing commander. After all, it had happened past quitting time, and nobody in Captain Piotrowski's chain of command apparently knew of his spectacular accomplishment. Then too, considering his job of weapons development and testing, combined with periodic (clandestine) combat assignments, the risk involved with a night weather flight for the dedicated air commando captain actually had been just another day at the office.

Still, it was this same skill combined with intelligence, courage, and humanitarianism that led him to greater career achievements: he became the Vice Chief of Staff of the US Air Force and later served four years as commander of US Space Command—ultimately retiring with thirty-eight years of service.

Chapter 14

Functional Check Flight

A quick test flight to verify operation of the F-105D
Thunderchief's pitch trim system proved to be challenging.

IT WAS MONDAY, MARCH 1, 1965, near quitting time at Seymour-Johnson AFB, North Carolina. Maintenance control had just called the quality control flight test section of the Fourth Tactical Fighter Wing to ask whether F-105D, tail number 91750, required a test flight. The aircraft was being used at low altitudes for weapons training and qualification on the Matagorda Island gunnery range. Pilots on the last three flights had reported an abnormal pitch-trim response.

Regulations at the time stipulated that any work done on the flight controls required a functional check flight (FCF). Yet the technicians were stumped. They simply couldn't find anything wrong. Thus, each of the complaints had been signed off as "could not duplicate."

At the time, I was the newly appointed chief of maintenance quality control. It was tempting to make an aircraft available to a squadron because we were always hurting for mission-capable airplanes. However, because this situation involved flight controls, my immediate response when asked if a flight test was required was *yes*. A trim and flight-control check could be performed in less than twenty minutes, but over time I concluded that functional checks of jet fighters should last at least an hour and include time in subzero temperatures at high altitude. Cold-soaking aloft often revealed problems that might otherwise go undetected. Therefore, except for a Mach-2 run, I planned to complete a full test flight as itemized by the test card (itemized list of systems tests).

A complete test involved verifying operation of the stability augmentation and autopilot systems, along with a check of engine parameters at ten-thousand-foot levels to forty thousand feet. Then, after slowing to 220 knots, the engine afterburner was selected to verify reliable ignition and to check for compressor stalls. This was followed by acceleration to Mach 1.48 to see that the air data computer (ADC) unlocked the engine inlet duct plugs.

Certain heavy maintenance actions, such as structural repair, required testing to Mach 2 in a clean configuration (no external pylon tanks or bomb racks). During a Mach-2 speed check, upon achieving Mach 1.48, the duct-plugs began moving forward slowly as the Mach number increased, and were fully forward upon reaching Mach 2. This kept the engine inlet airflow smooth and helped prevent compressor stalls upon reaching Mach 2.

Upon reaching Mach 2, the pilot was checking the engine for smooth operation and the engine inlet duct plugs for full forward movement in the airscoops. This was accomplished with the throttle against the forward stop, since a power reduction at that speed precipitated severe compressor stalls.

The supersonic run was performed at thirty-seven thousand feet in a designated high-speed corridor to prevent the shockwave hitting an inhabited area and breaking windows. The remaining test requirements were completed at low altitude with a high-speed check of the toss bomb computer (TBC), followed by an autopilot-coupled *Instrument Landing System (ILS)* approach and landing. The goal of the test, of course, was to provide the line pilot with a fully functioning combat-ready airplane.

The Thunderchief

The F-105D Thunderchief was one of the first of the sophisticated, nuclear-capable fighter-bombers. The aircraft's size, weight, and sophistication actually made it a weapons system rather than fighter-bomber. With a top speed in the upper atmosphere of Mach 2.13, and 810 knots at low altitude, its primary mission was to deliver a tactical nuclear weapon on relatively short-range targets in Europe and East Asia.

To accomplish this with a single crewmember, it had a multifunction autopilot and radar with several features, the most useful being the ground-map mode. For the nuclear mission, it had a bomb bay that provided internal carriage of a nuclear weapon, enclosed by automatic, hydraulically operated doors. Loaded with conventional weapons for an interdiction role, and two wing-pylon tanks with extra fuel, its takeoff weight was typically fifty-three thousand pounds. This included eight externally mounted 750-pound World War II–era bombs, along with a six-barrel twenty-millimeter M-61 cannon. With an astounding rate of fire of six thousand rounds per minute, the cannon was General Electric's modernized version of the Civil War–era Gatling gun.

The single J-75-P-19W engine produced 24,500 pounds of thrust in afterburner (2,000 pounds more if water injection was used). During a bomb run at low altitude, this routinely pushed a fully loaded airplane to 550 KIAS (633 mph) and up to 810 knots (930 mph) once the bombs were delivered.

After takeoff, the autopilot could fly automatically to the waypoints set in the Doppler navigation system. At high speed, using radar and the TBC, the autopilot could deliver a nuclear weapon with a 4-G toss and roll out on top of the half-loop—an Immelmann. Then, if desired, the autopilot would steer the aircraft to the escape waypoint set in the Doppler. Integrated with and controlled by the air data computer (ADC), the TBC could deliver the bomb to within seven hundred yards of the designated target. (A direct hit was deemed unnecessary because it was designed for a nuclear weapon. Later upgrades with Thunderstick II improved its accuracy considerably.) The ADC was actually the brain of the entire weapons system and processed, among other things, outside air temperature, ram air inlet pressure, and static inputs from the pitot tube to give calibrated airspeed to the TBC and the pilot's vertical-tape flight instruments.

Although there was a computing sight for dive-bombing with conventional weapons, it was never perfected or used. Instead, pilots relied on a manual sight, with depression preset based on the planned dive angle and anticipated release altitude.

F-105D cockpit shows the vertical tape flight instruments and its array of capabilities.

To deliver a nuclear weapon, the pilot would have a designated initial identification point (IP) that would show prominently on the radar some nine miles prior to the target. With "auto toss" selected on the TBC, and the engine afterburner engaged, upon acquiring the IP at the proper airspeed—normally 550 knots (633 mph)—the pilot pressed the bomb release button on the control stick. This started the TBC—indicated by a green light on the gunsight. At the proper time and range, the autopilot began a 4-G pull for the Immelmann/toss maneuver.

In auto-toss mode, the autopilot kept the cross pointers in the attitude director indicator (artificial horizon) centered like those in an ILS landing system. When performing a manual toss, the horizontal bar told the pilot how he was doing relative to the 4-G pull required by the TBC. The vertical steering bar indicated the ship's azimuth relative to the target. Ideally they were both kept centered as in an ILS (instrument landing system) approach until a red annunciator light and an easily felt *thump* indicated the bomb released. Once the bomb released, the autopilot rolled the aircraft wings level and, if desired, proceeded toward the escape waypoint set on the Doppler navigation system.

Back at home base, the autopilot could lock on to the instrument landing system and perform a coupled (automatic) ILS approach to weather minimums. At that point, the pilot took over for landing. With landing flaps set and about fifteen hundred pounds of fuel, the typical landing threshold speed was 190 knots—or, if you were heavier, 215 to 225 knots. Because of these landing speeds, getting stopped required a drag chute, or you'd end up in the hot-brake area with the risk to ground crews of exploding tires.

Flyer Beware

Over time I became wary when testing the Thunderchief. The aircraft's marvel of electronic systems produced all manner of strange and integrated problems. For example, the original pitch damper would occasionally cause a sudden un-commanded nose-down pitch. At high airspeed and low altitude, this was very disconcerting. For safety reasons, the air force and the manufacturer, Republic Aviation, quickly eliminated the feature from the system. The yaw damper could also—without warning—produce a hard full left or right rudder deflection. This flaw led to a number of ejections, and was suspected in a couple of fatal accidents.

Still other problems surfaced in the maintenance of the sophisticated airplane. After completing the high-altitude FCF requirements, I would typically descend to five thousand feet to check the TBC and practice a few aerobatic maneuvers. A loop was typically initiated using afterburner at five thousand feet altitude. With a 4-G pull at 550 knots, the aircraft usually topped out at around fifteen thousand feet and 150–175 knots. At this point the afterburner was disengaged, and with a 4–5-G pull in the recovery, the aircraft would be level again at five thousand feet.

Yet on occasion, at the very top of the loop, as the nose started down, the airspeed tape would pulsate wildly (an ADC malfunction) then settle on 550 knots instead of the actual 150 knots. This called for immediate action. With the ADC showing 550 knots, this repositioned the continuously variable mechanical advantage shifter (CVMAS). The CVMAS was designed to prevent inadvertent airframe overstress at high indicated airspeeds. It did so by proportionally limiting the available pitch authority of the horizontal stabilizers as the indicated airspeed increased. At 550 knots, the stabilizers were at their maximum limitation. But to recover from the top of a loop, full throw of the stabilizers could be required. (There were no elevators, only the solid horizontal stabilizers—the slabs—for pitch control.)

To recover from this airspeed malfunction, and avoid boring a large hole in the ground, required an immediate roll upright. Or, if you were already descending on the back side of the loop, you quickly reduced power to idle and, with speed brakes extended, pulled energetically on the control stick while cross-checking the altimeter.

A related malfunction, which quickly got your attention, involved the auto-toss maneuver. At 550 knots, as the pull-up began for the bomb delivery, the autopilot would sometimes begin "hunting" for the programmed 4-G pull—often with violent, rapid pitch oscillations. Because of the aircraft's high airspeed, this frequently caused the wing-pylon tanks to separate, usually resulting in major damage to the ship's aft section. This malfunction is thought to have killed a Republic Aviation test pilot flying a live weapons test out of Eglin AFB, Florida. Because of the hazard and the uncertainty of correcting the problem, most F-105D-equipped fighter wings forbade use of the auto-toss mode. Instead, nuclear-weapons delivery was practiced manually.

160

Yet another attention-getter on a Thunderchief maintenance flight test was the autopilot-coupled ILS landing approach. When it worked, the auto-ILS was a thing of beauty. But after extensive avionics maintenance, it sometimes malfunctioned. When engaged in the approach mode, the autopilot would take over the flight controls smoothly and proceed to intercept the centerline radial. Then, at fifteen hundred feet altitude in landing configuration (landing gear and flaps extended), as it captured the centerline radial and the glide-slope needle became active, it would suddenly roll the aircraft inverted. At such a low altitude this invariably doubled one's pulse rate and precipitated a loud exclamation (oath) or practice scream.

The Porpoise

On this clear March day, as I continued the FCF, the flight controls and trim on the aircraft—call sign Test 750—had functioned normally at low altitudes and high speeds. The climb to altitude had been routine. However, at forty thousand feet, while accelerating through Mach 0.98 for the supersonic run, I thought I felt a slight pitch undulation—a *porpoise*. Or was it my imagination? Maybe the pylon tanks caused it. I wasn't sure. As the aircraft continued accelerating to Mach 1.48, the flight controls felt normal. Once the duct plugs unlocked and began pulsating, I disengaged the afterburner. At cruise power, I allowed the aircraft slow to Mach 0.9.

With the test card complete, I descended to ten thousand feet with the intent of practicing some aerobatic maneuvers. At 450 knots, in level unaccelerated flight, the aircraft suddenly began to porpoise wildly. Simply touching the control stick caused the large horizontal stabilizers to audibly hit the stops in both the nose-up and nose-down position. My nylon seat belt had worked loose at the adjustment buckles. Consequently, the undulating pitch forces threw me wildly about the cockpit, with my helmet bouncing off the canopy and mercifully protecting my head.

Based on past experience, I suspected the autopilot was involved. After managing to locate the selector switches in the bucking bronco, I shut off all electrical power. Still, the wild oscillations continued, with the stabilizers still audibly slamming from stop to stop. Now the problem was isolated to the hydraulic flight controls. Obviously this was very serious.

I restored electrical power and informed the tower of my location and the problem. To activate the search and rescue helicopter, I advised them to notify the command post to expect an ejection. Emotionally I was in a state of disbelief. Despite flying a variety of aircraft with the hydraulically operated flight controls, I never before had one become uncontrollable. I checked the right-hand ejection seat lever to make certain I had removed the safety pin before takeoff. Then I just sat there, riding the bucking bronco, trying to think what else could be done.

In a last ditch effort to regain control, and with the airspeed tape still showing over four hundred knots, I deployed the speed brakes and decelerated to two hundred knots. Hopefully this would reduce the slabs' effectiveness and mollify the vicious pitching action. It worked: at two hundred knots the pitching became tolerable.

By experimenting, I discovered that the slightest back pressure on the control stick increased the pitching amplitude, with an audible *boom* in the aft section, as the slabs hit the *up* stops. Finally I tried the small stick-grip override toggle switch located on the left side console (an alternate trim switch). By making pitch adjustments with the toggle switch instead of the control stick, the oscillations ended, and the aircraft resumed flying smoothly. Now the problem was how to land the dangerous beast.

Since my only means of control was the small alternate trim toggle switch, I decided to try a large circling pattern with a long final approach. I radioed the tower: "Test 750 will attempt one landing approach, and if unsuccessful I'll eject when clear of the air base!"

Descending through eight thousand feet, I placed the landing gear handle down. As the gear extended, the center of gravity shift caused the nose to drop slightly. With my right hand still lightly gripping the control stick, I reflexively added a slight back pressure to the controls. The airplane immediately began to porpoise, with the slabs again audibly hitting the stops. To resist further such instinctive reactions, I removed my hand completely from the control stick and concentrated on the small override toggle switch. Once again the pitching subsided.

Seymour Johnson AFB (NC) tower had cleared the airfield for my landing attempt. In fact I could see the flashing red lights as the fire trucks and "meat wagon" (ambulance) moved into position near the runway.

With a high, wide, descending downwind leg, I flew a relatively flat, slightly fast, 200-knot final approach. The wide pattern allowed me the time needed to make the necessary pitch trim changes with the small toggle. Still, it was the landing flare that had me worried. My left hand was quite busy alternately managing the power lever, radio-transmitter button, speed-brake selector, and the small trim toggle switch. Once established in a landing attitude on the long final approach, the trim override was doing the job nicely as the runway's threshold stripes flashed by. Then, upon encountering ground effect close to the runway surface, the F-105D's nose dropped. Reflexively I tried to catch it with slight back pressure on control stick. Instantly the stabilizers hit the up stops with a loud *boom*. The aircraft pitched slightly, but the heavy fighter-bomber was out of energy.

Touchdown was smooth, and the drag chute deployed nicely and slowed the aircraft down. I taxied to the parking area surrounded by fire trucks and the ambulance. When I looked at the ship's clock I thought, *Nuts! I'll be late to dinner again.* Besides, I needed a shower and change of underwear.

Although it was now past quitting time, the maintenance quality control inspectors returned to examine my aircraft thoroughly. The problem was quickly identified as a frozen lubricator bolt in the stabilizer actuator bellcrank. This was exacerbated by internal failure of the stabilizer actuator servo pistons—probably the result of the long-term drag of the frozen bolt.

Because the airplane's flight controls were totally hydraulic, the pilot simply repositioned hydraulic valves to effect aerodynamic changes. To prevent over-controlling, an artificial feel system provided a normal flight control feel. However, in this case, once the aircraft cold-soaked at altitude, the frozen lubricator bolt caused the artificial feel system to drag, then release, resulting in over-positioning of the horizontal stabilizers.

The failed servo pistons were submitted for a design change through the air force's Emergency Unsatisfactory Report system. The frozen bolt was the result of mechanics skipping an item on the periodic maintenance checklist during several of the aircraft's required major inspections.

The author in an F-105D shortly after completing a successful maintenance test flight.

After the maintenance quality control inspectors had examined all eighty-two aircraft in the Fourth TFW fleet, three more were found with frozen lubricator bolts. The omitted checklist item was the result of undue pressure on the field maintenance squadron for a quick turn-around of the lengthy and detailed periodic maintenance inspection procedure.

The incident was best summarized by a saying in the maintenance organizations of that time: "If you want it bad, you get it bad."

Chapter 15

The Thunderchief at War

Dropping World War II–era iron bombs with the sophisticated F-105D was like hauling dirt in the back seat of a new Cadillac.

PICTURE IF YOU WILL THIS sleek Mach 2–capable all-weather fighter-bomber that flies one thousand feet above the ground on auto-pilot while a Doppler navigation system steers it to a target three to five hundred nautical miles distant. Then, at the proper time and airspeed, using inputs from the integrated air-data computer and toss-bomb computer, the ship's autopilot pulls it into a flawless 4-G Immelmann, whereupon the TBC tosses a nuclear weapon nine miles to strike within seven hundred yards of its designated target. Once the weapon releases, a silver-coated hood automatically snaps over the canopy to protect the pilot's eyes and face from the flash of the nuclear blast to follow.

Now picture this same sophisticated supersonic "tactical nuclear weapons delivery system," loaded externally with World War II bombs that were designed for *internal carriage* in four-engine World War II B-17s and B-24s. The pilot is to drop these bombs on a culvert—identified officially as a bridge—located within the heavily defended outskirts of Hanoi.

To avoid the enemy's defenses, the pilot flies the mission at very low altitude. Upon reaching a predesignated identification point (IP) at an airspeed of 550 knots, the pilot pulls the aircraft up through intense antiaircraft fire interspersed with surface-to-air SA-2 missiles, to a roll-in altitude of twelve thousand feet. Then he dive-bombs his assigned primary target—the *culvert*—located along a two-lane road within sight of a railroad yard where freight trains are bringing ammunition and missiles to resupply the enemy.

If the pilot attempts to shoot or destroy the trains, the enemy's antiaircraft gun emplacements, or the SA-2 missile sites, he will be court-martialed as a criminal. These are forbidden targets—to be hit only if and when specifically authorized by the president of the United States or his secretary of defense.

The nondescript targets—officially reported as directed by the Joint Chiefs of Staff—were usually selected at a weekly Tuesday luncheon attended only by President Lyndon Johnson, Defense Secretary Robert McNamara, Secretary of State Dean Rusk, and National Security Advisor McGeorge Bundy. The specific weapons to be used were selected by the secretary of defense, along with systems analysts and other civilian members of his own department and the Department of State. They devised their own strategy without benefit of advice from the military's Joint Chiefs, "who had the statutory responsibility as the nation's principal military advisors" (McMaster 1997, 88–90).

But that's not all: in an act of unbelievable treachery, in an interview with CBS correspondent Peter Arnett, for a documentary titled *The Ten Thousand Day War*, former Secretary of State Dean Rusk acknowledged that the administration was providing the forthcoming week's target list to the North Vietnamese because "we didn't want to harm the Vietnamese people." Thus, with technical and logistical assistance from the Soviets, the enemy could and did prepare for our arrival.

Sound unbelievable? It shouldn't, because it precisely describes the role, mission, and political treachery to which the F-105D Thunderchief and its pilots were subjected, in the bombing campaign against North Vietnam.

Background

As hostilities with North Vietnam escalated, fighter-bombers initially flew to their politically selected targets at around eighteen thousand feet then dive-bombed with relatively light resistance. Then the Soviet sponsors brought in their air defense system. This included a coordinated series of antiaircraft guns, radar-guided SA-2 surface-to-air missiles (SAMs) and MiG interceptors.

These antiaircraft assets were organized in a series of defensive rings, each about seventeen miles in diameter. The SAMs were located at the center, surrounded by a dense array of antiaircraft guns. An SA-2 battery usually contained two to six missiles. When and how these assets were used was orchestrated from a control van by a combat-ready interceptor pilot. This included Soviet-bloc, Chinese, Cuban, and North Korean "instructors."

Within the SAM ring, when the missiles were launching or antiaircraft artillery (AAA) was firing, every man or woman with a firearm was instructed to fire vertically into the air. This helped compensate for the fact that the SA-2s couldn't track a target below about fifteen hundred feet. Thus anything entering the circle at low altitude encountered a hailstorm of bullets emanating from the ground.

Then MiG interceptors were added to the mix. The controller in the van would instruct the guns and missiles to cease fire then direct the fighters into the SAM ring to intercept an intruding aircraft.

The air force leadership had repeatedly asked the Department of Defense (DoD) for permission to strike these new SAM sites before they became operational. But until the fall of 1965 the requests had been consistently denied. Finally, on October 31, 1965, two four-ship flights of F-105Ds, each carrying eight 750-pound bombs, and led by a navy A-4 armed with 500-pound bombs, were sent to destroy a *single* SAM-site near Hanoi. The navy aircraft was equipped with a rudimentary device that would home on the SA-2's "Fan Song" (search mode) radar emissions (Berger, n.d.). The A-4 pilot was to mark the site with his bombs, whereupon the F-105s would destroy the control van and missiles.

On this occasion, the A-4 pilot was Lieutenant Commander Trent R. Powers, executive officer of VA-164 squadron, flying from the USS *Oriskany*. Since it was a White House–directed mission, Powers knew it was dangerous. His plan was to fly directly across the site and skip-bomb the missiles. Since the F-105Ds had larger and more powerful bombs, the air force pilots preferred to pop up from low altitude at high speed, then dive-bomb the target.

Captain Gary Barnhill, flying the number-four aircraft in the second flight of that strike, remembers: "[During the run-in to the target,] I flew so low over a guy driving a tractor that he leapt to the ground. Then my plane was hit by small arms fire, causing some yellow caution lights to illuminate. Then Powers calmly transmitted, 'I've got 'em on my nose… starting my run.' He flew directly over the target at treetop level and was literally disintegrated by withering ground fire. I lit the [after] burner and popped up to about 7,500 feet with Powers emergency locator beacon screeching in my headset. During my brief dive-bomb run there was a sharp knocking sound, like a fist on a door. This was [more] enemy ground fire hitting the plane. The small arms fire caused multiple red [fire] and yellow emergency lights [on the annunciator panel] to blink incessantly."

With each pilot living his own individual hell and violently jinking (dodging from side to side) to get away from the unrelenting ground fire, Barnhill relates, "I departed the target area at 810 knots on the deck." Meanwhile, because of the fire warning lights, "I transmitted my intention to eject over the Gulf east of Haiphong" (Gary Barnhill, e-mail to author, September 14, 2004).

The enemy was clearly expecting the strike. Until that mission they had typically launched just one or two SA-2s at the fighter-bombers. Barnhill relates "They were firing SAMs like artillery. Fifteen is the number I remember. It's what they mean by *all hell broke loose*."

A SA-2 surface-to-air antiaircraft missile explodes and damages an F-105D in North Vietnam.

Fortunately, Captain Barnhill made it to the Gulf of Tonkin, where the navy would have surely rescued him. But the fire warning lights were now out, and after refueling from a KC-135 tanker, he made it back to home base.

Later examination of his aircraft found thirty-four small-arms bullet holes "all over the plane, except (miraculously) for the extremely vulnerable underbelly of the aft section. The aircraft required four thousand man-hours of work just to get it airworthy enough to ferry elsewhere for repair."

Battle Damage

Captain Barnhill had been exceptionally lucky because at the time there was no armor plate to protect the aircraft's critical underside. A single .30-caliber bullet in the ship's aft section could puncture a fuel or hydraulic line, or put a hole in the engine's hot turbine or compressor casing. Any one of these would produce an intense fire that would cause the hydraulic lines to the flight controls to burn through and rupture.

171

With hydraulic pressure gone, the horizontal stabilizers would flop to the full leading-edge-up position, and the aircraft would violently pitch down.

It happened regularly. In fact this flight control frailty caused Captain Lew Shattuck to eject twice, and his second ejection cost him seven years of freedom as a prisoner of war.

Shattuck's first experience with flight control failure occurred on July 1, 1966. (E-mail to author, 2004) Shattuck relates, "I went down to shoot up a tugboat that was apparently just leaving the dock. It was a trap. The 37s opened up [thirty-seven-millimeter antiaircraft cannons], and I took a hit in the lower aft section. The [annunciator] lights came on and the P-1 [primary flight control] hydraulic system went to zero. I was burning and headed out to sea with the engine running fine.

"Then my wingman said the fire was out. So I headed south for Da Nang [Da Nang Air Base, South Vietnam]. Then a minute or so later my wingman confirmed the [aft-section] fire had restarted, so I climbed for altitude as the P-2 [backup flight control] hydraulic system started to drop. Shortly thereafter the nose pitched down, and at 240 knots I punched out." He was picked up by the US Navy and returned to his home base in Thailand.

Just ten days later it happened again, but this time it was quick. The flight was well inland—their mission was to knock down a bridge. Shattuck had just pulled off the target in a climbing turn and looked back to check on his flight: "I was caught by two 37 mm rounds in the lower aft section. Almost immediately the controls froze and the nose started to pitch down. I punched out with the airspeed reading 540 knots and increasing." He was seriously injured and captured immediately.

During the high-speed ejection, windblast broke his left arm and dislocated his right shoulder. While being transported to Hanoi for interrogation and confinement, his captors stopped briefly at an army unit where a medic reset his dislocated shoulder. Once in Hanoi, his broken arm and shoulder were twisted during interrogation to force him to talk. It wasn't until several weeks after his capture that Captain

Shattuck was sent to a local hospital and put into a body cast—which was left on for a number of months.

First Lieutenant Donald William (Bill) Bruch Jr. also experienced a flight control failure. At the time, Bill was one of only two lieutenants in our newly formed 333rd Tactical Fighter Squadron at Takhli Air Base, Thailand. As his flight commander, I was immediately apprehensive. The average age in the squadron was thirty-one, with all members having at least five years' experience flying the Thunderchief. Bill was only twenty-six years old and just out of flight school and combat-crew training in the F-105D.

Based on our already significant loss rate, a lieutenant just out of flight school had little chance of surviving the one hundred missions we were expected to fly. (The hundred-mission rule changed when it became obvious to DoD that a shortage of fighter pilots would follow completion of our combat tour. So despite the high loss rate, missions in Laos were not counted in the hundred-mission total.)

Yet despite his youth and inexperience, Bill proved to be the best among us. We all missed the target on occasion, but despite the heavy antiaircraft artillery, Bill's bombs consistently made direct hits. In fact, his accuracy in dive-bombing worried me. He was releasing at low altitude, thus making himself vulnerable to both AAA and small-arms fire.

On one of our first missions together, he was flying the number-four position. Our assigned target was a highway bridge in a relatively remote section of North Vietnam. Upon reaching the target area, we found the entire countryside covered by a thick layer of clouds. But after circling the area, a break opened in the undercast. We dived through the opening in follow-the-leader fashion and bottomed out beneath the six-thousand-foot cloud layer. Then, thanks to our Doppler navigation system, we promptly spotted the bridge, located in a very steep ravine between two mountains, their peaks shrouded with clouds.

Because of the low clouds and steep terrain, it looked too risky for dive-bombing. Quickly, I made a decision. "Buick Flight, the target's at two o'clock, but we'll have to forget it. Instead let's cut the road up ahead."

Three of us hit the road successfully. Then, off to my right, the wooden bridge suddenly vaporized, as all six of Buick Four's bombs hit it dead center. Despite the cloud cover and steep terrain that limited his maneuvering space, Bill had obliterated the target. His courage and accuracy were commendable, but his daring was now of some concern. The other lieutenant in our squadron had just been lost while trying to strafe a truck in a steep ravine. He had hit the hillside during his dive recovery.

In our post-flight debriefing I attempted to explain my rationale for bypassing the target. Hopefully he would see the point and temper his future actions. Yet over the next few months he continued to be deadly accurate. Then came the big one.

Bill was flying as Dodge Two in the four-ship flight—wingman to another flight leader. The target was the Thai Nguyen Railroad yards, located about sixty miles north of Hanoi. We all quickly recognized this as one of the first truly worthy targets of the war. The intelligence officer emphasized, "Do not drop any bombs on the steel plant adjacent to the railroad yards. You are only after the rolling stock and the railroad itself."

When he briefed us on the target's defenses, its importance was immediately obvious. The entire area contained an unimaginable array of antiaircraft guns and SA-2 missiles. Even today, listening to the recording of that mission's radio transmissions raises the hair on the back of my neck. Our entire fighter wing went down through everything the enemy could throw at us.

On a typical lightly defended target, the bomb-release altitude was around four thousand feet. But in order to stay out of the small-arms fire and the AAA surrounding a heavily defended target, a release altitude of seventy-five hundred feet was necessary. While the higher release altitude was somewhat less accurate, it increased your chances of surviving the mission.

Dodge was the fifth flight into the target. By the time they attacked, the radio was alive with excited chatter and the sky full of deadly orange and black puffs of AAA. At 550 knots they popped up to around twelve thousand feet, and then each of the four Thunderchiefs dove on the target. During their dive, Dodge Three called, "Watch out for the SAM!" as an obviously unguided surface-to-air missile went hurtling past.

Their bombs were unerringly accurate, with Bill's destroying a freight train. The flight departed the target, desperately jinking left and right, through the unbelievable flak.

Then Dodge Three called, "Someone's hit—who is it?" An F-105 was burning badly. Dodge Four replied, "Dodge Four's with you." Then Dodge Leader said, "It must be Dodge Two." Only then did Lt. Bruch speak up in his calm, almost soft voice and say, "It's me. Dodge Two's hit."

With Dodge Leader now alongside, the two airplanes continued through murderous antiaircraft fire. Now indicating close to six hundred knots and only three thousand feet above the rice paddies, Dodge Leader called, "You're still torching quite a lot out the back." Suddenly Dodge Two's Thunderchief pitched down violently—the hydraulic lines to the flight controls had burned through. Bill crashed with no apparent effort to eject—likely the result of the tremendous negative G-forces caused by the downward force as the big slabs flopped up. The entire squadron grieved over his loss.

Survivability Modifications

The Thunderchief was contracted under the Cook-Craigie plan, wherein the very first plane built was considered a production aircraft. Subsequent modifications were made as tests and experience dictated. In essence, the aircraft was literally a continuous work in progress. Because it was designed primarily to deliver a tactical nuclear weapon, protection from battle damage had not been considered. Production costs were also a major consideration. Unfortunately, both the fuel and hydraulic lines were routed underneath the aircraft's fuselage-mounted engine which made the aft fuselage exceptionally vulnerable to small arms fire. Still, the aircraft did survive some unbelievable hits.

During 1966, the first full year of active combat, 126 F-105Ds were lost, 103 to the ever-widening coverage of North Vietnamese antiaircraft defenses (Visit to National Air and Space Museum, November 16, 2001). During the seven months of my combat tour—December 5, 1965, through June 1966, the 355th Tactical Fighter Wing lost twenty-six aircraft—roughly a third of the fleet. Our squadron, the 333rd TFS, lost twelve airplanes and seven pilots, with one spending seven years as a POW. Yet only a few of the targets we struck were of any significant value. Most were what we called "splinter missions"—making splinters out of trees while striking targets such as "suspected truck-park" or "possible rest area."

To increase the airplane's survivability, several modifications were made. One of the first was a system to lock the horizontal stabilizers in a fixed trim position when the hydraulic systems failed. This modification alone saved many lives. In addition, fuel and hydraulic lines were rerouted over the spine of the aircraft, and an additional hydraulic reservoir was added. The flap motors were modified so that with frozen controls the pilot could bank and maintain some directional control using differential flap deflections. In addition, armor plating was added to protect the airplane's vulnerable underbelly.

Finale

The last F-105D strike mission took place on October 6, 1970. However, the F-105G Wild Weasels that hunted the deadly SAM missile sites with their own Shrike missiles, remained in combat until war's end—the last plane departing Korat Air Base (Thailand) on October 29, 1974. A total of 382 F-105s were lost in the Vietnam War—almost half of the 833 aircraft manufactured. This cost the lives of 156 airmen.

This F-105D was hit by a Russian ATOLL missile that failed to explode.

Carrying World War II–era bombs externally on a Mach 2, nuclear-weapons-delivery system could be compared to hauling dirt in the back seat of a new Cadillac. Still, it was about all we had, and the dedicated Thunderchief air and ground crews made it work. More than 75 percent of the bombs dropped over North Vietnam were carried by F-105Ds.

As for the Vietnam debacle, never in our nation's history has the constitutionally required civilian leadership's control of the military been so severely mishandled. Never has it been so abused as it was during the reign of Secretary of Defense Robert F. McNamara and his collection of supposedly intellectual giants, known as the "whiz-kids." With the military services' joint chiefs functionally sidelined by Secretary McNamara, pseudo-tacticians with no more than academic credentials (history, political science, accounting, etc.) callously sacrificed our military warriors. Then our US Congress, some of whose members actively supported the enemy's agenda, stopped the funding of the South Vietnamese government at a critical time in history, an action that led to an unprecedented bloodbath in Southeast Asia—particularly in Cambodia.

Our ignominious withdrawal of support from South Vietnam and the subversive actions of some members of Congress denigrated the sacrifice of 58,148 service members who were killed, 75,000 who were severely disabled, and 23,214 who were totally disabled. It was in fact the most mishandled and incompetently planned and executed conflict in the history of warfare.

Chapter 16

In-Flight Refueling Nightmare

An F-105D loaded with bombs for a combat mission explodes as the pilot is aerial refueling.

Captain Barnhill is shown before departing for an especially hazardous combat mission.

IT WAS 0800 HOURS ON September 6, 1965, when the four members of Dodge Flight lifted off from Takhli Royal Thai Air Base. Their mission was colloquially called a "ball-buster"—a so-called JCS target into Route Pack Six—the area around North Vietnam's capital city of Hanoi. The four F-105D Thunderchiefs were each loaded with six 750-pound bombs on a centerline rack. The two wing stations held 430-gallon pylon fuel tanks, with a 390-gallon tank inside the bomb bay. For Captain Gary Barnhill, flying as Dodge Two, the day's mission would prove especially hazardous.

In the relative cool temperature of an early-morning departure, the fifty-three thousand-pound single-engine fighter-bombers required about eighty-five hundred feet of runway to get airborne. At this weight, with only about fifteen hundred feet of the ten-thousand-foot runway remaining, a high-speed aborted takeoff due to an engine abnormality or blown tire was deadly. To ensure adequate fuel to and from the target, shortly after takeoff, each flight of fighter-bombers typically refueled from a KC-135 tanker. Thus, once airborne, the four-ship flight joined up into fingertip formation and climbed toward the rendezvous point with the KC-135 tanker in central Thailand.

About fifteen minutes after departure and at fourteen thousand feet, flight leader Dodge One—Major Gayle Williams—sighted the tanker. Cautiously, he pulled up to the refueling boom, with the rest of the flight joining in echelon formation on the tanker's right wing. Flying between cloud layers, each aircraft duly received a full load of kerosene. Still, because of the time involved in refueling, Dodge One decided they should top off once again, to make certain that all four aircraft had full fuel loads.

Dodge One topped off then moved back into the flight's echelon formation. During their initial refueling, Dodge Three, flown by Captain John Betz, had noted that Capt. Barnhill's aircraft continuously siphoned fuel from the ship's so-called saber drain. This was the aft-section-mounted overflow drainpipe for the internal fuel tanks. While the siphoning seemed abnormal, it had stopped when he disconnected from the tanker's boom. But on this second refueling cycle, immediately after Dodge Two locked on the refueling boom nozzle, Dodge Three noted fuel spilling over the entire length of Capt. Barnhill's bomb-bay doors.

When advised he was gushing fuel, Dodge Two immediately backed off the tanker.

This meant only one thing: the tank's high-pressure fuel shutoff valves had failed and the bomb-bay tank had ruptured. With thinly disguised urgency Capt. Betz transmitted, "Dodge Two, you're gushing fuel." With that Captain Barnhill disconnected from the refueling boom and began backing away from the tanker.

Approximately six seconds later, an explosion blew off panels from the right underside of Barnhill's aircraft, and vaporized fuel from the bomb bay ignited all around the ship's aft section. Now with unmistakable urgency, Dodge Three transmitted, "Dodge Two, you're on fire. EJECT! EJECT!"

Motivated by the sound of the explosion and Capt. Betz's urgent call to eject, Barnhill retarded the throttle to be sure of clearing the tanker. Then, gritting his teeth for what was to come, he pulled the right armrest, and out he went. Roughly a second after his rocket-propelled seat cleared the cockpit rails the sleek fighter-bomber blew apart—falling in two separate pieces and disappearing into the clouds below.

Captain Barnhill relates: "Once I pulled up the seat handle it was literally like being shot from a cannon. Everything functioned as designed; the lap belt blew open and seat-man separator straps kicked me out of the seat." Because the seat-anchored low-altitude lanyard was connected to his parachute's D-ring (as required below fifteen thousand feet), the chute's canopy opened the instant he was flipped from the seat.

"The opening shock was violent, as I went from about 300 knots to a dead stop—just in time to see the two burning halves of my Thud disappear in the undercast." (So many F-105s were shot down or otherwise lost they were affectionately called "Thuds" because of the sound they made upon hitting the ground.)

While descending in his parachute, Barnhill activated his emergency handheld URC-4 radio and began talking to Dodge One. He relates, "I was descending in and out of cloud layers. During my descent, Dodge Flight thought I was on the ground already and darn near ran over me while tracking my emergency beacon."

While floating earthward, Barnhill recalled the survival-school instructor explaining the "four riser cut"—how to cut the parachute canopy's four aft suspension risers to make the otherwise unsteerable military parachute maneuverable like a skydiver's chute. In fact, everyone carried an orange-handled "riser cutter" (knife) in his flight-suit thigh pocket, with its hooked blade extended for use on just such an occasion.

Cutting the parachute's four aft risers released tension on the backside of the otherwise taut canopy. This allowed air to spill from the rear, giving the chute forward momentum. By pulling down on the left or right front risers the chute could be made to change headings.

Barnhill relates, "I was descending over a dense, nasty-looking forest. The week prior I knew of a pilot who was impaled in the crotch after parachuting into tall trees. I looked down at the dense, intimidating forest canopy and decided to try the 'four riser cut.' It worked beautifully, and I was able to glide to a small clearing." This later proved useful for his rescue, as the helicopter was able to use the clearing for Barnhill's pickup.

His parachute landing was uneventful, but Barnhill immediately heard machine-gun fire. With verification from Dodge One that he had landed in friendly territory, he decided it was the twenty-millimeter cannon rounds in his aircraft cooking off in the burning wreckage.

Sometime later, the remaining members of Dodge Flight reached BINGO (minimum fuel). As the flight prepared to leave, Major Williams reassured Barnhill that the rescue helicopter was inbound and homing on his emergency radio beacon.

Euphoric over having cheated certain death when his aircraft exploded, coupled with a successful ejection and parachute landing without injury, Captain Barnhill spread his chute's orange and white canopy on the dark green understory. Then in a celebratory act he began firing his emergency flares and orange smoke bombs into the air.

Ironically, as the air force rescue helicopter approached Barnhill's location, its UHF radio failed, and the pilot, Captain Bill Wirstrom, immediately lost the bearing to the downed pilot's position. But the orange smoke and bright flares saved the day. Wirstrom quickly spotted the pyrotechnics and skillfully landed in the small clearing among the tall trees.

Accident Board Findings

The cause of the accident was divided between the design of the Thunderchief's high-pressure fuel shutoff valves and the KC-135's refueling system. The primary cause was attributed to failure of the bomb-bay tank's high-pressure fuel-shutoff valve, which failed to stop the fuel flow once the tank filled. Then the continued high-pressure fuel from the KC-135 tanker ruptured the tank.

The board's report also faulted the tanker's refueling system design: "A contributing cause was a faulty fuel pressure regulator on the tanker aircraft which provided excessive fuel pressure, causing rupture of the bomb-bay tank."

Finale

The helicopter crew delivered Captain Barnhill to the fighter wing based at the Royal Thai Air Base at Nakhon Phanom, Thailand. Since there was no transportation available to his home base, Captain Barnhill headed for the Officers Club.

At the club he ran into Jim, a flight-school classmate who was currently employed as a pilot for the CIA's clandestine operation called Air America. Jim gave Barnhill a ride back to Takhli Air Base in an Air America T-28.

Following discussions with Jim about his Air America employment, Barnhill began mentally comparing his monthly air force salary of $995 with the $5,000 per month of his CIA counterpart. Having only recently survived major battle damage, wherein his aircraft absorbed thirty-four bullet strikes (see chapter 15), and now an in-flight fire and explosion, somehow the pay differential didn't seem logical.

Despite a stiff neck from his rocket-powered ejection and the sudden deceleration from the parachute's opening shock ("which nearly pushed my head under my armpit"), Captain Barnhill was airborne the next day on another so-called JCS-directed strike in Route Pack Six.

After completing his combat assignment, he was transferred to McConnell AFB, Kansas as an instructor in the F-105D crew-training wing. There, he immediately resigned his AF commission, and after making the proper contacts he was verbally hired by Air America. His starting date was to be February 7, 1966, in Vientiane, Laos, the center of clandestine activity in Southeast Asia. Alas, because of his multiple moves, the mail from his CIA contract and written orders never arrived. Upon calling his CIA contact, he discovered "the man would be out of the country for a long time." Thus, in desperation, Barnhill accepted a job with Trans World Airlines as First Officer on their Boeing 727s and became a very happy and wealthy airline pilot. Years later while awaiting his scheduled flight in a Philadelphia International coffee shop he was joined by another TWA crewmember. As they began talking, the conversation naturally began with a review of their pre-TWA days. Barnhill told of flying F-105Ds in Vietnam. His new friend told of flying rescue helicopters during the Vietnam War: then he mentioned being credited with recovering five F-105D pilots. He recalled one especially that had occurred on Labor Day, 1965, when an incredibly lucky pilot had ejected just seconds before his Thunderchief exploded while refueling. He then introduced himself as Bill Wirstrom. It is indeed a small world!

Chapter 17

The Fabulous Phantom

The F-4 Phantom ushers in the age of electronic and missile air warfare.

IT WAS MAY 10, 1972, when four air force F-4D Phantoms, using their AIM-7 Sparrow missiles, initiated a head-on engagement with a four-ship formation of MiG-21s. Unlike the Phantoms, the MiGs had no weapons that were capable of engaging from a frontal aspect.

Oyster Flight was part of a twenty-eight-ship F-4D prestrike combat air patrol (MiGCAP) configured to intercept any Vietnamese People's Air Force (VPAF) aircraft that might try to attack the ninety-two-plane strike force that followed.

A Phantom loaded for a MiGCAP Mission with AIM-9 and AIM-7 missiles and a SUU-16A gun pod.

The strike force's target was the Paul Doumer Bridge: this was a major structure on the highway network from China into Hanoi. Disco, an EC-121 radar aircraft, had warned of MiG-21 "Fishbeds" departing the VNAF's Kep Air Base near Hanoi. In addition, Red Crown, which provided radar coverage from the USS *Chicago*, manned at the time by Radioman Larry Nowell, reported four separate MiG elements just getting airborne.

After repeatedly feinting toward the Phantoms, at 0942 hours a four-ship flight of MiGs turned toward the area where the MiGCAP interceptors were orbiting. Forewarned by both Disco and Red Crown, Oyster Flight turned to meet them.

Oyster One, flown by Major Robert Lodge, and weapons systems officer (WSO) Captain Roger Locher—a crew with two previous kills—enjoyed a "missile-free" condition, wherein visual identification was not required. In addition, they were equipped with newly acquired Combat Tree capability. This electronic system allowed Oyster One to see the enemy's IFF (Identification Friend or Foe, called transponders in civilian aircraft) on their Phantom's radar. The IFF signal emitted by the MiGs was the electronic signature used by VPAF air defense controllers to identify their own aircraft. Our ability to see them electronically was thanks to covert acquisition by the Israelis of Soviet IFF transponders (Davies 2005).

At eight nautical miles and at Mach 1.4, Maj. Lodge fired a single AIM-7. The missile climbed and tracked but detonated early when its motor burned out. Quickly he "fired a second missile and saw it climbing about twenty degrees toward its still invisible target."

Almost simultaneously, from a position six hundred yards off Maj. Lodge's right wing, Oyster Two, piloted by Lt. John Markle and WSO Steve Eaves, fired two of their AIM-7s at the MiG leader's wingman. An instant later, a pair of orange explosions brightened the sky ahead, as both the MiG leader and his wingman disintegrated. The second element of MiGs flashed by, and Oyster Flight turned hard in pursuit. Major Lodge went after the number-four MiG. Oyster Three, piloted by Captain Steve Ritchie, pursued the surviving element leader. Ritchie related, "I managed to get a [radar] lock on one of the remaining planes and fired off two [Sparrow] missiles...at the minimum limit of the radar parameters. The second missile exploded under the third MiG... Smoking, venting fuel, and on fire...the pilot managed to eject." This marked the first aerial victory for the air force's soon-to-be (only) pilot ace.

As Oyster One continued in hot pursuit of the number-four Fishbed (NATO-code name), a flight of VPAF MiG-19s entered the milieu—initially overshooting the lead Phantom. Maj. Lodge's wingman and Oyster Three tried desperately to warn their leader as the lead MiG-19 repositioned to fire. But Lodge and Locher were fixated on that last MiG-21. Fire from the MiG 19's three thirty-millimeter cannons covered the Phantom, "and the machine was flipped over...Plummeting out of the sky upside down and on fire." For some reason Maj. Lodge delayed ejecting and died in the crash. Captain Locher ejected successfully, and despite being only five miles from the enemy's Yen Bai airfield, he managed to evade capture for twenty-three days and was rescued (Davies 2005, 29; Ritchie, n.d.; Ethel 1997).

New Age Warfare

As this war story documents, our Vietnam embroilment ushered in the technological era of aerial warfare. Electronic teamwork and air-to-air missiles began replacing mano-a-mano dog-fighting. The postwar study, "Red Baron Reports," (2008) showed that fighter-versus-fighter maneuvering occurred in only 13 percent of engagements. Thanks to support from our other electronic operations, in 66 percent of our aerial victories the US pilot "began from a position of advantage."

At the end of operation Rolling Thunder in 1968, our fighter forces had been severely handicapped "because the White House virtually gave air superiority back to them [the enemy], by placing severe restrictions on targeting." With their air defense network politically protected from attack, the MiGs began aerial engagements from a position of advantage 89 percent of the time. When starting from a neutral position, US fighters were lost only twice (Sayers 2008).

Phantom's Evolution

The F-4's design originated in 1954 when the navy selected McDonnell Aircraft to build a supersonic aircraft for fleet air defense. Intruders were to be countered with long-range missiles. An internally mounted gun was considered superfluous.

After prototype testing, on December 17, 1958, the navy purchased McDonnell's design, which was officially designated the F-4H-1. Meanwhile, during the early 1960s, in an effort to reduce expenses, the Department of Defense initiated a program to combine the military services—the so-called "purple suit" military. Uniforms and equipment of all three services were to be standardized. There was even talk of integrating the marines with the army.

Accordingly, in 1962, Secretary of Defense McNamara required the air force to evaluate the navy's F-4H-1 interceptor as a multirole fighter-bomber. In a competition with the F-106A and F-105D it *supposedly* proved superior in both armament and range (Wetterhahn 2000; Marrett 2008).

On January 17, 1962, the air force bought the Phantom—designated the F-110A—with a DoD caveat that only minor changes to the original navy design would be allowed. Essentially this included larger tires and antiskid brakes. Then on September 18, 1962, the aircraft designations were combined: navy Phantoms would be called the F-4B and the air force version the F-4C.

The Learning Curve

In the navy's high-speed interceptor role, the Phantom's accident rate was exceptionally good. However, as an air force fighter-bomber, including its then brief record of combat in Southeast Asia (SEA), the loss rate quickly became alarming. By 1967, the air force had lost ten Phantoms involving stall/spin accidents alone; and several combat losses were suspected as due to the same cause (Marrett 2008).

A key ingredient was the fighter pilots' deeply ingrained, hyper-aggressive "tiger" spirit. While engaging in simulated fighter-versus-fighter combat in earlier aircraft, it was common to pull hard into high-speed buffet, which reduced both airspeed and the aircraft's turn radius. Hopefully this allowed you to put your gunsight on your adversary. But it quickly became obvious that this high-G maneuvering overtaxed the much heavier, missile-equipped Phantoms.

There were also aerodynamic reasons to temper aggressive maneuvering. Loaded with fuel and weapons, a fifty-eight-thousand-pound F-4C had an inherent *aft* center of gravity (CG). This decreased its static stability (tendency to return to equilibrium). Because the externally mounted "drop tanks" continuously refilled the six internal fuselage tanks, the CG always remained aft, keeping the aircraft marginally stable. (A later modification provided a cutout switch to prevent the aft tank from refilling from the external fuel tanks.) Exacerbating the problem was that the Phantom's two fuselage-mounted engines moved its mass balance aft.

Other factors included the strong production of lift by the ship's fuselage. This was combined with the forward and inboard movement of the wings' aerodynamic center as airspeed decreased. As a result, the aircraft didn't stall all at once. During high-angle-of-attack maneuvers the combination of these characteristics created a strong tendency for the aircraft to pitch up and go out of control—i.e., to "depart" (Krings 1980, 116; Stuck 1980, 65).

Subsequent NASA tests demonstrated "an abrupt loss of directional stability (nose slice) near wing stall." Massive airflow separation on the swept-wings caused "adverse flow fields at the tail, thereby degrading the stabilizing influence of the vertical fin at high angles of attack." NASA also identified several potential spin modes in the F-4C. In a steep nose-down spin it was recoverable with normal anti-spin control inputs. However, it also "exhibited a relatively fast, flat spin, in which the aircraft descended vertically in a rapid spin motion…Recovery from the flat spin was found to be impossible" (NASA 2008).

McDonnell test pilot Don Stuck (1964) lamented, "It's ironic that the people who get into spin problems seldom use the recommended technique for recovery." Yet the problem was that air force Phantom pilots were untrained in the aircraft's unique spin recovery technique. They had simply read the recommended procedure in the Pilot's Dash One (pilot handbook). Unfortunately, the required recovery involved flight-control inputs that were opposite to a pilot's instinctive reactions. For example, in an accidental departure, the ailerons had to be placed *with the direction of spin* rather than against it.

The problem involved strong adverse yaw produced by a downward-deflected aileron. During high-angle-of-attack maneuvering and at landing-approach airspeeds, drag from a Phantom's deflected aileron produced very strong adverse yaw. Wind-tunnel tests showed this aileron drag to be *greater than the aerodynamic force of the rudder* (emphasis added), which NASA tests showed was masked by the wake of the wing. In fact, adverse yaw was so strong that once flaps were extended during landing approach, the aircraft had an aileron-rudder interconnect that automatically applied rudder anytime the ailerons were used.

While maneuvering at higher speeds, during an accidental "departure," pilots would instinctively apply aileron *against* the direction of roll-off—for instance, with a snap to the right, the control stick would instinctively be placed to the left in an effort to stop the right roll. This brought the Phantom's left spoiler "up" while the right aileron deflected downward thirty degrees. (The ailerons had only one degree of "up" travel with the spoiler being primary.) The resulting downward deflection of the right aileron generated strong adverse yaw on the right wing, almost guaranteeing a spin to the right.

Stuck's lament that pilots were using improper control inputs to recover was later verified by a special series of stall/spin tests of ten instructor pilots at Tactical Air Command's Nellis AFB Fighter Weapons School. These tests were conducted by the author of this book and Colonel John P. O'Gorman. Using a T-33, when asked to recover from a sudden departure with F-4C control inputs, each of these instructors invariably applied ailerons incorrectly. However, after some practice, the correct procedure became second nature. Because of similarities in spin-recovery techniques in other Century-series fighters, the T-33 spin training was unanimously recommended by TAC fighter-wing commanders for all fighter units.

Consequently, General Gabriel P. Disosway, commander of Tactical Air Command, promptly authorized establishment of a spin-training program for all command fighter pilots. Unfortunately, Gen. Disosway retired soon thereafter. When General William W. Momeyer assumed command, the spin-training program was quickly spiked as being too dangerous. However, it was adopted by the navy's Top Gun school and used successfully for several years. Meanwhile the postwar 1974 USAF "Red Baron III Report" found that inadequate training accounted for many of the air force losses (Sayers 2008)

Battle Damage

Early in its service life, the F-4's hydraulically operated flight controls proved especially problematic. In fact, between June 1966 and December 1967, the air force lost six aircraft due to defects in the aileron actuator cylinder barrels. This of course had implications for the aircraft's battle damage tolerance, which was not a consideration when the Phantom was designed in the 1950s.

The ailerons were operated by four actuator cylinders, each bored into a *single rectangular metal block*. Two of the cylinders powered the PC-1 hydraulic system; the other two provided pressure to the PC-2 system. (The utility hydraulic system was added later as a third backup.) Tests disclosed that a high-energy impact on the unit could cause a hairline fracture that crossed one or more cylinder barrels. Then, with any aileron movement, a fluid loss would occur through the crack.

This design flaw came to a head on the morning of March 31, 1967, at Da Nang Air Base, South Vietnam. An F-4C from the 366th TFW was downed in the traffic pattern by fragments from a single 12.7 millimeter (.50-caliber) bullet that hit the left aileron hydraulic actuator cylinder block.

Bear Flight had originated as a four-ship formation of F-4Cs tasked with escorting two EB-66 electronic countermeasures aircraft on a mission along the Red River Valley, northwest of Hanoi. Toward the end of these escort missions, the EB-66s typically separated. In consequence, Bear Flight was returning in two ship elements—Bear One and Two with the lead EB-66, with Bear Three and Four escorting the second one to safety.

As the second element neared home base, the element leader, Bear Three, called for landing information. Da Nang tower reported a two-ship flight on a twelve-mile radar final and requested that Bear Three and Four fly a short initial approach for traffic sequencing.

While descending through five thousand feet, with Bear Four (piloted by Major Kenny Cobb) tucked in close, Bear Three brought the two-ship element around in a fairly tight, descending turn. During the turn they passed directly over a four-thousand-foot mountain peak where the enemy reportedly had installed a pair of very active 12.7 millimeter (.50-caliber) machine guns.

As they entered initial approach, Maj. Cobb commented to his weapons system officer, First Lieutenant Lawrence Peterson, "We're not supposed to be over this peak." Almost simultaneously they experienced a solid jolt. Maj. Cobb loosened the formation to take a look. Seeing nothing abnormal and with no annunciator warning lights illuminated, he resumed the normal close-wing position. A minute later Bear Three made his "break" in the overhead traffic pattern.

As Bear Three broke to downwind, Maj. Cobb began a five-second count for spacing, whereupon he turned his attention to the cockpit. Instantly he was startled to see the master caution light glowing, along with *Check Hydraulic Gauges* on the telelight (annunciator) panel. A quick check of the gauges showed the flight control hydraulic pressures were both dangerously low.

Typically, the hydraulic-pressure gauges both showed three thousand psi; then as the controls moved they would dip and recover. However, PC-1 now indicated twenty-two hundred psi with PC-2 registering seventeen hundred psi. Worse yet, with every control movement, rather than recovering, the pressure on both systems continued to decay.

Quickly recognizing their predicament, Maj. Cobb made a twenty-degree right turn away from the highly congested town. Then he transmitted to Bear Three, "Don't land but keep us in sight: we'll be ejecting soon." He then asked the tower to scramble the rescue helicopter.

Maj. Cobb stated, "With essentially neutral controls, the ship's nose began to rise about thirty degrees above the horizon. In an effort to adjust the pitch, I used full nose down stick pressure—whereupon it began to very slowly fall; then full aft stick to get the nose to rise about fifteen degrees up. Then with the PC-1 reading six hundred psi and PC-2 reading zero, the aircraft abruptly pitched nose down."

Both crewmembers ejected successfully, but upon landing Maj. Cobb was badly injured: "My attempt at a successful PLF [parachute landing fall] failed. I knew I was screaming down, but assumed the appropriate position and looked outward from the direct landing spot. I hit the ground like a meteorite, stars and all, including numbness from my waist down for about one to two minutes, until my legs could be forced straight and I could rise up on my hands and arms. Slowly the feeling returned, but I did need help into the rescue chopper" (Colonel Cobb, pers. comm.).

Later tests showed the parachute canopies used in the F-4 Martin-Baker ejection seats were too small for the job. In this case, Maj. Cobb weighed 210 pounds and was wearing a flight suit and G-suit loaded with various items of equipment. In addition he was wearing a packed survival vest, along with a fifty-pound survival seat-pack attached to the bottom of his parachute harness—which included a rubber life raft. An engineer at Martin-Baker Industries (manufacturer of the ejection system) later estimated his descent rate to the ground as twenty-four hundred feet per minute—more than twice the standard parachute rate of descent.

Cobb recalls, "When the rescue helicopter arrived, the pilot made a sharp turn directly over six black-pajama-clad coolie-hat locals standing in a rice field about ninety meters away…Then [he made] an immediate left turn and landed next to me." After delivering both crewmembers to the military hospital, the helicopter crew returned to the crash site to recover the personal equipment items, such as the life raft and seat survival packs, but all were gone.

Maj. Cobb continued, "Shortly after being admitted to the hospital there were sounds of a war zone…artillery booming, with airplanes bombing and strafing right through the Da Nang traffic pattern." Later he was told that a marine sergeant, a lieutenant, and a captain had traveled to the crash site to secure the wreckage and were killed immediately. This precipitated a five-day battle off the end of the Da Nang Air Base runway. Ultimately, thirteen marines were killed along with 133 Republic of North Vietnamese (RNVN) soldiers.

Still, despite the battle, the aileron actuators from Major Cobb's aircraft were recovered. The left actuator showed an irregular gouge in one end made by shrapnel from a 12.7-millimeter bullet. On a hydraulic test stand, a power actuation stroke caused three of the four cylinders to emit a misty weeping from a hairline crack. This led to redesign of the actuator, along with tying in the utility hydraulic system as backup.

Phantom's Operational History

In April 1965, the Forty-fifth Tactical Fighter Squadron became the first unit in Southeast Asia (SEA) equipped with Phantoms. Their first F-4 MiG kills occurred on July 10 when, after some maneuvering, Mink 03, crewed by Captains Kenneth Holcombe and WSO Arthur Clark, destroyed a MiG-17 with an AIM-9 Sidewinder heat-seeking missile. Shortly thereafter, Mink 04, crewed by Captains Tom Roberts and WSO Ronald Anderson, downed another, also with Sidewinders (Davies 2004).

During the Vietnam War, thanks to teamwork with other agencies such as Red Crown, Disco, and Teaball (an all-source communications center that issued real-time MiG warnings), F-4C aircrews destroyed forty-four MiGs—thirty-six with missiles, four with gunfire from the externally mounted centerline SUU-16A gun pod, with four made to crash while maneuvering.

Thanks to Colonel F. C. "Boots" Blesse, the F-4Cs were fitted with external SUU-16A gun pods.

In May 1967, the 555th TFS became the first F-4D squadron in SEA. Equipped with an advanced avionics and fire-control system, the D-model was made famous by Eighth TFW Wing Commander Colonel Robin Olds, and his "Wolf Pack." On January 2, 1968, Colonel Olds led his Wolf Pack in what appeared to be a massive strike by unescorted F-105Ds. Instead, F-4D crews using missiles downed seven MiG-21s without a loss of their own. The ruse was called Operation Bolo. Four days later the same trick caught two more (Sayers 2008).

On August 28, 1972, Captain Steve Ritchie, flying an F-4D, became the air force's only pilot ace of the Vietnam War. Having heard that the MiG-21s had resumed flying at high altitude, Capt. Ritchie and WSO Captain Chuck DeBellevue were scanning the sky above them and spotted a pair approaching head on at around thirty thousand feet.

Ritchie pulled the F-4D into a steep climbing turn. Then, at an extreme range, he fired two Sparrow AIM-7E-2 missiles, hoping to force the enemy aircraft to turn. As he rolled out in a stern chase he fired his other two Sparrows. One of these missed; the other knocked the MiG down in flames, marking Steve's fifth kill. This made him the USAF's one and only pilot ace of the Vietnam War (Davies 2005).

While in SEA, the F-4D phantom accounted for forty-five enemy aircraft destroyed. Interestingly, all three of the Vietnam-era air force aces (one pilot and two WSOs) got their kills in the D-model during the Linebacker campaign of 1972.

The F-4E

Despite DoD's original prohibition of major modifications, the aircraft's accident history and NASA wind-tunnel tests documented a critical need for major aerodynamic changes to the fighter-bomber's design. On June 30, 1967, McDonnell-Douglas Aircraft flew the first Phantom modified to correct its known aerodynamic deficiencies. Designated the F-4E, it proved to be a Cadillac among fighters. Major modifications included a fuselage extended from fifty-eight to sixty-three feet, allowing space for additional fuel. Engine performance was upgraded; automatic wing leading-edge (maneuvering) slats greatly improved turning capability; and an internal nose-mounted M-61 cannon improved fighting capability. The F-4E was so well received that the USAF bought 1,389 of this model. (In production from 1957 until 1981, there were 5,137 Phantoms ultimately built.) (Boeing 2008).

The E-model arrived in Southeast Asia in November 1968, first replacing the F-105Ds of the 469th TFS of the 388th TFW at Korat Royal Thai Air Force Base, Thailand. While most of its missions were ground attack, ultimately the F-4E was credited with twenty-three MiG kills—ten downed by Sparrow missiles, four with Sidewinders, seven using the internal cannon, and two while maneuvering. (One MiG downed by Lieutenant Colonel Lyle Beckers and First Lieutenant Thomas Griffin was only damaged by an AIM-9 but finished with the cannon.)

Finale

Out of 2,254 air force aircraft lost in the Vietnam War, including 444 Phantoms, 382 of which were lost in combat action, the rest in accidents. (Note: the loss figure varies with the information source.) In November 1967, the 366th TFW, based at Da Nang Air Base, South Vietnam, lost eight F-4Es and sixteen crewmembers in rapid succession. This was due to premature bomb detonation—the result of a flawed design in newly introduced FMU-35 fuzes—and exacerbated by inept command leadership. Only the alertness and assertiveness of the wing's director of operation, then-colonel Frederick C. "Boots" Blesse prevented further losses (see chapter 18).

The Vietnam War forced us into the technological age, with new electronics, new weapons, and improved tactics. Perhaps the most valuable lesson we learned was that proper employment of modern electronic systems with high-speed, missile- and gun-equipped jet fighters demands teamwork among the services and related agencies—once again proving that waging war *must always be* a group effort.

Chapter 18

The Expendables

When the bombs began exploding prematurely, killing sixteen F–4E aircrew members, instead of investigating the cause, higher headquarters callously told the fighter wing, "Sometimes you get losses like that in combat."

—*Major General F. C. "Boots" Blesse, Check Six*

THE PROBLEM OF AIRCREW KILLED by premature bomb detonation began early in the Vietnam War. The first known occurrence was on November 12, 1965: Captain William "Nasty Ned" Miller was flying an F-105D to a target in North Vietnam. His flight of four Thunderchiefs was still over Thailand, and his six 750-pound bombs should have been secure. Yet, as he approached the KC-135 tanker to refuel, one of the proximity-fuzed bombs exploded.

The fuzes were supposed to arm only after being released from the bomb rack. But somehow one of the World War II–era VT-188 proximity fuzes had become armed before release. Then, as the fighter-bomber closed on the tanker, the small radar-beam emitted by the fuze detected the aircraft and detonated: Capt. Miller was killed instantly. In this case, the fuzes were withdrawn temporarily from service to determine the cause.

The task of identifying the problem was assigned to the 4525th Fighter Weapons Wing at Nellis Air Force Base, Nevada. The project was assigned to then-captain John Morrissey who conducted the tests that subsequently identified the problem.

The first thing Morrissey discovered was that the proximity fuzes had been designed during World War II for internal carriage by B-17s and B-24 bombers. (The applicable technical order was in fact dated in the early forties.) If carried externally—as they were on the F-105Ds—they were limited to a maximum speed of 240 mph (204 knots). Yet this speed was the typical *final approach landing speed* of the F-105D.

Until the advent of the Vietnam War, our national military policy had emphasized "mutual-assured destruction" with atomic weapons. Therefore development of new modernized conventional weapons lagged badly. In essence, the air force's Mach 2–capable fighters were forced to carry leftover World War II bombs and fuzes simply because there was nothing else available.

Typically the 750-pound M-117 bombs were carried externally at airspeeds of 550 knots or slightly greater. Lt. Colonel Bill Sparks reports, "They were very old and had a problem with detonation if dropped any distance, even without fuzes installed" (B. Sparks, e-mail to author, February 17, 2005).

The proximity fuze was designed to detonate the bomb in the air to suppress antiaircraft fire over a wide area. Once armed, the bomb detonated when the fuze's small radar unit detected anything that would reflect a radar beam, such as a ground target, or in Capt. Miller's case, the KC-135 tanker. These old fuzes were armed by a clock-like mechanism that counted the revolutions of the small propeller, with the arm-time set prior to departure. They operated by a set number of turns of a small propeller located on the nose of the fuze, which in turn armed the radar-activated detonator Only limited quantities of these World War II leftovers were available. Despite official denials to Congress by then-secretary of defense Robert S. McNamara, the limited supply of M-117 bombs was a critical problem too. In fact, as the war heated up in the spring of 1966, the inventory of bombs in Southeast Asia (SEA) was completely exhausted. Reportedly, the Department of Defense had our war reserve munitions (WRM) stockpiles on Guam purged—barged out to sea and dumped—to save storage costs. Consequently, the DoD was forced to purchase replacements from the WRM stockpiles of Allied nations. And despite our continuing losses to antiaircraft fire, for several weeks we flew fighter-bomber missions into heavily defended North Vietnam armed only with the airplane's single twenty-millimeter cannon and using training ammunition since high explosive incendiary (HEI) rounds were not available.

Capt. Morrissey's subsequent flight tests with the VT-188 proximity fuzes immediately identified the problem. It involved a combination of both high speed and the safety wire used to restrain the small arming propeller. Normally the safety wire was pulled when the bomb released. This allowed the propeller to spin and arm the proximity fuze. But at the high speeds typical of the F-105D, the safety wire vibrated and broke, which allowed the arming propeller to spin and arm the bomb prior to release. Once the problem was identified, changes were made to make them safe to carry.

Golden BB Losses

Unfortunately, the problem involved more than just one mishap. In November 1967, the F-4E-equipped 366th Tactical Fighter Wing, located at Da Nang Air Base, South Vietnam, lost eight aircraft and sixteen aircrew members in rapid succession. One pilot, Medal of Honor recipient Captain Lance P. Sijan, did survive the bomb explosion on his F-4; despite being severely wounded, he ejected successfully, only to be captured several days later and die of his untreated wounds as a POW (Colonel Howard Plunkett, e-mail, Feb. 17, 2005; Blesse 1987, 141).

At first these losses were attributed to so-called Golden BB hits, wherein an aircraft rolling into a dive is hit by a lucky shot from antiaircraft fire. "We had no proof that anything was wrong," said wing director of operations Colonel Frederick C. "Boots" Blesse. "We were told, 'Sometimes you get losses like those in combat'" (Blesse 1987, 142). Nonetheless, Blesse attempted to stop all bombing missions to investigate the cause. In his book, *Check Six*, Blesse told of a Skyspot mission that ultimately provided a clue to the mystery. When a target was covered by clouds, ground-based Skyspot radar was used to vector a flight of four or more fighters in close formation toward the target. The radar controller then started a countdown, and upon his command all aircraft released their bombs simultaneously. On this occasion, however, a hurry-up vector to the release point had left the flight's second element—ships number three and four—spread out by several hundred yards. As the flight leader released his bombs, crewmembers of the second element saw one of the leader's bombs explode a few feet beneath the aircraft. The explosion destroyed both aircraft in the lead element, killing all four crewmembers. Now, however, the wing knew where to look for the true cause of its "Golden BB" losses.

The problem involved the newly introduced electric long-delay FMU-35 fuzes. Something was causing these fuzes to activate prematurely. However, despite eyewitness support for the explanation, leadership in higher headquarters rejected the assessment and, with no alternative available, ordered the fighter wing to continue using the dangerous fuzes.

As Colonel Blesse observed, however, this order failed to specify that the fuzes had to be armed. He launched his subsequent missions with unarmed bombs, and the wing's losses stopped immediately (Blesse 1987, 144). Sometime later, the flawed fuzes were withdrawn and replaced by the newer FMU-72 (Col. John Morrissey, e-mail to author, March 27, 2005).

In 1968, the air force accepted for test a new electrically actuated FMU-57 proximity fuze. Designed specifically to counter the surface-to-air missile and antiaircraft fire that was taking a heavy toll on our fighters, the fuze was destined to replace the obsolete fuze that had cost Capt. Miller his life.

Testing of the new fuzes was assigned to the operations test and evaluation (OT&E) section of the 4525th Fighter Weapons Wing at Nellis AFB, Nevada. Again, Capt. Morrissey was appointed project officer. The wing had just received thirty-six live fuzes for test and evaluation from the manufacturer, Saunders Industries. To expedite the program, the fuzes were being tested with live bombs instead of first validating them with inert shapes. Capt. Morrissey had already tested more than half of them successfully when he was deployed to Southeast Asia as leader of a munitions introduction team for a related project. In his absence, another member of the OT&E section, Major Robert L. Chastain, was assigned to complete the tests (Colonel John Morrissey, e-mail, February 8, 2005).

Major Chastain (R) receives congratulation from his squadron commander for completing one hundred missions over North Vietnam.

Final Test

On December 17, 1968, the mission of the two-ship flight of F-105Ds (each loaded with six 750-pound M-117 bombs) was to complete the evaluation of the modernized electrical proximity fuzes (called the fuze munitions unit-57/B). Major Chastain—a recent graduate of the Air Force Aerospace Research Pilots School—was flying the number-two position (call sign Winder Flight) on Major John O. Rollins II. The flight departed at 1000 hours and entered the Nellis (weapons) Range III complex approximately five minutes later. The six bombs on each aircraft were set to be dropped individually. To ensure safe separation of the aircraft from the bomb blast, each electrically activated fuze had a safe-arm time set for six seconds.

The test fuzes had been installed and inspected by air force munitions specialists then checked by Major Rollins and a representative of the fuze manufacturer. The test plan called for a thirty-degree dive angle, with each bomb released at 470 Knots Calibrated Air Speed and five thousand feet above the ground. Six single "hot" passes were to be flown by each pilot against the designated target.

Major Rollins was first, and all six of his bomb drops were normal. The only discrepancy involved a bomb that was not an airburst. Instead it exploded upon ground contact. (It would have been a dud except for the tail fuse used as a safety measure.)

Then it was Major Chastain's turn. His first pass was a dry run to check bomb-release conditions. On the second pass, he released his first bomb. It hung up momentarily, then released cleanly three seconds late.

Three minutes later, while being tracked by radar and a series of four movie cameras, Major Chastain rolled in on his second hot pass. The air force accident report noted that this pass was normal in all respects. Film footage showed the bomb released normally, but at about four feet below the aircraft's fuselage it exploded, and the aircraft disintegrated. Major Chastain's body was found still strapped in his ejection seat (USAF Accident Report, January 16, 1969).

Background

When the thirty-six test fuzes had arrived at Nellis AFB for testing by OT&E, Capt. John Morrissey and Maj. Guy Pulliam immediately questioned the fail-safe circuitry. There appeared to be a fatal failure path that could lead to premature ignition. When they visited Saunders Industries in Hanscom Field, Massachusetts, for their initial briefing on the new proximity fuze, they voiced their suspicions. Subsequently they submitted a letter regarding their concerns through the Fighter Weapons Wing to Headquarters Tactical Air Command, then ultimately to Air Force Systems Command at the Eglin Test Center. Capt. Morrissey described the response they received as, "leave the heavy intellectual lifting to us. You just drop the bombs" (Col. John Morrissey, e-mail to author, April 6, 2005).

The first commandment for all bomb fuzes had always been that they would not arm until far enough from the airplane to prevent damage if they detonated. With this newly designed proximity fuze, the internal battery was inert until a connector was pulled as the weapon released from the bomb rack. Then, upon battery rise, the proximity fuze armed.

The problem they had identified with the new fuze was that following release, a single failure in the wiring, caused, for example, by faulty construction or damage in the field, could cause it to detonate as its internal battery came online—*approximately three or four feet below the aircraft.*

When Maj. Chastain had been tasked with completing the tests, he was briefed on the possible design flaw. While he was fully aware of the urgency surrounding the new fuzes, his university degree in geophysics gave him uncommon insight into the design and construction of the sophisticated electric proximity fuze he was about to test. In desperation, Chastain and an unidentified associate flew to Washington, DC, and visited the Pentagon. There they explained their concerns to the Hq. USAF deputy for operations, then-major general George Simler, a fighter pilot and former fighter wing commander.

The two officers showed General Simler how, upon release, there were two places where a short or bad wiring could cause the fuze to function instantaneously once the battery reached full voltage—*approximately three or four feet underneath the aircraft* (Col. Bill Sparks, e-mail, April 23, 2005).

Gen. Simler agreed, in theory. However, half of the fuzes had already been tested successfully, and there was nothing else available for the war in SEA. As a brigadier general and deputy for operations of the Second Air Division at Kadena Air Base, Okinawa, Simler had complained in a secret letter to Headquarters Pacific Air Forces (PACAF) about the lack of progress in improving fuzes for general-purpose bombs then being used on tactical aircraft. Now, however, as Hq. USAF deputy for operations, he was under severe pressure from above (Col. Howard Plunkett, e-mail, Feb. 17, 2005). In the end, he overruled the two officers' findings.

As they departed Gen. Simler's office, Maj. Chastain reportedly turned and said, "Boss you are wrong about this, and I'll prove it if it kills me." They departed "mad as hell" (Col. Bill Sparks, e-mail, April 23, 2005).

Analysis

On the day of Maj. Chastain's accident, the cameras tracking his dive were filming the event at one thousand frames per second. This allowed documentation of every six inches of bomb travel. Analysis of the film showed that the second bomb he dropped exploded four feet below the bomb rack. The project officers had been right, but they had been ignored. Major Chastain had to die to prove their point.

Conclusion

After redesign, and testing by the Fighter Weapons Wing Center's OT&E, the new fuze finally entered service in 1973. Meanwhile, great strides had been made in munitions and fuze design, including the smart weapons used so effectively today. The officers had spotted the problem and tried to be heard. Yet when they were rebuffed—put down, actually— they doggedly continued the tests despite the hazard.

Until this mishap, both the aircrew and airplanes had been treated as "expendables." But it was Maj. Chastain's dedication, integrity, and bravery that ultimately saved many others from a similar fate.

Chapter 19

The Downing of Strobe Zero One

*On his last combat mission of the Vietnam War, Air Force
Major General Robert F. Worley dies in a burning RF-4C.*

THE DATE WAS JULY 23, 1968, and their assigned target was to
perform a photoreconnaissance of an area northwest of Khe Sanh. The
flight was to be General Worley's last mission of the Vietnam War. In
fact, some six weeks hence he was slated to become deputy chief of

staff for operations of the Pacific Air Forces (PACAF). His aircraft was an RF-4C—call sign Strobe Zero One. Because most general officers didn't fly frequently enough to maintain proficiency, they were required to fly with an instructor pilot. But General Worley was an exception, and throughout his yearlong tenure as vice commander of Seventh Air Force, he had been flying missions regularly. Nevertheless, he was flying that day with Major Robert F. Brodman, an IP assigned to the 460th Tactical Reconnaissance Wing, based at Tan Son Nhut Air Base, Republic of Vietnam.

During a high-speed, low-level run on the target, their RF-4C was hit in the nose section by what apparently was a single 14.5 millimeter machine gun bullet—some of which were known to be explosive. Unfortunately, this round proved to be the explosive type. The projectile hit the nose-section camera bay, starting a very hot fire. In their Mayday call to Waterboy (a ground control radar site), Strobe Zero One reported that they had been hit, were losing hydraulic pressure, and had smoke in the rear cockpit (US Air Force Oral History Interview 1987, 49).

Meanwhile, Gen. Worley began an immediate climb and headed east toward the South China Sea to get "feet wet" (over water). An ejection over the jungle was dangerous because of the chance of getting hung up in one of the tall trees and the risk of being captured by North Vietnamese troops or guerilla forces scattered throughout the country. With an ejection over the sea, their rescue by helicopter would be assured.

Strobe Zero One's Mayday call was heard by Misty Four Zero, a so-called Fast FAC (forward air controller) flying an F-100F. A Fast FAC was a two-place F-100F that was flown very fast at low level, with the mission of spotting ground targets and troop movements in and around the so-called Ho Chi Minh Trail and near the demilitarized zone (DMZ). The FAC would then direct strikes by fighter-bombers against any targets they discovered.

Misty Four Zero was flown by Captain Don Harland in the front seat, with Captain Dick Rutan, the actual forward air controller, occupying the back seat. They had just completed in-flight refueling when they heard Strobe Zero One's Mayday call. Capt. Rutan quickly realized their heading was almost head on with Strobe Zero One. Consequently, he took control of the aircraft and asked Waterboy for vectors so they could join up and appraise the Phantom's battle damage. They quickly found the RF-4C and pulled up on the aircraft's left wing.

Capt. Rutan reported the aircraft looked OK, but the crew maintained they were losing hydraulic pressure and "getting a lot of heat in the rear cockpit" (Rutan 2002). By now they were "feet wet" and paralleling the coast at ten thousand feet.

Flying as a Fast FAC, Captain Rutan assumed control of the F-100F

With the aircraft now headed south for an emergency landing at Da Nang Air Base, Rutan relates, "I eased the Hun [F-100] in close underneath the big Phantom to check for damage. Harlan noticed them first—flames flickering in a small hole up inside the camera bay near the nose. He also spotted a little smoke coming out of the belly seams…Strobe Zero One acknowledged that he was on fire and said, 'OK, we're going to bail out.'"

Conditions for their ejection were ideal: the aircraft was under control with plenty of altitude, a reasonable airspeed of 230 knots, and a rescue helicopter awaiting their water landing. Having never watched an ejection before, Rutan took spacing on the doomed fighter to watch the forthcoming action.

After what seemed an eternity (but was actually less than two minutes) Maj. Brodman, the rear seat pilot, ejected. Rutan relates, "From my vantage point the rear cockpit ejection was 'textbook'…The aft canopy opened and separated cleanly, clearing the tail by at least 20 feet. Then the seat started up the rails. Just as the bottom of the seat cleared the canopy seal, the rocket motor ignited and burned for 1.2 seconds: then the seat went straight up—very stable. When the rocket stopped, the small drogue parachute came out, and the seat rotated backward ninety degrees as it cleared the tail. Then…I could see the main C-9 parachute canopy come out. As it started to open the seat separated…and kept right on going. With the parachute's canopy fully open, the pilot swung back underneath.

"When I looked back at the stricken aircraft I was horrified to see that the front cockpit was totally engulfed in fire. I saw an occasional flash from a white helmet that was barely visible through the smoke and flames. The general sat straight up as before, but he was motionless…Huge flames that looked like giant blow torches streamed from the rudder-pedal wells, through the front cockpit, around him and out through the open rear cockpit. Fire engulfed the Phantom's exterior and turned into a dense, black smoke trail that obscured the tail. Yet strangely the aircraft flew on."

Out of frustration and horror, Rutan began to holler over the radio to the stricken pilot, "Strobe Zero One! Bail out! Bail out!" But despite repeated calls, the general just sat there and didn't move. Capt. Harland then said, "Oh, my God! Look at it burn!" Rutan moved his aircraft in closer, but the pilot's white helmet was no longer visible—only a jet-black canopy. Then explosions blew panels off the nose, and the entire front end was a charcoal mass. Finally the orange and yellow flames subsided, and dense smoke streamed over the fuselage. At about five hundred feet above the shoreline, with the Misty F-100F still flying its wing, the Phantom pitched up a little then dove straight into the beach.

Rutan confesses, "I was horrified and just couldn't let go." Suddenly Harland screamed, "Pull up, Dick! Damn it, pull up!" With that, Rutan pulled back hard on the control stick, just missing some small trees behind the beach. With a choking voice he told Waterboy, "Strobe Zero One just impacted the beach." A few minutes later Waterboy asked if there was any chance of survival: To which Rutan replied, "Negative survival, negative survival!" But the action wasn't over yet.

Quickly they returned their attention to the backseat pilot, who was still floating down and was now about five thousand feet above the very rough sea. Then they spotted a motorized sampan flying a South Vietnam flag. It was plowing through the swells straight toward where the pilot would splash down. Rutan didn't like what he saw. Even if they were friendly, they might inadvertently run over and kill the pilot. "Conditions were that bad." Rutan made a low pass across the boats bow. But the sampan continued toward where the major was about to touch down. Rutan made another pass and put a long burst of twenty-millimeter cannon rounds across the boat's bow. That did it. The sampan crew got the message and made a quick 180-degree turn—just as the major's feet hit the water. Shortly thereafter, the USAF Jolly Green helicopter picked up the downed airman.

Later, Rutan asked Maj. Brodman why, after deciding to go, he had taken so long to eject. Brodman's reply was that the general hadn't wanted to eject and "argued about the position of the command ejection handle in the rear cockpit." Maj. Brodman wanted the handle in the "command" position, meaning that the back seat would go first, to prevent being burned by the front seat pilot's rocket exhaust plume. Then immediately thereafter the front seat ejection system would fire, so that no one—conscious or unconscious—would be left behind.

Still Gen. Worley refused to eject. After a brief argument about the position of the ejection selector handle, he specifically ordered, "Let's eject individually." Thus the major obeyed the general's order and left the handle in the "single initiated ejection" position. Then, after reading the checklist procedure to Gen. Worley, Maj. Brodman pulled the D-ring on his seat and ejected (US Air Force Oral History Interview 1987, 49).

For many years, Maj. Brodman reportedly felt guilty about leaving Gen. Worley behind. Yet he had no reason to feel responsible. By refusing to allow the automatic ejection sequence, the general sealed his own fate.

It was academic anyway: when the rear seat canopy blew off it released the cockpit's pressurization. This caused a chimney effect that literally sucked the very intense fire from the camera bay into the front cockpit with blast-furnace intensity. In fact, a subsequent laboratory analysis of Gen. Worley's parachute harness, conducted at the University of Tokyo, "could not duplicate the temperatures of that fire." Thus, because of the exceptional heat, had the general acquiesced to the dual automatic ejection, only his charred remains would have been ejected (US Air Force Oral History Interview 1987, 50).

In the end, Capt. Dick Rutan said it best: "General Bob Worley was a real, honest to goodness Tactical Fighter Pilot…His was a strong and much-needed voice for the fighter pilot." Anyone who knew this dedicated warrior-pilot would surely agree.

Captain Rutan examines battle damage from antiaircraft fire on his F-100F Fast FAC.

Above and Beyond the Call of Duty

Flying an F-4C, Colonel Ralph S. Parr, with backseater Captain Thomas McManus, defies unbelievable odds to thwart the siege of Khe Sanh.

THE MARINE FORWARD AIR controller (FAC) Fingerprint 54 was shouting, "Sharkbait Zero Two: you're receiving unbelievably heavy fire. Pull out! Pull out!" The F-4C Phantom's aircraft commander was Colonel Ralph S. Parr, a double jet ace from the Korean War. In the fighter-bomber's back seat was Captain Thomas McManus, who tells what he saw from the aircraft: "We flew down into the low, hazy visibility of the ravines, below the hilltops on both sides. I looked back and forth for the mortars that were, at that moment, pounding the marines at our Khe Sanh Fire Support Base [FSB]. Suddenly there was a mass of enemy troops upon the hill to my left, shooting down at our canopy. Several hundred enemy troops had been waiting, dead center of the FSB's only runway, to ambush and destroy the approaching C-130 resupply aircraft that we were escorting. In addition, we had stumbled onto an entrenchment of hidden heavy antiaircraft and machine guns."

Background

Khe Sanh is a township located among Bru Montagnard villages and coffee plantations in northwestern Quang Tri Province. Located on Route 9, it is the seat of the government for the Huong Hoa district and just seven miles from the Laotian border.

Route 9 is the northernmost road in South Vietnam, extending from the coastal region through the western highlands, ultimately crossing the border into Laos. At the time it was a major infiltration route used by the People's Army of Vietnam (PAVN) into the south.

Located originally at an old French fort just outside the village, Khe Sanh Combat Base (KSCB) originated in August 1962 as a US Army Special Forces airfield. Subsequently, it became the outpost for the Special Forces–organized civilian irregular defense groups. Their mission was to monitor infiltration along the border and protect the local population.

In November 1964, the Special Forces moved their camp to the Xom Cham Plateau, which ultimately became the Khe Sanh Combat Base. Sometime in 1966, the Special Forces unit moved off the plateau and established a smaller camp along Route 9, nearer the Laotian border at Lang Vei. Then, in 1967, the plateau was manned permanently by the US Marines. They had been given tactical responsibility for the five northernmost provinces that stretched below the DMZ, from the coast along Route 9 to Khe Sanh. The base was intended to serve as the western anchor for marine corps forces.

The battle for the KSCB took place during the People's Army of Vietnam's Tet offensive, between January 21 and April 8, 1968. The combatants consisted of elements of the US III Marine Amphibious Force along with elements of the Army of the Republic of Vietnam (ARVN). They were facing two divisions of the PAVN.

By March, five battalions (including the ARVN) at Khe Sanh required logistical support of 185 tons of supplies daily. Overland resupply had been essentially stopped by both the winter rainy season and the PAVN. This left the job to the air force C-130s and marine helicopters.

From the beginning of the siege until early March, low-hanging clouds and fog covered the area from early morning until around noon. Even then, the cloud cover rarely rose above two thousand feet. Air force C-130s were forced to make instrument approaches, using radar guidance from the base's ground control approach (GCA) unit—frequently through antiaircraft fire shot randomly into the clouds.

Once the big transports managed to land, they became targets of PAVN artillery and mortar rounds. Upon departing, they ran the gauntlet of fire during climb-out. Silencing the antiaircraft guns had thus far been unsuccessful, as the gunners would stop firing when fighter-bombers were in the area.

Breaking the Siege

The siege of Khe Sanh was an effort by the PAVN to repeat their devastating victory of May 7, 1954, against the French at Dien Bien Phu. The PAVN generals were using tactics that had been successful at that time, but at Khe Sanh they had failed to consider air power. The French had none; but at Khe Sanh the US Marines and ARVN Rangers had plenty.

Colonel Parr's close air support mission took place on March 16, 1968, just as the determined North Vietnamese Tet offensive was beginning to bog down. The mission of Sharkbait Zero One and Zero Two was to escort a large C-130 resupply effort, urgently needed to prevent Khe Sanh from being overrun and the marines and ARVN killed or captured.

PAVN antiaircraft fire was taking a devastating toll on the transports. This had prevented effective resupply of the outpost. To ensure that the C-130s could deliver their load and then depart safely, Colonel Parr's goal was to find and destroy as many antiaircraft guns as possible.

Sharkbait Flight had just rendezvoused with the transports when a call from the Khe Sanh battlefield commander diverted them to a close-support mission. From the jagged hills just off the Khe Sanh runway, PAVN mortars at that moment were shelling the base. The diversion proved to be of momentous importance.

Extremely heavy enemy fire had filled the area with smoke and haze. As the two Phantoms arrived, the marine FAC dropped a marker on the side of a ravine, close to the desired target, and less than a quarter mile from the runway. Sharkbait Zero Two was cleared in with napalm on what the FAC reported as two mortar positions that were actively shelling the base and runway. Because his external weapons consisted of napalm, Parr could work in close to the target, while his wingman, Sharkbait Zero One, held high with his fragmentation bombs, which could have caused injuries to nearby marines.

Captain McManus continues: "The first mortar was destroyed with a direct hit. Seemingly inches away from the gunners on the ridgeline we pulled up to the left, and our plane made a sloppy porpoise. I said to the Colonel, 'Check your gauges. Could you feel us being hit?' Quietly he responded, 'Don't know, I've never been hit.' Then I remarked, 'Well, there's large hole in our wing.'

"As we came around, Fingerprint 54 radioed that we'd been hit and should immediately head for home. He cancelled our mission, saying we couldn't survive any more passes at such a point-blank range. Then Colonel Parr said, 'Tom, we've been hit, but the transports will be sitting ducks against this. We are the only ones around who can help. *We gotta go back in*! We've been trying to find these guns for too long. We've got to destroy them before they are moved and hidden again.'

"Colonel Parr then radioed Fingerprint 54, refusing the cancellation, and said, 'Relay that to your Ground Commander and have him keep his marines undercover while you clear us back in. Tell him I realize I've been hit and I'm aware of the intense fire against us…But unless I can destroy their big guns our supply aircraft will fall like flies. So, when I call *ready*, 54…clear me back in!'

"Reluctantly, but quickly, approval was granted, and seven more attacks were made through withering fire at point-blank range. On our second pass our F-4 did another sloppy maneuver, and I knew we had again been hit really hard. But out we came with the gauges still checking OK. Once again Fingerprint 54 ordered us to cancel our mission.

But Colonel Parr countermanded, 'If we don't take out these guns and mortars the supply aircraft and your marines will be lost.'"

Again and again Colonel Parr returned to attack, with the enemy shooting from embedded positions from all sides with combined firepower. Fingerprint 54 was repeatedly screaming, "They're lighting you up like a Christmas tree!" Yet on each successive pass one more mortar and heavy gun position was destroyed.

Once again, the marine battle commander attempted to cancel the mission—because he judged the ground fire to be un-survivable. But again, because of the disastrous toll the gun emplacements would take of the approaching C-130s, Colonel Parr refused. Using the externally mounted SUU-16A twenty-millimeter Gatling gun, they made several more passes into the cauldron—with the enemy's firepower diminishing after each pass.

With his napalm and ammunition expended, Col. Parr was dangerously low on fuel but still within range of the antiaircraft fire. Nonetheless, he remained in the area, directing his wingman to target enemy troops located farther from our marines—thus assuring the greatest area of safe passage for the incoming transports.

Fingerprint 54 was finally able to fly down the landing approach without drawing fire. He radioed back, "There must be over a hundred enemy killed by air." The official marine tally, relayed through channels, was two mortars destroyed, five four-barreled heavy antiaircraft guns destroyed and one silenced, with ninety-six enemy troops killed.

The Aftermath

Shortly after this mission, marine intelligence noted an exodus of PAVN units from the Khe Sanh sector. The PAVN 325C Divisional Headquarters was first, followed by the 95C and 101D Regiments, all of which relocated west. Simultaneously, the PAVN 304th Division withdrew to the southwest.

From the opening of the PAVN's Tet offensive in late January 1968 through its termination at the end of March, the US Air Force flew more than twenty-two thousand sorties and dropped eighty-two thousand tons of bombs in support of this strategic combat support base. The Joint Chiefs of Staff estimated the enemy sustained ten thousand casualties, with the PAVN 304th and 325C Divisions decimated (Momyer 1978, 311).

Because Khe Sanh and the surrounding hilltop outposts were under almost constant artillery, mortar, and rocket fire, the air force turned to aerial delivery to avoid the hazard of ground operations. The result was that out of 14,356 tons of supplies delivered to Khe Sanh during the siege, 8,120 tons were para-dropped, with First Marine Aircraft Wing helicopters delivering 4,661 tons of cargo.

Finale

Colonel Parr's Phantom survived twenty-seven hits—remarkable for an aircraft built as an unarmored fighter-interceptor. Shortly thereafter the marine ground commander sent the commander of the Twelfth Tactical Fighter Wing a glowing report of the mission. His recommendation was that Colonel Parr, who was the Twelfth TFW director of operations, be submitted for the Medal of Honor (MOH) for his actions that day—which he emphasized were clearly and undoubtedly "above and beyond the call of duty."

When the recommendation was received by the newly arrived wing commander, he said to Colonel Parr, "Gee, Ralph, I've been here for three weeks and haven't even been awarded an air medal." Whereupon he tabled the recommendation (Colonel Ralph S. Parr, personal communication, March 2011). For several days news of the mission was the prime topic of conversation at Seventh AF Headquarters; a member of the Seventh Air Force awards board said they were expecting a MOH recommendation, since it certainly fulfilled the criteria. Sometime later a letter arrived at the Twelfth TFW from Colonel James Fogle, commander of the Direct Air Support Center at Da Nang Air Base, recommending the Air Force Cross for Colonel Parr. Still, no action was taken to process either award.

Captain McManus's full-time job was as duty officer in the fighter wing's operations center. Years later, in a letter to Vice President George H. W. Bush, dated October 1, 1987, wherein he was attempting to get Colonel Parr's Air Force Cross upgraded to the Medal of Honor, McManus tells of sensing the "strain of personalities emanating from our new Wing Commander's office and the Director of Operations. The Wing Commander simply refused to forward the recommendation for even the Air Force Cross." Finally, almost a year later, at the urging of his staff, "when many of those involved, including Colonel Parr, had been transferred…the recommendation itself was written and watered down…Those elements of the mission described in the marine ground commander's write-up, which qualified for consideration for the Medal of Honor, were omitted or diluted." The Air Force Cross was finally awarded a year and a half after the mission.

Meanwhile—in direct violation of air force regulations—Colonel Parr's written recommendation for a Silver Star award to Captain McManus was never forwarded to the Seventh Air Force Review Board. However, the award was made some years later through congressional action.

Colonel Ralph S. Parr finished his career as one of the most highly decorated officers in air force history. With sixty decorations for bravery, he had become a rated military pilot at age twenty, flown more than eight thousand hours in fighters, beginning with the P-38 in the Pacific theater toward the end of World War II and ending with two combat tours in the F-4 Phantom in Vietnam. He flew 641 combat missions in three wars, 427 of which were in the Vietnam War. During the Korean conflict, he flew his first combat tour in F-80 fighter-bombers. Then, on his second tour in Korea, while flying the F-86 Sabre, he became a double jet ace in less than thirty days, scoring his tenth victory on the last day of hostilities.

Other efforts through Congress have been made to upgrade Col. Parr's Air Force Cross to the Medal of Honor, but these requests have been denied each time by DoD. Meanwhile, his record serves as the pinnacle of combat leadership, courage, and technical competence to which future generations of air force warriors can aspire. It was an honor to have served with him as a junior officer-pilot.

Escape and Evasion

Shot down in southern Laos in their F-4C Phantom, Major John F. Clayton and his backseater faced the ultimate test of their survival skills.

THEIR MISSION THAT DAY WAS to interdict North Vietnamese army supply lines in southern Laos. Normally, during the day the antiaircraft defenses were spotty and inaccurate: but on February 28, 1967, they were spot-on. Leading the flight of four F-4C Phantoms was Major John F. Clayton. His "after action report" relates, "I was recovering from a 45-degree dive bomb pass at about 5,500-foot altitude, when over a two second time period I was hit [by antiaircraft fire] eight or ten times.

I recovered from the dive and established a ten-degree climb, then proceeded to try and get as far from the target area as possible. The right engine fire warning light suddenly illuminated and the engine began losing power. I retarded the right throttle to idle and the left engine fire warning light came on bright and steady. I was obviously too close to the target area for a successful evasion, so I jettisoned the external fuel tanks and my [remaining] bombs and put both throttles into afterburner."

Meanwhile, Clayton's wingman, flying in another F-4C, began urgently transmitting, "You're on fire! You're on fire. Eject! Eject!" However, in a desperate effort to distance themselves from the target area, the two stricken crewmembers stayed with their burning aircraft a while longer.

About four miles south of the target, the ship's hydraulic flight controls locked up solid, and its nose began to drop. Clayton remembered, "I called to my backseater to eject and we both left the aircraft at 450 knots and an altitude of 5,000 feet." Both our ejections were successful, "with a good deal of ground fire still audible from the hills northeast of our position."

In the jungle below, Clayton saw several farm plots and a few hooches (primitive dwellings). In an effort to steer the chute away from these signs of human habitation and land in the protective foliage of the jungle, he pulled hard on the parachute's risers. But a strong wind was blowing, which made steering the parachute almost impossible. "I was traveling sideways at about the same speed as my descent," the report stated.

As the wind pushed him roughly through the treetops he managed to grab onto a tree's trunk—absorbing the impact with his feet. "I finally landed in the top of a very tall [teak] tree." Then, as he looked around from his treetop position, he realized he was in full view of the hooches and a well-traveled footpath. "I could almost feel people watching, which gave me a strong motivation to move."

He quickly unlatched the chute's harness and the attached survival pack, then climbed down to the lowest limb on the tree. "I couldn't definitely see the ground [because of the dense vegetation], but could tell I was still over 100 feet high." With no other choice, he "bear-hugged" the tree trunk and started down. However, after sliding about fifty feet, "The tree trunk became so large I was unable to control my descent...As my descent rate increased I could just barely hang onto the tree with my arms and really accelerated during the last 20 feet or so before hitting the ground." As he slid rapidly through the jungle canopy, he unwrapped his legs from around the tree in order to land on his feet. His report stated, "On impact I almost blacked out, but after a few moments I regained my vision and was able to stand up."

He promptly abandoned his parachute harness and started moving southeast, since from the treetop level it had looked like the thickest jungle. After traveling about sixty feet, he discovered some unfinished hooches that looked to be just several weeks old. "I then realized I was on an old trail and was afraid of encountering someone."

After looking around for the best place to hide, he crawled through one of the hooches trying to leave as little trail as possible. On a slight rise about eighty feet behind and out of sight of the hooches, he stopped crawling, lay flat in a small depression, and took out his small handheld survival radio and attempted to make contact with his wingman. But the radio was damaged, and it took considerable "tinkering" to get it to work. And when it worked all he could hear was the emergency beeper signal from his companion's parachute.

Clayton's report stated, "The wind would alternately blow, making considerable rustling noises with the dry leaves, then suddenly stop and become deathly still...The radio made so much noise I tried to turn it off when the wind stopped and back on when the wind blew."

He had been on the ground about fifteen minutes when he heard someone on his left whistle. Then someone on his right whistled. He then turned off his radio, and like the animals he had hunted as a youth in Texas, covered himself with leaves and lay very still. Several minutes later he heard voices talking excitedly near the tree in which he had landed. Soon the voices stopped, but he continued to remain motionless for another fifteen minutes; then resumed trying to use his survival radio.

"I discovered I could regulate the radio's loud volume by holding my hand over the speaker and varying the pressure applied." Using this method he was able to monitor the radio and to attempt to transmit while the wind was blowing. "Then I heard someone say the rescue choppers would arrive in about 45 minutes to an hour.

After about thirty-five minutes on the ground, Clayton was able to make radio contact with his backseater. "I instructed him to turn off his [parachute's] beeper.

"An hour and twenty minutes after ejection I heard the rescue choppers and attempted to vector one to my position; but the Jolly Green Giant's reply was unreadable." Clayton then fired a smoke flare, and the Jolly Green hovered about one hundred feet downwind of where the smoke was clearing the jungle canopy.

"I then popped a second flare and the chopper moved to within 20 feet of me. I learned later that that although I was holding the smoke flare and could see the hoist operator, he couldn't see me. I tried to signal the hoist operator by shaking and jerking on the cable but to no avail…Then the jungle penetrator began moving farther away from me. I chased the penetrator through 15 to 20 feet of thick brush, and it finally came to rest in the center of a small bamboo thicket. Then, I got in the sling and seat and waited expectantly to be reeled up to the chopper. But the hoist remained limp.

"I tried signaling the hoist operator by shaking and jerking the cable but nothing happened." Then the hoist operator decided Clayton had had enough time and began retrieving the jungle penetrator. But while the cable was limp, it had somehow become wrapped around his left ankle; and for the next fifteen feet, he was being reeled-in upside down. Thanks to the penetrator's safety strap, he didn't fall as the cable unwound from his leg and he righted himself.

As he cleared the bamboo, near the top of the foliage the cable became entangled with the tree branches. Fortunately, with the hoist operator's help, he finally worked clear of the larger limbs. Then he gave the hoist operator the thumbs-up, ducked his head and grabbed the cable with both hands, and the operator pulled him free. Although he received numerous superficial cuts and scratches on his right hand, cheek, and neck, he had no more further problem getting into the chopper. The helicopter crew then moved over and retrieved his backseater from the jungle, and they headed for home base.

The mission was Major Clayton's fiftieth, and he subsequently went on to finish his combat tour with a total of 145 missions in the Phantom, logging 252 hours in combat.

Chapter 22

Those We Left Behind

The story of our cowardly abandonment of captured service personnel in the interest of "political considerations."

DURING THE COLD WAR WITH the Soviet Union and its acolyte states, the documented record of our airmen shot down and captured alive but abandoned by our government in the name of "political expediency" is a heartbreaking chapter in our nation's history. Following the Korean War, fifty-nine captured aircrew are known to have been transferred to various Soviet locations—including Moscow—for "intelligence exploitation." In fact, during a meeting in December 1991, Russian President Boris Yeltsin acknowledged the transfer of some POWs to Russian territory. But our Departments of State and Defense were too busy with other areas of containment to get involved.

In the 1950s and 1960s, 171 USAF aircrew members aboard sixteen reconnaissance aircraft were shot down while flying electronic intelligence ferret missions over international waters, along the borders of the Soviet Union. Many of these airmen are known to have parachuted to safety. While twenty-nine bodies have since been recovered, a few individuals have been identified as alive and in Russian captivity. Our government, however, has made no obvious effort to secure their return (Boyne 2012).

Although still officially denied by the Department of Defense, there is *overwhelming evidence* that at the conclusion of the Vietnam War the US government knowingly abandoned several hundred of our captured servicemen. This statement is backed by the Defense Intelligence

Agency's "Tighe Report" (May 27, 1986) that states in chapter XI, Observations: "Although live sightings through 1985 continued to flow into DIA, the evidence is compelling that at least between 1975 and 1979, American Military personnel were held in captivity in Laos by Vietnamese troops."

In hearings conducted by then-congressman Robert K. Dornan, Czech General Jan Sejna, who defected to the United States in 1968, said that between 1961 and his defection in 1968, his office was responsible "for organizing the shipment of [American] POWs and their housing in Prague before they were shipped to the Soviet Union" (Hoar 1998; Miller 2012, 50). He stated, "I was personally present when American POWs were unloaded from planes, put on buses whose windows had been painted black, and then driven to Prague, where they were placed in various military intelligence barracks and other secure buildings, until they were shipped to the Soviet Union…Czech intelligence [also] learned that the North Vietnamese provided US prisoners to Red China" (Hoar 1998).

In the early 1990s, the Russians opened their archives for American scholars to peruse. Documentation was found showing that the North Vietnamese acknowledged capturing 1,205 of our airmen alive, but only 591 were repatriated. The 1,205 figure was later verified by Mr. Le Dinh, a member of the Democratic Republic of Vietnam's Politbureau, who defected to the West in 1979. He revealed that, as of 1975, the Vietnamese still possessed about 700 American POWs.

Worse yet, the Cubans are reported to have taken seventeen of our airmen to Havana for medical experiments in torture techniques. Of course, none of these were repatriated. And, as you will read, both the Russians and Cubans had POW camps in the southern part of North Vietnam and Laos. None of our men imprisoned there were acknowledged or repatriated (Benge 1999). To this day, despite a plethora of declassified evidence showing the continued imprisonment of US servicemen, the official position of the US government remains that all of our airmen captured during the Vietnam War were returned.

Korean War POWs

Following the Korean War, the Soviets purposely held back fifty-nine airmen for "intelligence exploitation." They are known to have been transferred to the Soviet Ministry for State Security (Ministerstvo Gosudarstvennoy Bezopasnosti, or MGB) interrogation center at Khabarovsk, Russian Siberia, the regional capital of the Soviet Far East Military District, very near the Soviet-Manchurian border. There they underwent further interrogation and, if they survived, were later transferred to destinations within the Soviet Union.

At the time, the supersonic F-86 Sabre was the fastest fighter in the US Air Force. In fact, it was the only operational aircraft capable of breaking the sound barrier (exceeding Mach 1 in a dive). This made the capture of Sabre pilots a high Russian priority. Former RAND researcher Dr. Paul Cole said in an e-mail on November 2, 2008, that he found evidence that most of the thirty still-missing Sabrejet pilots are known to have been captured alive, with some taken for intelligence exploitation by engineers at the Russian design bureau in Moscow. None was ever repatriated, and their fate remains unexplained.

In a September 28, 1993, article in the now defunct newspaper, *The Sacramento Union,* writer Robert Burns wrote that the name of First Lieutenant Robert Frank Niemann appeared on a document provided by the Russians called the "List of 59." This document, compiled in 1991 and 1992 from original Soviet military archives, identified fifty-nine airmen who were shot down in Korea, "and who transited through a [Soviet] interrogation point" (Jolidon 1995, 188–189). A later Pentagon study concluded that only fifty were taken to the Soviet Union. (Associated Press 1994.) (Cole 1993 & 1994)The principal interrogation points for captured US airmen have been identified as Siniuiju, North Korea; and Khabarovsk, USSR. For those captured in North Korea, they were first interrogated in Siniuiju then turned over to the Russians and sent to the interrogation center at Khabarovsk (Associated Press 1994).

In a September 1992 interview, retired Soviet Colonel Viktor A. Bushuyev, deputy chief of intelligence for the MiG-15 equipped Soviet

64th Fighter Aviation Corps (FAC) based at Antung, China, was quoted as saying that he remembered an F-86 pilot named "Neiman or Naiman." The 64th FAC commander, General Georgii A. Lobov, remembered Niemann, too. Lieutenant Niemann was a Sabrejet pilot assigned to the 334th Fighter Interceptor squadron based at K-14 (Kimpo Air Base), South Korea. He had been shot down during a dogfight with MiGs on April 12, 1953. General Lobov recalled questioning Niemann while he was recovering from wounds in a warzone hospital—identified elsewhere as Antung, China.

Lt. Niemann is dressed and ready to ride out to his aircraft on what would be his last combat mission.

The reports from his captors—three of whom remembered Lt. Niemann by name after more than forty years—show he was a man of his word. It is clear that his adamant adherence to the military code of conduct impressed his interrogators. This also may have been the reason for his transfer to the MGB interrogation center at Khabarovsk.

Colonel Bushuyev confirmed that Niemann was alive and in Soviet custody for some time. A later notation on the Soviet list of fifty-nine airmen noted that he had died. Given his refusal to be interrogated and his apparent presence at the special Khabarovsk interrogation center, we can only imagine *how* he died. Alternatively, this report of his death could have been cover for his transfer to Russia.

According to General Lobov, around April 1951, a special secret unit was formed, consisting of nine top MiG-15 pilots from the Moscow air defense area. Their mission Both Gen. Lobov and Col. Bushuyev recalled that Lt. Niemann refused to answer *any* of their questions. Instead he chastised them, saying that it was a violation of international law to attempt to interrogate a wounded POW.

Lt. Niemann's reported resistance to interrogation was consistent with the author's earlier conversations with him. A recent graduate of the US Military Academy at West Point, on several occasions he had talked fervently about the necessity of resisting interrogation if we were captured. I felt sure his intensity on the subject was the result of his Academy training, since the rest of us had been given no specific instructions or indoctrination. There was simply a poster in squadron operations that cautioned, if captured provide only, "name, rank, and serial number."

According to General Lobov, around April 1951 a special secret unit was formed, consisting of nine top MiG-15 pilots from the Moscow air defense area. Their mission was to force down an F-86 and not only capture the pilot but also obtain his airplane's radar-ranging gunsight, which Russian designers wanted to replicate. Unfortunately for the Soviets, several of their special pilots were quickly shot down and killed, with the survivors returning to Moscow empty-handed.

While the unit's special mission was unsuccessful, on October 6, 1951, Colonel Evgenie Pepelyayev shot down an F-86, which crash-landed onto a sandbar on the Yellow Sea coast. The pilot was quickly rescued by an air force SA-16 amphibian. However, the Sabre's wreckage was recovered by the Soviets and sent to Moscow.

Academic Research

Until around 1994, the Russians were relatively generous in allowing access to their heretofore-classified files. For example, they provided a "Summary of Combat Activities of Corps Units on 12 April 53," the day Lt. Niemann was shot down and captured. (Also discussed was a MiG pilot's downing of soon-to-be triple ace Captain Joe McConnell, who fortunately was rescued from the Yellow Sea by an H-19 helicopter.) In this report, the MiG engagement with Niemann's flight is fully described:

"Captain Lazarev, flying as wing of his pair, noticed a pair of F-86s, which were pursuing a pair of MiG-15s. He went into an attack. The pair of MiGs, which were being attacked, went into the cloud cover while the pair of F-86s turned left and began heading for the bay. Banking left and closing to a distance of 800–900 meters, Captain Lazarev fired a short burst from an angle of 2/4. The pair of F-86s rolled over from a left into a right turn and entered a right bank. Having completed 3–4 banks and descended, Captain Lazarev closed on the F-86 to a distance of 600 meters, and on an attack angle of 1/4, fired three bursts. After a third burst the F-86 turned over onto its back and began to smoke. Captain Lazarev began to quickly close and pass above him [the F-86]. He [Lazarev] pulled out of the battle by going into the cloud cover." (Daily operational summaries, 12 April 1953, Soviet 64th Fighter Aviation Corps) (Note: in May 1953, Captain Lazarev was shot down and killed by Lt. Walter Fellman Jr.)

Unfortunately, in 1995 the Russian government closed access to their files. Still, they had allowed us to acquire much valuable information on our Korean-era MIAs.

The POW/MIA Policy

In 1955, Pentagon analyst James Kelleher wrote, "If we are in for fifty years of peripheral 'firefights' we may be forced to adopt a rather cynical attitude on this [unreturned POW/MIA issue] for political reasons." Two years later in 1957, the Pentagon adopted this policy of "cynical thinking" because, they reasoned, we could never be certain that all American POWs had been released. "In other words, some disposable assets [captured servicemen] might have to be written off as combat losses" (Anton 1997, 184). Our war in Vietnam saw that policy utilized in painful detail.

Sometime in February or March of 1973, when 591 of our servicemen were repatriated from Hanoi in Operation Homecoming, Secretary of State Dr. Henry Kissinger informed President Nixon that, "US intelligence officials believed that the list of prisoners captured in Laos was incomplete." The president responded by directing that the prisoner exchange continue and stating that Hanoi's "failure to account for the additional prisoners after Operation Homecoming would lead to a resumption of bombing." However, even though the government knew of three hundred unrepatriated POWs still in Laos "the president was later unwilling to carry through on his threat" (Schanberg 2010).

In March 1973, as Operation Homecoming was ending, President Nixon had become involved in the Watergate scandal and was unwilling to prolong our withdrawal from Southeast Asia. Thus, despite voluminous intelligence information to the contrary, he "summarily declared that all prisoners had been returned, and anyone who was still missing was dead." That became, and remains, the official US policy (Anton 1997, 184–187; Schanberg 2004, 3).

Recently declassified documents show that the North Vietnamese held back many of our airmen with the intent of collecting "reparations" for each one, as they had with the French in the 1950s. Bodies of deceased captives also were to be offered for ransom (Jensen-Stevenson and Stevenson 1990, 172; Schanberg 2004; Anton 1997, 182).

In a desperate effort to end the war in Vietnam, Secretary Kissinger, on behalf of President Nixon, sent a secret letter to the North Vietnamese agreeing to $4 billion in reconstruction and other "unconditional assistance." But the money was never paid because the State Department and National Security Council knew of our POWs who had not been released (Schanberg 2004).

In 1981, a special Senate committee headed by Senator John Kerry heard sworn testimony about yet another ransom offer from President Reagan's national security advisor, Richard Allen. In a detailed account, Allen told of an offer by Hanoi to repatriate fifty live POWs for a ransom of $4 billion. Later, in an *unsworn letter*, Allen recanted his testimony, saying "his memory had played tricks on him" (Schanberg 2004). But part of his testimony was overheard by Secret Service Agent John Syphrit, who verified hearing about Hanoi's ransom proposal. Syphrit, however, was forbidden to testify voluntarily by his Treasury Department superiors, and Senator Kerry refused to issue a subpoena.

Ultimately, Senator Kerry brushed off the reported ransom offer by saying, "The committee found no creditable evidence of any such offer being made" (Schanberg 2004). However, later on we did in fact pay ransom for the return of some remains. In the summer 1985, a large amount of money was flown to Hanoi aboard an air force C-141, and the remains of several airmen returned for forensic examination and burial. The aircraft's commander was a student in the author's night college course being taught at Travis AFB, California. Although the remains were not identified to the author, considering the time frame, they probably included those of US Navy Lieutenant Clemmie McKenney. As will be detailed, McKenney was shot down and captured alive near the DMZ in April 1972.

In September 1992, three former defense secretaries who had served during the Vietnam War acknowledged to a Senate POW committee that there were American POWs who had not been returned. James Schlesinger, Elliot Richardson, and Melvin Laird, speaking at a public session and under oath, said they based their conclusions on strong intelligence data—"letters, eyewitness reports, even direct radio contacts" (Schanberg 2010).

Cuban Involvement

Unknown to most Americans, the incumbent Cuban leadership was deeply involved in the Vietnam War. Among their more brazen actions was to provide an engineering battalion, called the Girón Brigade, to maintain Route 9, a major supply line from North Vietnam into Laos, Cambodia and into South Vietnam—the so-called Ho Chi Minh trail. "The Cuban contingent was so large they established a consulate in the jungle" (Benge 1999, 7).

Many American servicemen were involved in this area, and many were either killed or captured by the Cubans" (Benge 1999, 7). The Cubans had both a POW camp and field hospital in North Vietnam, very near the demilitarized zone—the border of North and South Vietnam. Their brutal torture of nineteen of our POWs in Hanoi is well known. But their abduction of seventeen American service-men who were taken to Havana for medical experimentation in torture techniques has been ignored by the mainstream media (Benge 1999).

The Soviets also were physically present and involved in the war. They too had a prison camp for American servicemen in southern Laos. The US government knew this from both human and pho-tographic evidence, but the names of our servicemen captured and held in the Soviet and Cuban compounds failed to appear on the Operation Homecoming list (Anton 1997, 179). "Air Force General Eugene Tighe, who later headed the Defense Intelligence Agency, said the discovery left US intelligence agents in a state of 'shock and sadness'" (Anton 1997, 181; Defense Intelligence Agency 1986, 27, 32).

Declassified documents reveal that those of our airmen captured in North Vietnam and Laos, and fortunate enough to have been repatri-ated, received unbelievably cruel and inhuman treatment. Several who were in especially bad physical condition were not released. Instead, they simply disappeared and remain officially "unknown" or their fate was officially obfuscated.

During 1967–68, in Hanoi's POW compound called the Zoo, at least nineteen US airmen were severely brutalized in the so-called Cuban Program. This involved torture administered by Cuban military attachés, tentatively identified as Brigadier General Edwardo Morjon Esteves, Luis

Perez Jaen, and Major Fernando Vecino Alegret—nicknamed by our captured airmen as Pancho, Chico, and Fidel. "The objective of the interrogators was to obtain total submission of the prisoners" (Benge 1997, 99).

An injured and catatonic Major Willard S. Gideon is shown shortly after being shot down in an F-105D and captured in the Hanoi area.

Major Jack Bomar, a surviving POW, told of how Fidel (Alegret) had beaten air force Captain Earl G. Cobeil to the point that "he was completely catatonic...His body was ripped and torn everywhere... 'Hell-cuffs' appeared almost to have severed his wrists...Slivers of bamboo were imbedded in his bloodied shins, he was bleeding everywhere, terribly swollen, a dirty yellowish black and purple from head to toe."

In one instance, Fidel became enraged because he felt Cobeil was faking his catatonic state. In an effort to force Cobeil to talk, "Fidel smashed a fist into the man's face, driving him against the wall. Then he was brought to the center of the room and made to get down onto his knees. Screaming in rage, Fidel took a length of rubber hose from a guard and lashed it as hard as he could into the man's face. The prisoner did not react; he did not cry out or even blink an eye. Again and again, a dozen times, [Fidel] smashed the man's face with the hose."

Major Bomar also told of how Fidel beat Major James Kasler across the buttocks with a large truck fan belt. "For one three-day period, Kasler was beaten with the fan belt every hour from 6:00 a.m. to 10:00 p.m. and kept awake at night…After one beating Kasler's buttocks, lower back, and legs, hung in shreds."

Miraculously, Maj. Kasler not only successfully resisted the Cubans but lived to tell about it. Capt. Cobeil was not so fortunate. Because of his physical and mental condition, to prevent embarrassing the North Vietnamese government, instead of being repatriated Capt. Cobeil was listed as "died in captivity" (Tamayo 1999; Benge 1999).

The Castro Connection

During the same period, two unrelated documents tell of the seventeen captured US airmen who were sent to Cuba for medical experimentation and intelligence exploitation. The POWs were held in Havana's Los Maristas, "a secret Cuban prison run by Castro's G-2 intelligence service," and the Mazorra [Psychiatric] Hospital. The motive was to develop improved methods of extracting information through "torture and drugs to induce [American] prisoners to cooperate" (Benge 1999, 5; Benge 1997, 1–2).

Meanwhile, in southern Laos and the DMZ area, a National Security Agency SigNet reported, "18 American POWs 'are being detained at the Phom Thong Camp…' in Laos, and are being closely guarded by Soviet and Cuban personnel, with [North] Vietnamese soldiers outside the camp" (Benge 1999, 7).

Other declassified documents show that just before the war ended, American prisoners in the Cuban POW camp near Work Site Five (Cong Truong Five), just north of the DMZ, along with those in two other Cuban-run camps, simply disappeared.

Then, during April 1972, in an in-your-face gesture to the United States, Fidel Castro visited the Cuban field hospital in North Vietnam, adjacent to the Work Site Five camp. In fact, he wanted to go into Laos to visit his troops there, but his security detail forbade it (Benge 1999, 8).

During this time period, navy F-4 pilot Lieutenant Clemmie McKinney, an African-American, was shot down, captured and imprisoned near Work Site Five. More than fourteen years later, on August 14, 1985, the North Vietnamese returned Lt. McKinney's remains. They reported he died in November 1972. However, US Army forensic anthropologists established the "time of death as not earlier than 1975 and probably several years later." It was *speculated* that he had been a guest at Havana's Las Maristas prison and his remains returned to Vietnam for repatriation (Benge 1999, 8; Tamayo 1999). But the official speculation is more truth than guesswork.

A medically retired CIA operative who was active in the area of Work Site Five during the early 1970s tells of seeing a photograph of Lt. McKinney, made after his capture, standing alongside Fidel Castro. The photograph came from an official CIA publication and is closely held by our government.

Another CIA document tells of two Cuban journalists, Raul Valdes Vivo and Marta Rojas Rodriguez, who "visited areas liberated by the NVA in South Vietnam." In 1967 at the Bertram Russell mock war crimes tribunal held in Denmark, Rodriguez told of their POW interviews. "Photographs of some of the American prisoners and related articles appeared in Cuban and various Communist media. Specifically shown and identified were "POWs Charles Crafts, Smith, McClure, Schumann and Cook." Others shown alive during a taped interview included Lieutenant Colonel Fred Haeffner, Majors Ernst Olds, and Donald McKeller (Benge 1999, 7). Still, nothing was done by our Departments of Defense or State to follow up on this information.

Incredibly, after the POWs were released they were instructed "not to tell of their torture by the Cubans." Chief warrant Officer Frank Anton, an army helicopter pilot who survived unbelievable treatment, tells of having his continued service in the army threatened by a brigadier general from the Pentagon. He was told, if he wanted to complete a career in the army, to stop talking about the POW issue (Anton 1997, 181).

Meanwhile, during 1977 and 1978, General Esteves (Pancho) reportedly served with the Cuban delegation to the United Nations in New York. At last report, Alegret (Fidel) was Cuba's minister of education (Benge 1999, 8).

Article 110 of the Geneva Conventions requires immediate repatriation of seriously wounded POWs. Yet in Vietnam, as in Korea, our adversaries ignored this completely. For propaganda purposes, the North Vietnamese gave *early release* only to healthy and compliant individuals. Medal of Honor recipient Lt. Lance Sijan was captured partially paralyzed and in severe pain with a broken back; yet he was denied both adequate medical care and prompt repatriation. Instead he was left to die a slow agonizing death, unattended, in a dank, bug-infested cell.

Finale

In his best-selling book, *An Enormous Crime, the Definitive Account of American POWs Abandoned in Southeast Asia* (2007), former US representative Bill Hendon (R-NC) documents the disturbing details of what we learned years after the war about our unreturned POWs. Bolstered by creditable defector information, combined with recent intercepts of Pathet Lao radio transmissions, on December 3, 1979, Defense Intelligence Agency (DIA) Director General Eugene F. Tighe Jr. (Lieutenant General, USAF) stated that "there was no longer any doubt that American POWs were still alive and in captivity."(Hendon, 205)

In the fall of 1980, General Tighe and DIA Vice Deputy Director Rear Admiral Jerry O. Tuttle, USN, began developing plans for a rescue attempt (Hendon and Stewart 2007, 206). On December 30, Tighe proposed to the CIA that the agency send an overland team to conduct ground reconnaissance on an identified POW camp in Laos. General

Tighe reported the CIA representatives "were openly hostile to his briefing and the proposition that any living American POWs were being held in Laos." Adm. Tuttle commented later, "With friends like these who needs enemies" (Hendon, 212).

In his 2002 book, *Inside Delta Force,* retired army Command Sergeant Major Eric Haney provides the rest of the above story. He writes that in 1981, his Special Forces unit endured rigorous training for the anticipated rescue of 125 unreturned POWs being held in Laos (Haney, "Inside Delta Force," 314). But the mission was inexplicably aborted, then revived a year later, and aborted again." Haney laments that this abandonment of captured soldiers ate at him for years and left him disillusioned about his service's creed "to leave no man behind."

Years later, Haney writes, he spoke at length with a former highly placed member of the North Vietnamese diplomatic corps. The former diplomat asked him point blank, "Why did the Americans never attempt to recover their remaining POWs after conclusion of the war?" (Haney, 318).

Section II, Article 118 of the Geneva Conventions reads, "Prisoners of war shall be released and repatriated without delay after cessation of hostilities." Yet following the Vietnam debacle, an academic researcher found Soviet Central Committee International Department Archives showing at war's end "705 American POWs were kept behind by the North Vietnamese." Henry Kissinger admitted to National Security Advisor Richard Allen that "he knew about Americans still in captivity when the Paris peace agreements were signed" (Jensen-Stevenson and Stevenson 1990, 157).

In late February 1993, while researching Soviet-North Vietnamese relations during the Vietnam War at the Russian Research Center in Moscow, Harvard scholar Dr. Steve Morris unearthed the Russian translation of a report presented on September 15, 1972, by the deputy chief of the North Vietnamese General Staff, General Tran Van Quang, to a session of the Politburo Central Committee. This was only five months *before* the prisoner release began in February 1973. General Quang confirmed that 1,205 American POWs were currently held in North Vietnam. He stated, "For now we have officially published a list of 368 POWs, the rest are not acknowledged." Subsequently, 591 were repatriated. Incredibly, this Russian document stated, "We have not told the world the truth about the number of the prisoners" (US Senate 1993, 42).

Major Willard S. Gideon, one of the fortunate ones, shakes hands with an air force colonel upon his release.

During a December 1991 US-Russia summit in Washington, DC, Russian President Boris Yeltsin met with members of our Senate Select Committee on POW/MIAs. They decided that the two countries should form a joint commission "to investigate the loss of American Servicemen in or around Soviet territory from 1945 to 1991." It was during that meeting that President Yeltsin acknowledged that "US POWs had been transferred to the Soviet Union."

Ultimately, a 1994 study by Dr. Paul Cole, then of the RAND Corporation, found that "a small number of unnamed Americans, possibly around 50, were taken to the former Soviet Union during the Korean War." Yet no apparent follow-up by our government took place.

Based on post–World War II history, it is obvious that only our military, CIA, and allies even attempt to honor the Geneva Conventions. It is the Soviet bloc nations—specifically the Russians, Chinese, North Koreans, North Vietnamese, and Cubans—whose heinous crimes against humanity have never been addressed on the international stage. Yet our politicians and media pundits are worried about "water boarding" and "naked night" at Abu Ghraib prison.

As for Cuba, it should be noted that Raul Castro was chief of Cuban armed forces during the Vietnam War and now heads their government. He in particular owes the United States and the civilized world an accounting for the seventeen US POWs who were taken from North Vietnam to Havana, Cuba, and subjected to hideous medical experimentation in torture techniques—and who were never repatriated.

Chapter 23

Project "Have Doughnut"

The heretofore top-secret story of our test and evaluation of an Israeli-acquired Iraqi MiG-21F-13, "Fishbed E."

IT WAS AUGUST 16, 1966, when Iraqi Air Force Captain Munir Radfa defected to Israel in a MiG-21F-13 jet fighter. At the time, this was a state-of-the-art Soviet aircraft and the pride of Russia's aircraft industry. Code named "Fishbed E" by NATO, the Mach-2.05 fighter posed a serious threat to Israel's air superiority. In the air order of battle, the Israelis faced eighteen Fishbeds in Syria, ten in Iraq, and thirty-four in Egypt (Weiss 2007). At the time, the Israeli Air Force (IAF) was equipped with slower French-made Vautours and Mirage IIIC fighters. A twenty-year embargo imposed by the US Congress had denied Israel the modern aircraft they needed, such as the Lockheed F-104 Starfighter or the newer McDonnell-Douglas Aircraft F-4 Phantom (Weiss 2007, 2).

Following approval of then-prime minister Levy Eshkol, Israel's ultra-secret Mossad had orchestrated the Iraqi pilot's defection, exploiting his frustration with an Iraqi military who had forced him to drop napalm on Kurdish civilians but passed him over for promotion because of his Christianity. Mossad agents had also learned that, following completion of a US military training course, Radfa had "become excited about life in the West" (Weiss 2007, 2).

245

On the morning of his fateful "training flight," Captain Radfa's MiG-21 was fitted with a 108-gallon (490-liter) auxiliary fuel tank. While the external tank was meant to allow increased flight-training time, on this occasion it served to ensure adequate fuel for Radfa's 560-mile flight to an Israeli air base.

After climbing to thirty thousand feet, he departed Iraqi airspace with no problem. But over Jordan he was intercepted by two Royal Jordanian Air Force Hawker Hunters, which attempted to make radio contact. Despite receiving no reply, the Jordanians allowed him to continue, undoubtedly because of his Iraqi insignia. As prearranged, Radfa was met at the Israeli border by four IAF Mirage IIIs whose pilots escorted him to a safe landing. With Radfa's assistance, Israeli test pilot Dani Shapira began a detailed evaluation of this intelligence bonanza. After a month of testing in Israel, the aircraft—accompanied by Shapira—was transferred to the US Air Force and US Navy for testing and further intelligence analysis (Weiss 2007).

Groom Lake

Because the MiG-21 had entered the fray in Vietnam, the US military urgently needed to develop defensive and offensive tactics for maneuvering against the aircraft. This required learning how its performance compared with the principal US fighters. The tests would seek to understand first the airplane's effectiveness as a day fighter-interceptor, and second, its capability as a ground-attack aircraft (Defense Intelligence Agency 1969, 1-1–1-13).

To ensure total secrecy of the highly classified project, the aircraft was moved to Groom Lake. This hidden Nevada airfield—officially called Area 51—was the birthplace of the Mach-3 SR-71 Blackbird and the stealthy F-117 fighter. Designated the YF-110, the Fishbed's test and evaluation project was code-named "Have Doughnut" (Eger, n.d.).

Mig-21 is shown with US identification after arriving at Groom Lake for further testing.

Mission Capability

As a fighter-interceptor, its basic weapons included a thirty-millimeter cannon loaded with sixty rounds of ammunition, along with two AA-2 Atoll heat-seeking missiles. The missiles were copies of a US-made AIM-9 Sidewinder, obtained when a Nationalist Chinese F-86F fired one at a MiG-17. Unfortunately, it failed to explode, and it lodged in the aircraft's fuselage. Using reverse engineering, it was copied by the Soviets and became the basis for their air-to-air missiles ("AA-2 Atoll" 2008).

While its armament was adequate for an interceptor, the gunsight was found deficient. "The tracking index drifts off the bottom of the windscreen when tracking targets in excess of 3Gs" (Defense Intelligence Agency 1969, 1–41).

A noteworthy aerodynamic characteristic of the delta-wing aircraft was the rapid airspeed bleed-off during high-G turns. This reduced its turn radius, and unlike our own delta-wing aircraft, the Fishbed could maintain the G-force at the slower speeds. Obviously, in a turning fight, this gave the Fishbed a significant tactical advantage. For the air-to-ground role it had the thirty-millimeter cannon, which proved potentially lethal against tanks. From wing stations it could carry two pods of thirty-two fifty-seven-millimeter FFAR rockets. However, when strafing with the cannon, "there was considerable pipper (gun sight) jitter during firing," (Defense Intelligence Agency 1969, 1–41).

Air force test pilot Maj. Fred Cuthill straps into the Fishbed's cockpit assisted by Maj. Jerry Larsen, both key members of the flight evaluation team.

Flight Characteristics

Four major aerodynamic limitations were identified:

- Exceptionally heavy pitch force required above 510 KIAS

- Severe buffeting below fifteen thousand feet when approaching 595 knots or 0.98 indicated Mach number

- Exceptionally slow engine acceleration from idle to full military power

- Poor directional stability in turbulence

The exceptionally heavy pitch force at high speed was a severe limitation to a pilot's ability to recover from a diving ground attack, or to maneuver while approaching and departing the target area. While this served to prevent overstress problems when pulling up from a target, for a fighter-bomber it made "high pitch rates difficult or impossible to achieve" (Defense Intelligence Agency 1969, 1–6). Thus recovery during dive-bombing, strafing, or air-to-ground rocket firing was problematic. This was exacerbated by the airplane's poor directional stability in rough air.

One of the most significant findings was that below fifteen thousand feet the aircraft could not go supersonic. Exceeding airspeeds of 595 KIAS or 0.98 indicated Mach caused severe buffeting. This airspeed limitation was a major exploitable design flaw. During the Vietnam conflict, those of us flying F-105Ds and F-4s typically approached a target at 550 knots; then, once the bombs were released, we departed well in excess of 610 knots—often supersonic.

As for the Fishbed's exceptionally slow engine acceleration, spool-up time from idle to full military power required fourteen seconds, "with a tendency to hang-up in the process." During tests, this slow acceleration led to occasional hot compressor stalls and engine over-temperature, a characteristic corrected in American jet engines during the late 1940s and early 1950s. The afterburner, too, when engaged or disengaged, marked the aircraft's location by producing highly visible white puffs of unburned fuel (Defense Intelligence Agency 1969, 1–7).

Flight tests revealed that the MiG-21 was not supersonic below fifteen thousand feet and was unstable in turbulent air.

A special limitation for this "day-visual-conditions fighter-interceptor" was its front and rear visibility. Forward visibility was restricted by the gunsight (combining glass) and bulletproof (glass slab) windshield. A protective seat flap over the pilot's head restricted visibility in the fifty-degree tail cone, a problem exacerbated by the narrow design of the ship's canopy and fuselage structure.

It is noteworthy, however, that during the Vietnam War, the Soviet and Chinese sponsors, along with North Vietnamese air force commanders, very effectively planned and controlled the aircraft around its limitations. They never committed their fighters unless there was a good chance of success and subsequent escape. In fact, in 80 percent of the Vietnamese People's Air Force (VPAF) kills, the victims were unaware they were under attack, and "the winner initiated the combat from a position of nearly unbeatable advantage" (Sayers 2008, 2). This was before we obtained effective radar coverage in the North.

Typically the Fishbeds were "vectored into the rear hemisphere for a high speed, single-pass attack," generally from a cross-course intercept. For example when our fighters were bombing targets such as the Doumer Bridge north of Hanoi, the MiG-21s, flying at high speed, would be vectored by their GCI radar from protected Chinese airspace to a position behind the Phantoms. As the F-4s either rolled in or pulled up from their target, the MiGs would launch their Atoll missiles then zoom back to political sanctuary in China. "Blow-throughs," these were called (Davies 2005; Sayers 2008, 4).

Because of target restrictions dictated by our political leadership, during the late 1960s, VPAF airfields, parked aircraft, command centers, and main radar installations were forbidden targets. Consequently, the MiGs enjoyed a superior kill/loss ratio over our F-4s and F-105s (Sayers 2008).

High Altitude

One of the major advantages the aircraft enjoyed was that at high altitude its small size made it very difficult to visually acquire or keep in sight while maneuvering. In a frontal or trailing attack, its slight silhouette also made it difficult to acquire on radar.

Still, despite its sleek shape, the MiG-21's performance at high altitude was found inferior to the F-4's, F-105D's, and F-104's. At high altitude its top speed was Mach 2.05, whereas the F-4s and F-105Ds were both capable of about Mach 2.14 (Davies 2005). The F-104 Starfighter was limited only by the skin temperature rise at about Mach 2.21.

Overall Evaluation

Despite being heavier, both the F-105D Thunderchief and F-4 Phantom were found superior to the MiG-21. Maintaining a high airspeed and avoiding a turning engagement was the key to success during air-to-air encounters. However, the F-4 *was* found aerodynamically superior in a vertical contest.

Tests showed the Phantom had the capability to control an engagement below fifteen thousand feet by exploiting the MiG-21's subsonic airspeed limitation and its rapid airspeed bleed-off during high-G maneuvers. In a visual encounter, "By orienting an attack towards the

Fishbed E's blind cone…and by operating in the vertical during ACM (air combat maneuvering), the F-4 can defeat the MiG-21" (Defense Intelligence Agency 1969, 1–10).

When flying formation, the Fishbed's slow engine spool-up was a special handicap. To stay in position, the pilot had to constantly use speed brakes and rapid throttle movements. Top airspeed comparisons in full military power showed that up to about thirty thousand feet the F-4 was much faster than the MiG-21, but only slightly faster in afterburner. Below fifteen thousand feet the F-4 would *easily* accelerate to airspeeds well above the Fishbed's 595 knots (.98 indicated Mach) limitation.

Using full military power in zoom-maneuver comparisons, from low altitude to thirty thousand feet, the Phantom had a significant advantage over the Fishbed E. In a zoom climb to twenty thousand feet, with engine afterburners engaged, it held only a slight advantage.

It was in the instantaneous hard (high-G) turn that the MiG-21's delta wing proved superior to all our major fighters. While the delta-wing Fishbed typically lost airspeed more rapidly while turning, it could retain its G-force to a slower speed. This reduced its turn radius significantly. As a result, the study warned against "prolonged maneuvering engagements" (dog-fighting) by US fighters. It recommended that pilots press an attack only if they had an initial "rear hemisphere advantage." In essence, from an advantageous position, a Thunderchief pilot or Phantom aircrew should use the same hit-and-run tactics used by the MiG-21s.

One VPAF MiG ace, Luu Huy Chao, told author and veteran fighter-pilot Ralph Wetterhahn, "The American fighters flew faster than ours: We had to force them to turn…When they turned the [superior] speed did not matter…We just made use of the appropriate angle to cut their [circle] and our guns became effective" (Wetterhahn 2000, 48).

The F-105Ds performance against the Fishbed E also proved surprisingly good. Below fifteen thousand feet it had the capability to greatly exceed the MiG's limiting airspeed. Thunderchief pilots routinely departed heavily defended targets at supersonic airspeed (650 knots). Maintaining a high speed at low altitude was the key to survival.

Last Kill

The last MiG-21 downed by a Phantom during the Vietnam War occurred in the early hours of January 8, 1973. The engagement took place in Route Pack III, eighty miles southwest of Hanoi, well after the cessation of the Christmas bombing in the north under Operation *Linebacker II*. Captain Paul Howman with WSO First Lieutenant Lawrence Kullman of the Fourth TFS/432nd TFW was leading Crafty Flight on a predawn MiGCAP—protecting B-52s that were bombing SAM sites around Vinh (Davies 2005, 84).

Red Crown, the US Navy's ship-borne radar control, had identified a MiG-21 some sixty-five miles to the northeast: "Whereupon the Phantoms were vectored to a position twenty-six miles from the bandit." Crafty One was a combat tree–equipped F-4D. This made it possible for the WSO to see the MiG's Identification Friend or Foe (IFF), which, as mentioned earlier, they used to prevent friendly fire destruction of their own aircraft.

Crafty Flight had been loitering at twenty-six thousand feet, whereupon Captain Howman decided to descend to just above the eight-thousand-foot undercast so they could look up on their radar and thus eliminate some of the scope's ground clutter (Davies 2005, 84).

Red Crown gave them a heading to fly of three hundred degrees. But this took the MiG off their radar scope. "When we turned back on the MiG, we had indications that it was out there, but Larry Kullman couldn't find it." Then, in the predawn darkness, Captain Howman spotted the yellow-blue flame of its afterburner, and "put it in the center of my windscreen, caged my radar straight ahead, and got a lock-on. The radar locked, I shot [an AIM-7E-2] and remembered you had to shoot two for best probability of a kill.

"Looking at the MiG's afterburner when the first missile detonated, I could see the delta shape of the aircraft. The second missile looked as if it hit the MiG in the belly. There was a momentary hesitation, then the MiG blew up—with the fuselage breaking in half and the right wing coming off. The 432nd TFW Wing Commander saw the explosions and radioed 'Tally ho' on the burning wreckage. It fell through the 8,000 foot undercast right in front of an F-111 on a strike mission" (Davies 2005, 84).

Finale

Despite severe political restrictions, the USAF finished the war on January 29, 1973, with a 2/1 air-to-air kill/loss ratio: 137 MiGs downed with 65 US aircraft (including bombers) lost to the enemy fighters. The navy did better with a 4.3/1 ratio: 56 MiGs destroyed while losing 13 of their own. It is noteworthy too that the navy's success included more of the MiG-17s. Their higher success rate was credited to the superior training in air-combat maneuvering delivered by their Top Gun program, which was started in 1968.

Air force missions covered a larger area with longer ingress and egress routes. This allowed the VPAF's air defense network more time to position their assets and set up for a kill. Political limitations, however, were the most significant factor contributing to the air force's tepid showing. Also relevant were the lack of adequate counter-air training, and derelict command initiative and imagination (Sayers 2008).

Unlike the North Korean and Chinese student-pilots we encountered during the Korean War, the VPAF fighter pilots were carefully trained and competent warriors. They finished the war with sixteen aces to our one air force pilot ace and one navy ace. Their top ace was Nguyen Van Coc, credited with seven aircraft and two Firebees (UAVs). His aircraft victories included two F-4Ds, one navy F-4B, two F-105Fs (Wild Weasels), one F-105D, and the only F-102A lost in the war (Wetterhahn 2000). The F-102A, flown by Wallace Wiggins, was downed on February 3, 1968 (Zampini 2002). The VPAF's command and control of its aircraft was excellent too. They very effectively used the Soviet Air Defense system to counter our forces. "Because the USAF did not attack the main radar installations and command centers [the politicians worried about killing Russian and Chinese advisors], the Vietnamese flew their interceptors with superb guidance from ground controllers, who positioned the MiGs in perfect ambush battle stations…Such tactics were sometimes helped by sophomoric American practices. For example, in late 1966 the F-105 formations would fly every day at the same time, in the same flight paths, and use the same call signs over and over again" (Zampini 2002.). For a time, Colonel Robin Olds helped correct these ridiculous "tactics," when he sponsored Operation Bolo, described in chapter 17 (Davies 2005; Sayers 2008).

Overall, the VPAF and their Soviet and Chinese "advisors" proved to be skilled and worthy opponents. They richly deserve credit for their ability to adapt their strategy and tactics to the realities of their aircraft capabilities. Fortunately, today we have all become friends.

Chapter 24

Acceptance Test

A routine production flight test of a new supersonic F-106A interceptor identifies a major design flaw.

IT WAS JUST AFTER NOON on October 27, 1958, and the weather over the expansive Mojave Desert was as usual CAVU—clear and visibility unlimited. After a short takeoff roll, air force Captain Edward C. Jones rotated the new delta-wing Convair JF-106A into the air. Popularly tagged the Delta Dart, the aircraft was a virtual rocket ship, especially with the limited fuel load typical of test flights. This was to be the airplane's twentieth trip aloft. The first fifteen flights had been company developmental flight tests, followed by four conformity tests to determine its suitability for integration into the air force inventory. Captain Jones had departed from Palmdale Air Force Plant Forty-Two on acceptance test number five to validate correction of previously identified radar and damper (gyro-stabilization system) malfunctions. The final radar check would utilize a B-57 target aircraft. If the radar worked in all modes, the aircraft would belong to the air force.

As one of the first thirty-seven airframes built, the aircraft had been utilized to perfect the new state-of-the-art electronic and fire control systems. Hence it's temporary designation as a JF-106A. If Jones accepted the airplane it would be delivered to nearby Edwards AFB, where Convair would update all systems to the standard air force configuration. It would then be assigned to an air force fighter squadron with the *J* designation dropped.

Acceptance test flights were usually flown in a clean configuration (i.e., no external fuel tanks). When lightly loaded, the interceptor approached the magic one-to-one thrust-to-weight ratio so coveted by fighter pilots everywhere. The single Pratt & Whitney J-75-P-17 engine, producing 24,500 pounds of afterburner thrust, pushed the only slightly heavier airframe to record speeds and altitudes. In fact, this 1950s-era airplane had an official airspeed of 1298 knots (1525 mph), with a rate of climb of 42,800 feet per minute and a service ceiling of 52,700 feet. However, because of the "thermal barrier" (heat-rise due to friction heat on the ship's skin and Plexiglas canopy) it was limited to Mach 2.31. Although it never saw combat, for many years the Delta Dart was the fastest fighter in the air force inventory.

As he rocketed through ten thousand feet, Capt. Jones was suddenly startled as the flight controls began pulsating and became sloppy. Inexplicably there was no centering position on the control stick. Worse yet, there were no breakout forces—no artificial feel—to the hydraulically operated flight controls. Thoroughly alarmed, he now began experiencing random control stick movements, causing control surface oscillations. Following established procedures, he called flight test operations, a company tower—call sign Convair Three—to report the control problems and ask for technical advice from Convair engineering. Their first question to him was, "What's your problem, Ed?"

Climbing through twenty thousand feet, Jones reported the aircraft was rolling intermittently up to one hundred degrees, and at times up to 180 degrees. Simultaneously, it was oscillating in pitch through an arc of twenty-five to occasionally forty-five degrees. The B-57 pilot, who by now had joined him, reported the elevons (a combination of elevators and ailerons unique to delta-winged aircraft) were continuously in motion.

Like all modern jet fighters, the F-106 was equipped with irreversible hydraulic flight controls, which were powered by both the primary and secondary hydraulic systems. In related cases involving the F-102A, which shared the same system design, Convair engineers had found that when one hydraulic system malfunctioned, it caused un-commanded control stick and surface movement. Company tests showed that overheated hydraulic fluid flowing into the hydraulic elevon package—called the HEP valve—which fed the flight controls, resulted in sporadic flight control movement.

The new aircraft was rolling uncontrollably, sometimes as much as 180 degrees.

Several causes of the hot hydraulic fluid were possible. For example, a cavitating hydraulic pump (due to air in the system or a lack of hydraulic fluid) would cause overheating. Contaminated hydraulic fluid below the ten-micron range resulted in silting, which increased friction within the HEP-valve. This too produced undesired control movements. A low-pressure setting on the thermal venting and pressure relief valve also could be involved. Yet if the pilot could make the malfunctioning hydraulic system fail, the uncommanded control movements stopped.

To get into denser air, which would hopefully dampen the oscillations, Jones descended to ten thousand feet. Then, in a desperate attempt to fail one of the hydraulic systems, he began bleeding off pressure by opening and closing the speed brakes and cycling the yaw and pitch dampers off and on. None of these actions helped. He fought to maintain control, but the pitch and roll oscillations continued unabated.

Then a company engineer recommended that Jones climb back to at least eighteen thousand feet. There, in a last-ditch effort to bleed off and hopefully fail the secondary hydraulic system, he was instructed to cycle the speed brakes and simultaneously lower the landing gear—both of which were powered by the secondary system. (This of course assumed the secondary system was the problem.) If it worked he'd be able to land using just the primary hydraulic system.

Once back at eighteen thousand feet, the aircraft continued to oscillate wildly. As instructed, he cycled the speed brakes several times. Capt. Jones told Convair Three, "It caused some uncomfortable attitudes... At one time I attempted to freeze the stick by bracing it with my hands and knees, but that was unsuccessful. By releasing the [control] stick completely, the aircraft would begin uncontrollable oscillations (USAF Accident Report 1958).

By now Jones's flight suit was soaked with sweat, and he was physically exhausted from wrestling three thousand psi of uncontrolled hydraulic pressure. On advice of Convair Three, he made one last effort to bleed down the secondary system by extending the landing gear. As the landing gear handle went down, the aircraft instantly rolled inverted. Quickly he retracted the gear, but he had lost it, and the beautiful delta-wing fighter was now totally out of control. He told investigators "I was in an inverted spin...with the [control] stick still oscillating."

Upon passing through fifteen thousand feet, with the airspeed showing eighty knots, Captain Jones ejected. Following the ejection, the aircraft flipped upright and crashed in the desert just north of Edwards AFB.

The F-106 wreckage shows a classic pattern of an upright flat spin.

Background

Development of the Delta Dart began in 1949 as project WS-201A—a weapons system that ultimately became the F-106A and later the F-106B two-place trainer. The concept called for a fighter-interceptor capable of supersonic flight, equipped with an all-weather search and fire-control radar and armed with air-to-air guided missiles (later models had a gun too). It was slated to be the air force's "1954 Ultimate Interceptor."

Because Convair's proposal was closely related to their efforts in 1948 on a delta-winged test bed, designated XF-92A, they were awarded the airframe development contract. Their design evolved from the work of Dr. Alexander Lippish, who had pioneered the delta-wing concept in

Germany during World War II. By December 1951, it became apparent that neither the engine nor the MA-1 fire-control system would be ready by the 1954 deadline. Thus the air force proceeded with an interim version, pending later availability of the fully developed system. The interim aircraft was designated the F-102A. The fully developed version would be called the F-102B, later re-designated the F-106A.

Design and development of the electronic systems was the first priority. And in October 1950, Hughes Aircraft Company was awarded the armament and electronics contract for what was later designated the MA-1 fire-control system. It was designed to fire a nuclear-tipped Genie missile and four radar-homing, infrared, heat-seeking Falcon missiles. The air force wanted the Interceptor to be operationally available by August 1958—four years later than planned originally. Its radius of action was to be at least 430 miles, with an altitude capability of seventy thousand feet. In addition, at thirty-five thousand feet it had to be capable of interceptions at speeds up to Mach 2.

In November 1955, the air force ordered the first seventeen F-106s, all of which would be used for systems testing. The first one was ready in December 1956, with the remainder delivered in January 1957.

To achieve the required performance, Convair made several changes to the basic F-102 airframe. While the delta wing remained essentially unchanged (the first few test aircraft had the same leading-edge fence found on the F-102A), the newer version had leading-edge slots that replaced the fixed leading-edge and wing fence. The fuselage too was more streamlined, with the engine's air inlets moved well aft of the nose and closer to the engine. The air inlets were fitted with automatic variable inlet ramps. These moved fore and aft with Mach number changes to keep the engine inlet air subsonic as the aircraft approached Mach 2. These aerodynamic changes worked.

(Three years later on December 15, 1959, Major Joseph W. Rogers, flying a stock air force F-106A, set the world's absolute speed record for single-engine aircraft of 1525.96 mph [1,297 knots]—Mach 2.31—at 40,500 feet. With a service ceiling of 52,700 feet, it could climb to its combat ceiling of 51,800 feet in 6.9 minutes.)

The fire-control system was designed to be compatible with the semiautomatic ground environment (SAGE) continental air defense network. The design concept had the MA-1 system taking control of the aircraft after takeoff, with a SAGE ground controller guiding the airplane to intercept the target, whereupon the pilot locked on the intruder aircraft and fired the weapons. The SAGE controller then resumed control until the airplane returned to the vicinity of the air base, where the pilot again took control and landed.

Ejection System

Captain Jones's JF-106A had an advanced version of the Weber-built ejection seat used in the F-102A. With a pyrotechnic lap-belt release, this interim seat was fitted with a MK-1 rocket/catapult (ROCAT) ejection system. This two-stage rocket design was similar to the improved zero-zero capable (zero altitude and zero airspeed) version that ultimately was installed in all the Interceptors. Earlier technology required both altitude and airspeed for a pilot to successfully eject.

When Capt. Jones ejected, it was a one-step procedure: He simply raised the armrests. This jettisoned the canopy then ignited the first stage of the two-stage rocket catapult. This booster phase started the seat up the rails. Then, just prior to the seat-ship separation, the sustainer rocket ignited. The sustainer rocket nozzle provided an upward and forward thrust to the seat, allowing both seat and pilot to clear the tail.

An automatic lap-belt release was included, but to allow the parachute to deploy, the pilot had to manually kick free of the seat. Unfortunately, in the euphoria of an ejection, pilots were forgetting to kick free of the seat. Capt. Jones's otherwise textbook ejection highlighted the problem of this manual seat-man separation procedure.

Because of high mountains west of the Palmdale, California, area, Jones's parachute's barometer was set to automatically deploy at sixteen thousand feet. Having ejected at around fifteen thousand feet, as he tumbled through the sky he began to wonder why his BA-18 parachute had not yet deployed. Then he looked down and discovered he had a death grip on the armrests' handles, and was still firmly in the seat. Quickly he released the armrests and kicked free, and his parachute deployed immediately.

Jones then encountered yet another problem. As the chute's canopy popped open, the freefalling seat tumbled through it, tearing out three panels. Fortunately, the seat missed hitting him, and while the missing panels increased his descent rate, he managed to land without injury.

Meanwhile, there were problems air force–wide, with the delayed pilot-seat separation, including canopy-panel damage and entanglement of the freefalling seat with the shroud-lines, resulting in serious injury to pilots. In 1965, the air force tasked Weber Aircraft Corporation with designing a "zero-zero-capable" seat that would eliminate these problems. This included an automatic-opening lap belt combined with a seat-man separator—popularly called a "butt-snapper." Upon ejection, the lap belt would open automatically; one second after the seat left the aircraft, the separator actuated and flipped the pilot out. Then, at the preset altitude, a ballistic charge forcefully deployed the parachute. Weber delivered the first seat in just forty-five days, and it proved highly effective. In short order the entire F-106 fleet was retrofitted.

Finale

The Air Force Accident Board quickly exonerated Capt. Jones of any responsibility for the mishap. But the manufacturer was faulted for an inadequate "fail-safe" design of the hydraulic flight-control system. Subsequently, Convair took several immediate corrective actions.

Ultimately, the air force acquired 340 of the Delta Darts, which included 277 F-106As and 63 of the two-place B models. The last of these air defense fighters was delivered on July 20, 1961. In late 1961, Secretary of Defense Robert S. McNamara briefly considered reopening the production line to build an additional thirty-six aircraft. However, during that era there was a DoD push to get commonality among the services in everything from socks to satellites. The goal was to simplify logistics and reduce costs. Thus, in the future, there would be only one type of fighter, and the navy and air force would use the same type of aircraft.

Convair's plant manager Bill Martin presents Capt. Jones with the Delta Dart's control wheel.

The result was a USAF competition called Project High Speed, which pitted the F-106A against the navy's McDonnell F-4 Phantom II interceptor and F-105D Thunderchief. While the F-106A bested the Phantom II in energy-maneuverability (visual dog-fighting), the consensus was that the Phantom's APQ-72 radar was more reliable and had longer detection and lock-on ranges than the competing aircraft. In December 1961, the USAF announced that Tactical Air Command would acquire the F-4 Phantom II—a lighter-weight version designed for the air force. Although the F-106A would remain in the inventory, Air Defense Command would get no new Interceptors.

In 1972, more than a decade later, this policy changed, and the air force began replacing the Delta Dart inventory with the McDonnell-Douglas F-15. While the spectacular F-106A never saw combat, it served overseas for short periods in Germany and during the *USS Pueblo* crisis in South Korea. The final F-106A was retired from the 119th FIS of the New Jersey Air National Guard in August 1988.

During its long service life, the F-106A had the distinction of recording the lowest single-engine-aircraft accident record in USAF history. Still, during its twenty-nine-year career, out of a total production of 340 aircraft delivered, one third (112 including 17 two-seat F-106Bs) were lost in accidents or ground fires.

Even today, the Delta Dart's superior performance could hold its own in both the fighter-training and combat arenas. And Maj. Joseph W. Rogers's speed record for single-engine jet airplanes, established in aircraft number 56-467, still stands: 1525.96 mph, or Mach 2.31, at 40,500 feet. The aircraft was truly a design ahead of its time.

Chapter 25

Death by Hypothermia

A fishing trip mishap takes the lives of Lieutenant General Glen R. Birchard, commander-in-chief of USAF's Alaska Command, and his pilot.

WITH SOME HIGH CLOUDS TO the west and a light breeze putting useful ripples on the lake's surface, the float-equipped de Havilland Beaver—designated a U-6A by the military—departed King Salmon Air Force Station, an outpost located on the upper Alaskan Peninsula. It was 0600 hours on June 3, 1967, when they lifted off from Naknek Lake, with the irreverent blast of the 450-horsepower Pratt & Whitney "Wasp Junior" engine roaring across the water's expansive surface.

Aboard was a party of four, intent on enjoying some of Alaska's renowned fishing. Included were Lieutenant General Glen R. Birchard, Alaskan Command commander-in-chief; Major General Joseph A. Cunningham, Twenty-second Air Force commander; the Command's conservation officer, Mr. Edward A. Bellringer; and flying the aircraft was the general's pilot, Major Norman C. Miller. For once, the fickle Alaskan weather seemed to be cooperating, and it promised to be a beautiful day for their undertaking.

At 0715 they landed on Upper Ugashik Lake. Major Miller beached the aircraft, and they all promptly began fishing. As advertised, the action was superb, and after five hours of landing silver salmon, it was time for lunch. They boarded the aircraft to return to the Air Force Station's Naknek Lake camp and taxied out for takeoff.

Unfortunately, by now the wind had become mean—so mean, in fact, it was causing four to seven foot waves on the open water. While the surface wind velocity was unavailable in the Alaskan outback, light float-equipped aircraft, such as the Cessna and Super Cub models, typically cease all flying once the wind gets to around eighteen to twenty miles per hour. This much wind causes whitecaps on a lake's surface, a visual signal of a dangerous condition known as "rough water." This water condition can trigger failure of certain structural components, as a floatplane bounces from wave to wave while accelerating for takeoff or during landing. Specifically, impact with large waves subjects pontoon attach-points and strut and engine mounts to extreme pounding. On a windy day, when a pilot has challenged rough water, it is not uncommon to see a floatplane taxi in with its engine drooping and the propeller slicing the top of the floats.

The Beaver, of course, is a bit heftier and can handle somewhat worse conditions. US Army Field Manual 1-106 (dated 1973)—the only source of information on the subject—identifies rough water as beginning at a wind speed of twenty-one mph (eighteen knots). The manual cautions, "Although the pilot can do much to ease the punishment the floatplane absorbs, in rough water the best advice is: *When in doubt, don't try it* [emphasis added]." Then, as if to encourage pilots to take a chance, the manual states, "If the waves are large each bounce will push the nose up. Forward stick should be applied promptly to avoid crashing into the next wave in a stall…Taking off is often a succession of bounces from wave crest to wave crest until flying speed is attained." Maj. Miller was undoubtedly taught this during his initial training in the aircraft.

In a 1966 book titled *Flying with Floats*, author Alan Hoffsommer states, "It has often been said that if the height of the waves from crest to trough is more than 20 percent of the length of the floats, takeoff on water should not be attempted." In this case, the Beaver's straight Edo 4930 floats measured about twenty-three feet in length. Using Hoffsommer's rule, the maximum wave height Miller should have challenged was about four and a half feet.

Based on the reported four-to-seven-foot waves, Maj. Miller faced a close judgment call. Both Hoffsommer and the army field manual emphasize that the pilot's skill is the most important factor. As an air force general's personal pilot, Maj. Miller was unlikely to have had extensive experience in floatplane operations.

Normally, when rough water conditions exist, for both passenger comfort and safety, the experienced pilot looks for an area sheltered from the wind. And to his credit Maj. Miller appears to have done this. The air force accident report reads, "The first takeoff was aborted because the pilot encountered a crosswind and rough water prior to attaining liftoff speed." This was an entirely prudent decision. But his subsequent actions imply either a case of "compulsion" or possibly undue pressure from one of his two high-ranking passengers.

Although the wind direction was not mentioned, apparently it was highly variable. The report states, "The second takeoff was started into the wind. As the aircraft approached the lake's shore, a left turn was made to parallel the shoreline. The aircraft again encountered rough water and continued through a series of hard bounces and turns." While it's difficult to envision, the report says the turns and bounces eventually placed the aircraft "in its final takeoff path with a quartering tailwind." Yet instead of aborting due to the extremely rough bounces, this time Miller doggedly continued at full power The accident report stated, "The aircraft bounced high into the air several times, but lacked sufficient airspeed to remain airborne…the aircraft crashed when the floats contacted the water with a tremendous force after the final bounce…the float and strut assemblies collapsed, and the aircraft nosed down into the water." As the aircraft rolled over and began sinking, the uninjured occupants successfully escaped.

Water Survival

All four of the occupants were dutifully wearing life vests, which, once out of the aircraft, they quickly inflated. In the cold water, approximately 55 degrees Fahrenheit, they initially stayed together, but Gen. Birchard seemed to be having trouble. The strong wind was now blowing them parallel to and about two miles out from the shoreline.

Recognizing the danger of their slow progress, in desperation, Gen. Cunningham struck out alone and managed to reach the shore "in a totally exhausted state." The Command's conservation officer, Edward Bellringer, stayed with Gen. Birchard and Maj. Miller until they were within about two hundred yards of the shore. After an estimated hour and a half in the cold water and when it looked like the two officers could make it to shore alone, Bellringer, too, swam ashore.

But for some reason Gen. Birchard and Maj. Miller failed to follow. As they lingered, the cold water slowly sapped their strength and consciousness. One after the other, they tipped over face-down in the cold water and drowned.

An hour later, the rescue coordination center at Elmendorf AFB reported Gen. Birchard and his party overdue and immediately launched a rescue team from King Salmon. When the rescue team arrived in the area, the helicopter pilot, Captain Stuart J. Silvers, reported high winds and limited visibility. The team members immediately spotted the bodies of Gen. Birchard and Maj. Miller, floating face down in the turbulent water. After first retrieving Mr. Bellringer and Gen. Cunningham, Capt. Silvers returned to the bodies and hovered. Then, using the helicopter's winch, Sgt. Freddie Gunn and Airman Second Class Kurt Stedingh laboriously reeled them aboard.

Finale

Key aspects of this tragedy involve decisions made under borderline conditions. As previously mentioned, the four-to-seven-foot wave action was clearly a no-go situation. To his credit, Maj. Miller's initial takeoff attempt was apparently started from a sheltered area. Then, upon encountering the immense waves and strong crosswind, he wisely aborted the attempt. Four-to-seven-foot waves look intimidating to any rational seaplane pilot. But on his second attempt, with the nose of the aircraft bobbing up and down at extreme angles, and with the pontoons heavily pounding the aircraft each time they dropped off the crest of a wave and hit the next swell, Miller stayed at full power and failed to abort.

The change in the aircraft's direction to a cross-tailwind in the extremely rough water only adds to the incredibility of the scene. Based on Miller's initial good judgment to terminate the first takeoff attempt, followed by an apparently doggedly determined—irrational, actually—effort to continue in the incredibly rough water, implies that he was being intimidated by one of the senior officers aboard

As for the two deaths from hypothermia and drowning, both would have survived had they been wearing immersion suits. Although not addressed in the report, at the time of this incident air force personnel flying over water that was 50 degrees Fahrenheit (10 degrees Celsius) or colder were required to wear immersion suits. These insulated rubber suits were developed for aircrew late in the Korean War to protect those forced to ditch or bailout into the sea during winter. In this case the crew and passengers were never far from land—and they were on leave and just enjoying the outing. Still, they *were* in an air force airplane.

If they had just waited for the wind to die down…

Although water temperature was not given in the part of the accident report made available, based on events we can assume it was between 50 and 60 degrees Fahrenheit (see Table 24-1). Had they been wearing immersion suits, both officers would have survived.

COLD WATER INDUCED HYPOTHERMIA

Water temp in ° Fahrenheit	Exhaustion / Unconciousness	Expected Time of Survival
Up to 32.5°	Under 15 minutes	15 to 45 minutes
32.5 to 40°	15 to 30 minutes	30 to 90 minutes
40 to 50°	30 to 60 minutes	1 to 3 hours
50 to 60°	1 to 2 hours	1 to 6 hours
60 to 70°	2 to 7 hours	2 to 40 hours
70 to 80°	2 to 12 hours	3 hours to indefinitely
Over 80°	Deferred indefinitely	Indefinitely
Information from Underwriters Laboratories, Inc.		AC91-69, 11/19/99

Table 24-1

As this accident shows, the life vests were only one part of the survival equation. A Canadian bush pilot reports that in spring it is common to find the bodies of fishermen who have fallen out of their boat floating in their life vest but dead from hypothermia. Because of the cold-water threat, the north-slope oil companies require immersion suits for all employees who transit the lake country via helicopter or work on the oil rigs in the Arctic Ocean.

There is also the question of why Maj. Miller, the youngest member of the group, failed to save himself. A study conducted in the 1960s of fighter-pilot fatalities that occurred due to tardy ejections in pilot-induced loss of control accidents might be applicable here. The study found that if the loss of control was due to an obvious error by the pilot—such as an accidental spin—in a desperate attempt to salvage the situation, he tended to stick with the aircraft too long. In this case, there could have been no doubt in Miller's mind that he was responsible for the accident. Then, too, he undoubtedly felt a special loyalty to Gen. Birchard. After all, an aide-pilot enjoys a close personal relationship. Thus, both his culpability and loyalty kept him by the general's side—until hypothermia snuffed out the spark of life.

Chapter 26

Reach for the Stars

His burning ambition was to become an astronaut and participate in space flight; but a zoom-climb maneuver in USAF's test-pilot school claimed the life of the talented student.

IT WAS A CLEAR AND cool morning at Edwards AFB, California. The date was November 22, 1968, and Major Kermit L. Haderlie, a student in the air force's prestigious Aerospace Research Pilot School (ARPS), was scheduled to fly a Lockheed F-104C Starfighter on a zoom-climb mission to the edge of the earth's atmosphere. For all ARPS students, the zoom maneuver was a rehearsal for future spaceflight, and that was certainly Haderlie's long-held goal.

The high-speed Mach 2 mission took the airplane so high that the thin air would no longer support the jet engine's combustion. Consequently, to prevent engine over-temperature damage, the pilot was forced to shut it down in the upper atmosphere; or sometimes it simply flamed out for lack of oxygen. Then, upon recovering from the apogee of the zoom-climb, like a returning spaceship, the pilot steered the supersonic glider to a lower altitude where he then restarted the engine. If the restart was unsuccessful, he could make an X-15-like landing on the base's fifteen-thousand-foot runway. If for some reason he was short of the main runway, the lakebed runway was always available.

Since many of the graduates would join NASA's space flight program, the zoom-climb mission was an important part of the test-pilot school's curriculum. It had been designed to familiarize students with the problems of operating in the upper atmosphere. The actual climb angle and apogee altitude for each of these missions was calculated by the student based on current atmospheric conditions. In order to maintain control at the top of the zoom-climb, the pilot needed at least thirty-five pounds per square foot of dynamic pressure on the aerodynamic surfaces. Otherwise, the aircraft would tumble out of the top into a potentially unrecoverable spin. Maj. Haderlie's calculations called for a thirty-degree angle for his zoom-climb. His projected apogee altitude was not reported, but it was probably around eighty thousand feet.

The ARPS used the Lockheed F-104C for some phases of student training.

Nearing the end of the course, Maj. Haderlie was already enthused over the possibility of becoming an astronaut. Indeed, several of his classmates would later become part of NASA's space program. On a routine training flight the previous week, he had shown the "right stuff" when a pressurization duct ruptured in the F-104C he was flying. He was instantly engulfed in searing hot air, as the cockpit reached a near-incinerating temperature. Yet he endured the intense pain from burns on his arms and recovered the aircraft at Edwards AFB.

Freedom's Cowboy

His path to this point had been challenging. He was born and raised on a ranch near the small rural town of Freedom, Wyoming. His staunch Mormon parents were hardworking ranchers, and a childhood of riding horses, herding cattle, and pitching hay had imbued him with a strong work ethic. He paid his college tuition by working summers driving bulldozers and other heavy equipment. When he later obtained a commercial pilot's certificate, he supplemented his income by working as a flight instructor, teaching fellow students to fly light airplanes. In 1952, he graduated from Utah State University. Thanks to their Reserve Officer Training Corps program, he was commissioned a second lieutenant in the US Air Force.

In the air force he found his niche. He graduated from flight school first in his class, was designated a distinguished graduate, and won the Commander's Trophy for superior performance. Flying the famed F-86 Sabre at fighter gunnery school, he again finished first in his class—graduating with the Top Gun award.

Assigned to the 36th Tactical Fighter Wing in Germany as a fighter pilot, flying the F-100C, he quickly earned the coveted Select Crew award. Subsequently, he was picked as a member of the wing's aerobatic team, the Skyblazers. This was the European version of the famous Thunderbirds.

After completing the overseas assignment, he was sent to Luke AFB, Arizona, as an instructor teaching new air force pilots to fly the North American Aviation F-100 Super Sabre. There he nurtured plans to become an astronaut.

Lt. Haderlie was selected to be a member of the USAF's European version of the Thunderbirds — the Skyblazers.

A year later he applied for test-pilot school, but the competition was too tough, and he wasn't selected. An advisor told him he had the wrong education. He had graduated with a bachelor of science degree, but for test-pilot school, he was told, a degree in engineering or astrophysics was highly desirable. So he went back to school and earned a degree in aeronautical engineering from the University of Arizona. At the next selection board meeting he was accepted for the Aerospace Research Pilot School (ARPS). At age thirty-four, Major Kermit Lloyd Haderlie was approaching his lifelong dream of space flight.

Zoom-Climb Mission

The zoom mission capped the final phase of ARPS, a program that took a seasoned operational pilot and gradually helped him develop the skill and confidence needed to perform at the edge of the earth's atmosphere. The day prior to his zoom flight, Major Haderlie flew with an instructor pilot and practiced the procedures applicable to a solo zoom-climb mission.

His aircraft for the zoom mission was one of the school's single-seat F-104Cs—call sign Zoom Three. A chase plane, a dual-seat F-104D crewed by two of the school's student test pilots—call sign Zoom Chase—was used to monitor all such flights.

Mission Preflight

Protocol at the time had the student-pilot don the pressure suit in a special room that housed all the school's protective equipment. After fitting and pressure-checking the suit, the student went through a denitrogenation procedure to eliminate nitrogen from his blood and body tissue. This required breathing 100 percent oxygen for at least thirty minutes prior to the flight. Then, carrying and breathing from a portable oxygen bottle, he was escorted to the airplane by life sciences personnel.

Unlike the usual air force procedure, to relieve the pressure-suited and tightly constrained pilot from the aircraft preflight inspection, the chase pilot performed it for him. Then, after dutifully completing the walk-around inspection he signed the ship's log book—Air Force Form 781. A suit technician then helped the pilot enter the small cockpit and made the suit-to-ship connections for him. Finally, the life sciences officer in charge rechecked the connections and again pressure-checked the suit. Both pressure checks simulated a pressure differential much greater than that to be expected in flight.

A suit technician checks the pilot's equipment, then helps him into the cockpit.

After the pilot is seated a suit technician makes the suit-to-ship connections and a Life Sciences officer then rechecks.

Life Support

Before being certified for the job, a technician qualified to manage pressure suits was carefully trained and supervised for several weeks by both a life sciences officer and NCO. This included proficiency in tasks pertinent to a specific type of mission. The zoom-climb was one such mission. Other tasks included fitting the pressure suits, checking for proper suit operation, detection of malfunctions, preflight check of aircraft components connected with the suit operation, and finally preflight check of the ship-to-suit connections with the pilot seated in the cockpit. All these activities were closely monitored by senior life sciences personnel.

The specific factor that doomed Major Haderlie's mission was that the suit-donning procedure no longer required taping the gloves' locking slides after they had been attached. Using tape to secure the glove-suit connection had previously been a routine part of the donning procedure. The purpose of the tape was to increase the force required to move the sliding lock out of the detent, thereby reducing the possibility of inadvertent unlocking.

But in the spring of 1968, just a few months prior to Major Haderlie's flight, the glove taping requirement was removed from the donning procedure. This was intended to make it easier for the pilot to intentionally unlock the glove and relieve suit pressure at low altitude if the suit malfunctioned.

At the time, air force regulations required a full pressure suit for all flights above fifty thousand feet. This had been found necessary because in the upper atmosphere the oxygen pressure needed to keep blood-oxygen saturation in the normal sea-level range of 98–100 percent caused severe eye and sinus pain and collapsed the lung alveoli. This prevented the alveoli from absorbing oxygen and transferring it to the red blood cells.

The pressure-demand oxygen regulator used in air force aircraft provided a mix of oxygen and ambient air up to thirty-four thousand feet. At that modest altitude the system produced 100 percent oxygen in order to keep the pilot's blood-oxygen saturation normal. If the unpressurized aircraft continued to climb, the system would begin to produce 100 percent oxygen under increasing pressure. At forty-five thousand feet the oxygen pressure peaked at about 30 millimeters of mercury (mm Hg), which provided only 76 percent blood saturation. This was considered marginal for safety. In addition the pilot's breathing pattern was altered. Because the pressure automatically filled his lungs, he was forced to exhale; "reverse breathing," it was called (USAF Manual 160-5, 5-1).

With an emergency depressurization, air force flight surgeons found the maximum altitude at which the pilot could function normally with the standard pressure-demand oxygen system was forty-three thousand feet. (This was later changed to twenty-five thousand feet.) There, 100 percent oxygen was supplied under 30 mm Hg of pressure to provide 82 percent blood saturation.

Among the problems involved with high oxygen-mask pressures were that above 25 mm Hg, it was difficult to get a good seal on the mask. In addition, air force flight surgeons found that human lungs could tolerate a maximum oxygen-regulator pressure of 30 mm Hg—but just barely—and only for short periods. Pressures greater than 30 mm Hg produced a variety of problems. With a pressure of 40 mm Hg, eye and sinus pain became intolerable. But the most significant effect was a disturbance of the blood oxygen flow through the lungs. This could rapidly lead to shock and loss of consciousness.

To overcome these deleterious effects it was necessary to counterbalance the high oxygen pressure in the lungs with external pressure. This was the function of the full-body pressure suit. In order to protect the pilot's eyes and ears from high oxygen pressure, his entire head was enclosed in a pressurized helmet. Counterpressuring the entire body to prevent circulatory disturbances necessitated either mechanical or pneumatic pressure (equal to helmet pressure). Thus outfitted, the pressure-suited pilot could receive oxygen under very high pressure at extreme altitudes without ill effects. In fact the standard air force pressure suits were found effective even in the vacuum of outer space.

The full pressure suit worn by Maj. Haderlie (suit model, A/P22S-2) was designed to provide counter-pressure on the human body beginning at thirty-five thousand feet. This was accomplished by surrounding the user with an envelope of pressurized air.

Takeoff

Major Haderlie's scheduled takeoff time was 0930 hours; however, he and Zoom Chase were airborne at 0915. After departure, Zoom Three contacted the Edwards Space Positioning Facility—call sign Sport—which would control his flight. Immediately, Sport began radar and optical tracking of Haderlie's flight. Meanwhile, the entire ARPS Class 68A was watching his mission on closed-circuit TV.

As planned, Zoom Three and Zoom Chase climbed in a northeasterly direction. During this outbound phase, at an altitude of thirty-five thousand feet, certain checklist items peculiar to the zoom mission were completed. These included depressurization of the cockpit to activate and check the pressure suit, along with a check of the angle-of-attack indicator and electronics-bay pressurization. About seventy nautical miles from Edwards AFB, Zoom Three began a right climbing turn to forty-five thousand feet. During the climb, additional checks of electronics-bay pressurization were accomplished, along with another check for proper functioning of the pilot's pressure suit. Everything appeared normal, and Major Haderlie transmitted this information to Zoom Chase.

For the acceleration run to Mach 2, Zoom Three was cleared into the supersonic corridor by Edwards RAPCON (radar approach control). This speed run would culminate in the zoom maneuver. Once established on the corridor's inbound track, Zoom Three accelerated to the target airspeed.

Once again, Haderlie acknowledged to Zoom Chase that all checks were complete. Then he requested a call from Sport prior to reaching the geographical abort point. This was the westernmost position along the acceleration track from which a zoom maneuver could be initiated, and if the engine failed to restart, the aircraft could still be recovered on the Edwards AFB runway.

Prior to the abort point, Sport gave Zoom Three the requested calls at twenty seconds, then ten seconds. Immediately after the ten-seconds-to-go warning, and now tracked at Mach 2 and 47,500 feet, Haderlie initiated the zoom-climb maneuver. Upon reaching 50,000 feet, as required by mission protocol, he confirmed that his pressure suit was properly inflating.

At sixty-one thousand feet, Zoom Three reported established at the preplanned thirty-degree climb angle. At sixty-three thousand feet, Sport transmitted the standard call for afterburner shut down. But this call was not acknowledged. Then, on the closed circuit television monitor in the Space Positioning Facility, the Starfighter was observed to roll inverted. Four seconds later, Major Haderlie transmitted, "I lost my glove." The aircraft had now passed through sixty-six thousand feet.

Loss of the glove caused total loss of air pressure within the suit and helmet. With this explosive decompression his body was instantly at the same altitude as the depressurized cockpit. He would stay conscious for only seconds.

Test pilot and accident-board member Colonel Fred Nordin stated that because of the Starfighter's snug cockpit, Haderlie's inflated pressure suit made movement difficult. His attempt to reach the throttle and shut down the afterburner, while keeping the aircraft on its programmed flight path, caused the glove-locking collar to rotate to the unlocked position. (USAF, Accident Report, November 22, 1968.)

In an effort to communicate with Zoom Three, Zoom Chase transmitted, "How do you read?" There was an immediate but garbled reply, then silence.

The accident report shows that Zoom Three attained an apogee altitude of 69,400 feet. Then, three seconds later—still in full afterburner—the beautiful Starfighter began an inverted descent. As the sleek fighter descended through the chase aircraft's altitude of forty-four thousand feet, the chase crew began transmitting, "Zoom Three, pull out! Pull Out!" Then "Eject! Eject!" Even Sport repeated their calls to eject.

Students typically zoomed the F-104C to around 80,000. The NF-104, equipped with a supplemental rocket engine could reach the outer edges of the earth's atmosphere.

Hurtling down at an extreme airspeed, the aircraft exceeded by a large margin the so-called thermal-barrier limitation, and the F-104's skin and canopy became dangerously hot. Then, with both space-positioning personnel and his classmates watching on close circuit TV, as the aircraft reached denser air at the lower altitudes the beautiful Starfighter disintegrated.

There was no in-flight explosion, but a post-impact fire consumed the fuselage and cockpit area. Westerly winds from the altitude at which the aircraft disintegrated down to ground level caused significant dispersion of the lighter pieces of wreckage. From the time of Maj. Haderlie's last garbled transmission at sixty-nine thousand feet until ground impact was only sixty-one seconds. Investigators said the ejection system had not been activated. Nor could the pilot's body have survived an ejection at greater than 1,750 mph.

Finale

The Air Force Accident Board blamed the mishap on "design deficiency of the forearm-to-glove locking mechanism…[which] allowed inadvertent disconnection of the right glove from the suit." Thus the discontinued procedure of taping the lock-ring was reinstated until modifications could be made.

Tragically, Major Kermit Lloyd Haderlie—the youthful and talented cowboy from Freedom, Wyoming—was within sight of fulfilling his all-consuming dream to reach for the stars as an astronaut. But fate had other plans. On the day of his death, he had been married exactly one week.

Chapter 27

Pushing the Envelope

Air force Colonel Emil (Ted) Sturmthal spent a career developing and testing the latest aviation technology.

Air Force experimental test pilot Col. Ted Sturmthal

ON FEBRUARY 4, 1969, AIR force test pilot Colonel Emil (Ted) Sturmthal and NASA research test pilot Fitzhugh Fulton landed the cobra-shaped Mach 3.1 delta-winged XB-70A Valkyrie at Wright

Patterson AFB, Ohio. Although they had conducted some structural dynamic tests on the flight, the aircraft was to be officially decommissioned. Because of its unique design and capabilities it was destined for display at the National Museum of the Air Force.

With the Cold War still simmering, nuclear-weapons-capable aircraft of the era typically were programmed to fly to their target at very low altitude to avoid radar detection and at subsonic airspeeds. Then, nearing the target they made a high-speed dash to and from the target to deliver the weapon and escape the nuclear blast.

Conversely, the XB-70A had been designed for continuous cruise at Mach 3—three times the speed of sound, or 2,056 mph—and at a stratospheric altitude of seventy-three thousand feet. Both the speed and exceptionally high cruise altitude provided certain advantages over the Soviet radar and their surface-to-air missiles.

During supersonic tests, the Valkyrie had been found to produce a severe sonic boom pattern on the surface. Thus, on this final flight to Ohio, to prevent shockwave damage to structures on the ground, the two test pilots had flown at a modest subsonic Mach 0.93 (707 mph).

The introduction of intercontinental missiles had lessened the importance of long-range bombers. And too, more advanced technology was now available in other classified projects, such as the Lockheed YF-12C and SR-71 Blackbirds, which were already operational. Although two prototypes of the Valkyrie had been completed, the number-two aircraft had been lost in a midair collision with an F-104 chase plane during a photo shoot. Thus President Kennedy canceled the program and reassigned the remaining XB-70A to NASA as a research aircraft— its primary mission to collect data useful for the supersonic transport (SST) design and to gather information for the National Sonic Boom Program. Now it was being relegated to national monument status. Still, for Colonel Ted Sturmthal, it was just another day at the office.

Background

Seemingly born with an obsession to fly airplanes, young Sturmthal began to actively fly at age fifteen. In 1944 at age sixteen, he joined the Civil Air Patrol (CAP), an auxiliary of the Army Air Corps. Upon joining the CAP, he pointedly expressed a desire for a career in military aviation. In the CAP, he was provided an in-depth ground school then allowed to fly and handle the controls of various aircraft.

On January 16, 1946, at age seventeen—exactly four days after being promoted to cadet-commander of the Los Angeles CAP squadron—with only five hours of dual instruction, he soloed a Piper J-3 Cub. This was the foundation of his subsequent extensive flying career. After qualifying for a private pilot's certificate, his uncle gave him a military surplus BT-13A trainer, used during World War II to train air corps pilots. Still, despite his increasing civilian credentials, his stated goal was a career as an air force pilot.

Enrolled in the University of California, Los Angeles (UCLA), studying aeronautical engineering, he continued his flying activities and signed up with the Air Force Reserve Officer Training Corps (AFROTC). Then, before starting his junior year, he took a six-month sabbatical to accompany two air force ROTC officers (active duty instructors) who had arranged to meet with the French military in Vietnam—their mission unknown, but it did not involve flying.

Returning to school, he changed his major to physics and finished in the spring of 1952 as a distinguished graduate of his AFROTC class. Awarded a regular commission as second lieutenant and immediately called to active duty as a nonflying maintenance officer, he promptly applied for flight school. But after his flight physical he was told his eyesight didn't meet the standards for flying; and only the Air Force Chief of Staff, General Hoyt S. Vandenberg, could grant a waiver for the vision requirement.

His first application for an eyesight waiver, submitted through normal air force channels, was predictably returned disapproved. Still determined, he flew his BT-13A to Washington, DC, brazenly walked into General Vandenberg's office complex, and asked to see the general.

General Vandenberg's secretary told him the general would be busy all day. Undeterred, the determined second lieutenant sat down and waited all day until the general was leaving at day's end. He then quickly explained his problem and that he'd been told only the Chief of Staff could grant him the eyesight waver. The general replied that if a second lieutenant had the guts to personally approach the chief to ask for a waiver he would give it to him. Thus he signed the waiver, and four months later Lt. Sturmthal received orders to USAF pilot training Class 54D.

His basic flight training began in February 1953 flying the T-6 Texan, an aircraft similar to his BT-13A, but with retractable landing gear. Although he wanted to fly fighters, because he was tall and wore glasses, for the advanced phase he was sent to Reese AFB, Texas, where he completed the program flying the twin-engine B-25 bomber—and graduated in the top 10 percent of the class.

In June 1954, his first operational assignment was to the B-57B Canberra jet-bomber equipped Third Bombardment Wing, based at Johnson Air Base, Japan. However, he was to fly World War II–era RB-26s in the wing's detached squadron, deployed to K-8 air base South Korea, flying night-intruder and electronic ferret missions along the coasts of North Korea. After almost a year in Korea, and with his Far East assignment nearing completion, instead of returning to the United States, he extended his overseas tour for two more years, joining the Wing's Eighth Bomb Squadron flying their B-57Bs. After a short time flying Canberras, he was recognized as one of the Wing's top pilots in bombing competitions.

After a few months as line pilot, he volunteered to be the squadron's maintenance officer and Wing Quality Control flight-test maintenance officer. These two jobs doubled his chances to fly since now he could both schedule and perform all the maintenance functional test flights and still participate in the squadron's operational missions. This also gave him in-depth knowledge of the aircraft's systems, with hands-on experience flight testing the bombers. Hopefully, this would lead toward his next goal: test pilot school at Edwards AFB, California.

Then came opportunities to ferry new bombers from Warner-Robins AFB, Georgia, to the Sacramento depot at McClellan AFB, California, and fly them across the Pacific Ocean to units in both Korea and his own Third Bomb Wing in Japan. It was while en route on one such trip to pick up a new airplane that he met Alice Doty, a very attractive American Airlines flight attendant. During the course of their subsequent whirlwind courtship, on one trip back to the United States, he took her to Edwards AFB and told her that someday he would be a test pilot there. Then, as they were returning to Los Angeles, he proposed marriage; in short order, American Airlines lost a flight attendant and Mrs. Alice Sturmthal became a resident of base housing at Johnson AB, Japan.

After two years of flying B-57s in Japan, the Sturmthals returned to the United States and Edwards Air Force Base. Despite being only four years out of flight school, his degree in physics and his varied civilian and military flying background combined with several outstanding performance reports as both a pilot and maintenance officer to get him selected to Class 58C of the prestigious USAF Experimental Test Pilot School.

Graduating on April 24, 1959—as he had promised his bride—he became a test pilot in Bomber Operations at the then remote desert air base. And ironically, he was to spend almost his entire air force career there, testing a variety of new airplanes and weapons systems. Some of these projects included the air force T-37B trainer; the navy's ski-equipped C-130BL, to be used in the Antarctic; the B-52G and H models; and flight control modifications made on the Mach-2, B-58 Hustler.

His assignment to Edwards AFB was interrupted only twice. In October 1962, he transferred to Fort Worth, Texas, where for three years he was chief of the Flight Test Branch of the Air Force Special Projects Office at General Dynamics, developing the highly classified RB-57F. Designed as a high altitude reconnaissance aircraft, the project involved equipping two B-57Bs with greatly enlarged wings and doubling engine thrust by replacing the two 7,200-pound-thrust Wright J65 engines with 15,500-pound-thrust Pratt & Whitney TF33 turbofan engines. When needed for missions above forty-thousand feet, two additional P&W J60 turbojets could be mounted on outboard wing pods, increasing its attainable altitude by several thousand feet. The ship's wing also had four additional hard points where various camera and air sampling pods could be mounted.

The nose of the aircraft was lengthened to house sophisticated navigational equipment, along with sensitive detection equipment for gathering electronic and signal intelligence. The addition of high-altitude cameras gave the aircraft the capability of taking oblique shots at 45-degree angles, with a sixty-mile range.

On June 23, 1963, Major Sturmthal accomplished the first flight of this new and unique reconnaissance aircraft. Then in late 1963, he flew one of the two aircraft to West Germany for reconnaissance trials along the East German border and over the Baltic Sea, making classified flights above sixty-thousand feet. The tests were highly successful, and the air force awarded General Dynamics a contract for construction of nineteen more.

Promoted to lieutenant colonel, in 1969–70 Sturmthal was sent for a combat tour in South Vietnam as commander of Detachment 1, of the 460th Tactical Reconnaissance Wing. Yet the record shows that even this assignment was a service test of new prototype equipment under actual combat conditions. The unit was flying the secret RB-57E in the Patricia Lynn Project, using the new systems Sturmthal had tested and also trained the crews to use while working with General Dynamics at Ft Worth.

The aircraft were equipped with special cameras used previously on the Lockheed U-2, and an infrared scanner and terrain-following radar. A video display allowed the back seater to monitor the IR scanner and spot Viet Cong river traffic at night along the Mekong Delta. Then instead of returning to base and getting the images developed—by which time the enemy would have moved—the crew could call in airstrikes on targets in real time.

Assigned the call sign Moonglow, they conducted both day and night missions, not just in South Vietnam but in North Vietnam, Laos, and Cambodia. Their high and low level day and nighttime imagery revealed enemy training and base camps, hidden factories, and storage dumps that the daytime equipment in RF-101 and RF-4C reconnaissance aircraft had failed to reveal.

During the course of flying 196 combat missions, Sturmthal was awarded a Bronze Star for the unit's effectiveness under combat conditions, and the Distinguished Flying Cross. Subsequently, he was transferred back to Edwards AFB and appointed Project Director for the B-1 Joint Test Force. Then in October 1973, he was promoted to colonel.

On December 23, 1974, Colonel Sturmthal made history as test pilot on the maiden flight of the first of four prototypes of Rockwell International's swing-wing B-1A—a Mach 2.2 (1,685 mph) multirole strategic bomber. The three-man test crew consisted of Rockwell's B-1 Division chief test pilot and aircraft commander Charles C. Bock Jr., with Sturmthal serving as copilot and Richard Abrams the flight test engineer. They lifted off from Palmdale's USAF Plant 42 in B-1A, serial number 62-0001 on what was a basic flight evaluation that would also reposition the aircraft to nearby Edwards AFB.

Colonel Sturmthal was test pilot on all of the first six flights of the number one B-1A. Their first series of tests were to prove the aircraft's primary mission capability as a low-level high-speed penetrator. Secondary emphasis was on the bomber's high-altitude, supersonic penetration performance.

Test flight number sixteen was the first flight of the experimental bomber with an all air force crew. With Sturmthal as aircraft commander, Lt. Col. Ed McDowell as copilot, and Mr. Pat Sharp as flight test engineer, their mission was to validate a flight control modification designed to improve the ship's pitch-control response.

First flight of the B-1A was accomplished with Rockwell's Chief test pilot Charles C. Bock Jr. (L), Richard Abrams (C) the flight test engineer, and Sturmthal (R) serving as copilot.

Flight number twenty-four involved refueling to maximum in-flight gross weight for the first time. Then at thirty-four thousand feet they took the aircraft to Mach 1.6 (1,218 mph). This was the maximum speed allowed because the aircraft's computer controlled variable engine inlet air ducts had not yet been activated. Thus, above this speed, the engine compressors could be damaged by the building shockwave. They completed the flight at low altitude, simulating terrain-following at five hundred feet and Mach 0.85 (650 mph).

Although the air force leadership was pleased with the airplane's performance, as a cost-saving measure a decision was made to have only fixed engine inlets on production airplanes, while still developing the high altitude Mach 2+ capability on the prototypes. This ensured the high altitude speed capability could be added later via retrofit. Thus on the twenty-eighth flight, with the automatic engine inlet ducts activated, Sturmthal took the aircraft to Mach 1.9 at forty-three thousand feet. On the thirty-first flight, he pushed the aircraft to Mach 2.12 at fifty thousand feet. He concluded the flight by refueling from five different tankers, taking on over two hundred thousand pounds of fuel.

Ultimately, their tests proved conclusively that the B-1A had demonstrated the capability to accomplish its design mission at both low and high altitudes. Strategic Air Command could be assured of having a viable penetrating bomber far into the future.

Then on June 30, 1977, President Carter cancelled the B-1A program. The Defense Department wanted to focus instead on cruise missiles that could be carried aboard less expensive aircraft such as the B-52. And in 1978, the B-1A program was halted with the funds transferred to cruise missiles, such as the air-launched cruise missile (ALCM), short-range attack missile (SRAM), and Tomahawk. Still, some research continued on the B-1, but at a greatly reduced level.

Then Sturmthal was told of a possible promotion to brigadier general. This of course meant the end of flight testing and probably flying itself. Consequently, in 1978 he retired from the air force and joined Flight Systems Inc. as director of commercial aircraft programs, based at Mojave Airport, California.

With Flight Systems Inc., he was in his element, flying a number of high-performance aircraft such as the Canadair F-86E-Mark Six Sabre and the North American Aviation F-100F and F-100D Super Sabres in both civilian and military test programs. In late 1980 and early 1981, he also conducted extensive certification tests of the now popular corporate Canadair CL-600 Challenger with company test pilot Dave Gollings. In May 1981, he traveled to Italy where he accomplished production test on Aermacchi's MB-339, a second-generation trainer and light-attack aircraft.

One of his signature programs was designing and developing an icing tanker for use in certifying new civilian aircraft for flight in known icing conditions (FAR 25, Appendix C). The manufacturers had found it expensive and dangerous to spend excess time looking for clouds with the right combination of temperature, liquid water content, and water droplet size. In addition, it was hazardous to totally immerse a new aircraft into an icing cloud without first evaluating the effectiveness of the new aircraft's icing-protection system. This was accomplished by modifying the two 230-gallon wingtip fuel tanks of a Canadair military T-33 jet trainer to supply the required water cloud needed for certifying aircraft's anti-ice systems.

Then, in the spring of 1981 his medical examiner found a suspicious mole on Sturmthal's cheek. It was removed surgically at the UCLA Medical Center and unfortunately found to be melanoma. This required removal of the lymph glands on the side of his face and neck, followed by treatment with a new experimental procedure being developed at UCLA. He was then scheduled for periodic checks every three months and allowed to resume flying.

On October 22, 1982, he flew an F-100D to Edwards AFB for a static display, returning the aircraft to Mojave Airport on October 25. But it was to be the dedicated test pilot's last flight. He had begun feeling bad and having vicious headaches. His coworkers would often see him sitting at his desk with his head in his hands.

With the urging of his loyal friends and help of his wife, he returned to the UCLA Medical Center where they quickly confirmed the melanoma had returned, this time to his brain. The university's experimental procedure had failed and radiation therapy was started. After a bout of radiation treatment he reportedly asked his doctor how long before he could resume flying. But on November 24, following yet another dose of radiation, he was hospitalized. Then, during the evening of November 25, at age 53, he died—leaving behind a record of service to the air force and civilian aviation that has seldom been equaled. He had literally spent his life as a test pilot, pursuing the latest in aviation technology in both military and civil aviation.

Chapter 28

Life on the Leading Edge

Air Force combat veteran and engineering test pilot Addison S. Thompson spent a career studying, developing, and testing the latest aviation technology.

WITH LOTS OF STABILATOR TRIM deflection already applied, and a hefty pull on the control stick, Rockwell International test pilot Addison Thompson was determining the high-speed stability and angle-of-attack limitations of the new supersonic B-1B strategic bomber. The unique airplane, with variable-sweep wings and four GE F101-102 turbo-jet engines, each producing thirty-thousand pounds of thrust, was basically the same as the B-1A: but now it was being certified for a 20 percent increase in gross weight. The additional eighty-two-thousand-pound increase included eight thousand pounds of structure needed to carry fifty-thousand pounds more payload and twenty-four thousand pounds more fuel. With the ship's wings swept at various angles, Thompson was forcefully pulling the heavy bomber through turns at the very limit of its aerodynamic capability and structural integrity. His tests would establish the aircraft's operational capabilities and flight limitations for air force crews.

At the heavier gross weight, the airplane was found limited in longitudinal stability rather than in lift (i.e., angle of attack). To better utilize all of the available lift, the flight-control system was modified to allow an increased maximum angle of attack. And while there was adequate control power, there was no pre-stall warning and no natural cue to warn pilots of the bomber's approach to its stability limit.

The test flights were specifically to evaluate the aircraft's new stability enhancement function (SEF) and stall inhibitor system (SIS) at various wing-angle settings to determine their capability of preventing a loss of control with the increased gross weight. If the two systems were validated, the operational capabilities and safety of the heavier bomber would be improved significantly.

As the lead crew of the lengthy and detailed test series, most of the flights were flown by Thompson and air force Lieutenant Colonel Randy Gaston. On this particular flight, Thompson was the pilot in command, with Gaston serving as copilot. In back were Franz Dewillis, the offensive systems operator, and flight test engineer Jim Leasure running the onboard data systems.

Although the tests were quite hazardous for both the airplane and crew, the SIS and SEF proved effective, and the heavier aircraft was accepted by the air force. In recognition of their outstanding accomplishments in expanding the B-1B flight envelope, in 1989 the Society of Experimental Test Pilots presented both Thompson and Gaston with the Iven C. Kincheloe Award for their outstanding contribution to our aerospace program.

From left to right posing shortly before flight, the B-1B test crew of ship number one consisted of Rockwell test pilot Thompson, AF Lt. Col. Randy Gaston, Capt. Franz Dewillis and Rockwell Flight Test Engineer Jim Leasure.

Background

Thompson's aviation career began in 1957, when the Honor Society student from the small town of Ridgefield Park, New Jersey, was one of 306 high-school graduates selected from a nationwide pool of applicants for the third class at the newly established Air Force Academy. There he excelled in the highly structured environment. Graduating in 1961, he was commissioned a second lieutenant in the USAF and immediately opted for pilot training.

Upon completing flight training at Reese Air Force Base, Texas, in Class 63B, he asked for jet fighters; but only two assignments were available for his class, and he wasn't selected. He then opted for Air Defense Command and Otis AFB, Massachusetts, flying the Lockheed EC-121 early warning radar surveillance aircraft. Since Otis also was home to an air defense squadron with F-101 fighters, he felt he could somehow wrangle a checkout and transfer to the fighter squadron. But it wasn't to happen, so he promptly began formulating an escape plan.

This ultimately led him to Air Training Command at Laredo AFB, Texas. His first year was spent teaching new students to fly the T-37 jet trainer; then he was made check pilot in the standardization and evaluation section.

Promoted to captain, he began aggressively pursuing assignment to a class in the Aerospace Research Pilot School (ARPS). To be accepted he was told that a multiengine background would be beneficial, and a combat tour in Vietnam mandatory. With the help of a friend in the Military Personnel Center, he received orders to fly B-57s in Southeast Asia. But in reality the assignment was a test program, as he was one of three pilots sent TDY (temporary duty) to the Tactical Air Warfare Center at Eglin AFB, Florida, for rushed operational testing and evaluation of an entirely new version of the Glen L. Martin Company's Canberra bomber—the B-57G. Known as Tropic Moon III, the program involved a redesigned nosecone housing a new sensor package and associated electronics. This included a moving target radar, forward looking infrared (FLIR) (thermal imaging), low-light TV and laser ranging for use with newly developed "smart weapons."

In September 1970, the three pilots joined the rest of their squadron-mates in the newly constituted Thirteenth Tactical Bomb Squadron of the Eighth Tactical Fighter Wing; and on October 17 they deployed across the Pacific to Ubon Royal Thailand Air Force Base. Their mission was a real-world operational test of the new electronic equipment, flying single-ship night armed reconnaissance over the Ho Chi Minh trail in Laos.

The aircraft proved quite effective, but ultimately was eclipsed by the much larger AC-130 Gunship. After completing one hundred missions, and awarded two Distinguished Flying Crosses for specific missions that were especially effective, in the summer of 1971 he was selected for Air Command and Staff College. There he again excelled, finishing as a distinguished graduate and with a promotion to major.

Now in his last year of eligibility for Aerospace Research Pilot School (ARPS), Thompson was finally selected for Class 72B at the USAF ARPS. Following a very detailed ten-day physical exam, he entered the program. There the students studied advanced aerodynamics, along with flight-test theory and techniques, while also flying a variety of aircraft. This included the Mach-2, Lockheed F-104C Starfighter, which students used to perform a zoom-climb maneuver to the edge of the earth's atmosphere. The mission was designed to prepare them for possible space flight.

Upon graduating, Thompson was assigned to flight test operations at Wright-Patterson AFB, Ohio. There he flew the NC-141, an experimental version of the Lockheed Starlifter, along with the C-131 and T-37. In this assignment he was involved with testing several futuristic programs; one being a joint USAF/FAA project titled, "The All Weather Landing System." The goal was to obtain data and experience during weather as low as zero ceiling and visibility.

After developing a customized avionics suite, he and his team of flight crew, mechanics, and engineers tested the new system at various major airports around the country, first in good weather, then seeking serious fog. This led to landings in winter fog and below-minimums weather at Baltimore-Washington International Airport. Upon beginning an approach, Thompson called a landing-gear check for a touch-and-go landing. Shortly thereafter, an airliner called in for landing. The approach controller replied that the field was below minimums, whereupon the airline crew questioned how the air force jet was giving a gear check if the field was below minimums. The tower responded, "He's OK. He's just doing touch-and-go landings." After a long pause, the airline crew simply asked for clearance to their alternate airport.

The system proved itself again during landings at then-active McClellan AFB, located in Sacramento, California. After his initial landing there, the fog was so dense Thompson required a "follow-me" truck for guidance off the runway and to lead the large aircraft back for another takeoff.

Another futuristic project was the fly-by-wire side-stick controller being developed by the Flight Dynamics Laboratory. Installed on the copilot's (right) side of the NC-141, the left side retained the conventional control yoke. The flight-control computers and engineers' stations were in the jet's expansive cargo compartment. Their test flights with the system were to determine the proper computer settings that would provide the control deflections required for large jets. Thompson recalls, "During approaches in gusty conditions we found the aircraft noticeably more stable and smoother using the side stick, as the flight control system handled the gust upsets much faster and more accurately than the basic aircraft." But funding for the project finally stopped, and development ended. However, data gained in developing the fly-by-wire flight-control systems is used in today's airliners.

Promoted to lieutenant colonel, Thompson was reassigned to Edwards AFB, California, as deputy director of the Advanced Medium STOL (short takeoff and landing) transport program. In this job he became one of two Edwards test pilots checked out in both the twin-engine Boeing YC-14 and four-engine McDonnell-Douglas YC-15. These prototype aircraft were entrants into the air force's Advanced Medium STOL competition, the winner to replace the C-130 as the standard tactical transport. The goal was an aircraft capable of carrying a twenty-seven-thousand-pound payload while operating from a two-thousand-foot semiprepared airfield, with a mission radius of four hundred nautical miles.

The aircraft were tested from dirt runways carrying heavy loads such as army trucks. And after completing the six-hundred-hour test program, both designs were found to have met or exceeded specifications. However, the increasing importance of strategic versus tactical missions eventually led to the demise of the program. Air Force Chief of Staff General David C. Jones asked Air Force Systems Command to evaluate the possibility of having a single model for both the long-range strategic and shorter range tactical airlift roles. This led to development of the McDonnell-Douglas (now Boeing) C-17 Globemaster III. Conceived using information gained from the two smaller prototypes, today it is a crucial component of the USAF worldwide logistics operations.

Following that project, Thompson was appointed director of operations and programs for the Air Force Flight Test Center (AFFTC) at Edwards AFB. Although basically a headquarters desk job, he was able to continue flying the A-37 and T-38. Then, during the late 1970s, with cruise-missile testing well underway at Edwards AFB, its integration with the B-52 had not yet begun. The test center commander decided to appoint him to set up a detachment at the Boeing Wichita (Kansas) facility to oversee the upgrade of the B-52 offensive avionics systems and the integration of cruise missile capability. Concurrently, he was selected for Air War College (AWC). But the center commander had his school attendance delayed until 1981; and he was off for a quick five-day checkout in the B-52.

In early 1981, with the B-52 Avionics upgrade and cruise missile integration program progressing, he received orders to Air War College (AWC). Because the AWC would lead to a promotion to colonel and a headquarters desk job, this meant his flight test career was about to end. Thus he elected to retire from the air force and continue testing aircraft.

Civilian Test Pilot

Upon leaving the air force, he received job offers from two major manufacturers and another from the smaller firm of Tracor Flight Systems Incorporated (FSI). Based at Mojave Airport, California, FSI held the possibility of again being involved in a variety of test programs and of flying several types of air force and navy airplanes; so he accepted their offer. In mid-July 1981, he began work there, his first projects being Pershing missile guidance tests conducted in FSI's highly modified corporate jet Sabreliner 40. Then, using the company's F-86, T-33, and navy A-4, he began tests on prototype weapons, such as cruise missile submunitions, and several types of towed targets and decoys, and began evaluating ship-borne defensive systems for a major ship manufacturer.

Another project involved certifying the handling qualities of a highly modified navy P-3C Orion, a long-range maritime surveillance/antisubmarine warfare aircraft. After getting a quick checkout in the aircraft, he and fellow FSI test pilot Joe Guthrie completed about twenty test flights to verify the original P-3C handling qualities. Then, while evaluating the modified aircraft, they detected it was less directionally stable than the original aircraft. During their dynamic sideslip tests at three thousand feet, the aircraft suddenly "departed," with Thompson quickly recovering from the ensuing snap-roll. Their startled chase pilot asked, "What the hell was that?"

In 1985, his last year with FSI, he was made program manager for the USAF QF-100 drone production program. While he still continued flying, he was tasked with starting a production program for modifying 210 Super Sabre F-100s, to make them remotely controlled targets for air force weapons training and live fire tests.

After four years with FSI, Thompson accepted a job with Rockwell International Corporation (which later became part of The Boeing Company) as test pilot on several leading edge programs. In addition to the B-1B certification, he worked on several black programs, including the X-30 National Aerospace Plane, and worked as director of flight test for the X-32, Boeing's entry in the Joint Strike Fighter program.

Development of the X-30 was first called for by President Reagan in his 1986 State of the Union address to Congress. Designated "a new Orient Express," it was to depart from Washington-Dulles Airport, accelerate to twenty-five times the speed of sound, attain low earth orbit, and fly to Tokyo in two hours.

Under the direction of Rockwell International, the X-30 was to be powered by scramjet engines. Its shovel-shaped forward fuselage generated most of the lift and formed a shockwave that compressed the air prior to it entering the engine. The aft fuselage formed an integrated nozzle to expand the exhaust. The wings were small fins that provided trim and control. Although efficient at high speed, it would have had trouble at slow speeds during takeoff and landing. Despite progress in developing the necessary structural and propulsion technology, the requirement to carry people made the cost of resolving the many technical problems prohibitive: in early 1990s the program was dropped.

In 1992, Rockwell's chief test pilot, Ken Dyson, retired, and Thompson became chief test pilot and director of flight test. In 1996, Rockwell International merged with Boeing, and six months later with McDonnell-Douglas. This gave Thompson oversight of test pilots involved with programs at both Edwards AFB and Palmdale's Production Flight Plant.

In November 1996, both Boeing and Lockheed Martin were awarded contracts authorizing them to build two each of their concept for the Joint Strike Fighter competition. This included representative aircraft systems and weapon systems. In 1998, with the project underway, Thompson was appointed test director for the X-32 program.

Boeing Lockheed Martin's concept of the Joint Strike Fighter lands at the Palmdale Plant.

Boeing's concept was an aircraft capable of conventional takeoff and landing (CTOL) and one with short takeoff and vertical landing capability (STOVL). First flight of their X-32A, CTOL prototype, was on September 18, 2000, from their Palmdale plant to Edwards AFB. Their

X-32B, STOVL made its maiden flight in March 2001. For the vertical landing, it used engine-thrust vectoring, as found on the marine AV-8B Harrier II: both prototypes were successful.

With their X-35, the Lockheed Martin team chose a riskier alternative for vertical takeoff and landing and opted for a shaft-driven lift fan powered by the main engine. The X-35's lift fan could generate more thrust than the Boeing X-32B's vectored thrust. In addition it could carry a greater payload and had longer range than Boeing's vectored thrust turbofan. And it didn't require two versions of the aircraft. Consequently, Boeing's entries were rejected and Lockheed Martin's X-35 became the F-35 Lightning II.

Following his company's loss of the Joint Strike Fighter competition, Thompson, now sixty-two, retired. His last flight was in the B-1B, an airplane he knew so well. The flight included "flying at supersonic speed with some barrel rolls, followed by terrain following at Mach 0.9 (684 mph) and 200 feet through the Sierras. Then a 'greaser' landing at McConnell AFB, Kansas"—ironically, the same place he had made his last landing as an active duty air force pilot twenty years earlier.

For over forty years of his extensive flight test career he was a member and fellow of the Society of Experimental Test Pilots (SETP), serving as society president 1998–99. For thirty of those years he was also a trustee and chairman of the SETP Scholarship Foundation. Concurrently, he was a member of the Board of Directors, and now a trustee, of the Flight Test Historical Foundation and founding task force for the city of Palmdale Memorial Air Park, where the foundation arranged a display of aircraft and artifacts commemorating the history of aircraft development at USAF Plant 42 at Palmdale airport.

From Palmdale, he and his wife moved to Santa Barbara, California, where he quickly became a member, then chairman, of the Airports Commission; and three years later he became a member of the city planning commission. The quiet, soft-spoken, unpretentious, experimental engineering test pilot spent his entire adult life in the service of his fellow man—with an amazing flying career that was always on the leading edge of aviation technology.

Chapter 29

The Warrior General

In a thirty-eight-year career, John L. Piotrowski, the son of Polish immigrants, rose from airman basic radar technician to commanding general of US Space Command.

IT WAS DUSK WHEN THE heavily armed AT-28s were scrambled from the short thirty-three hundred-foot runway at their newly established encampment at Bien Hoa, South Vietnam. It was January 1962, and the US Air Force Air Commando pilots had been launched in support of Special Forces (Green Berets) embedded with company from the Army of the Republic of Vietnam (ARVN) that was under attack. The Green Berets were there to train the ARVN and to make sure they stood their ground when the fighting started.

Upon reaching the target area they found the Viet Cong (VC) had started grass fires, which created dense gray smoke. In the fading light this significantly reduced visibility, making the mission especially difficult. The ARVN troopers were located in a triangular shaped fort, designed to protect an adjoining village. To point out the enemy's location, one of the Green Berets marked the attackers location with a white phosphorous rocket. Then, in a series of passes, the AT-28s delivered four cans of napalm and raked the area with their machine guns. Later they learned their ordnance had driven off the attacking force and saved both the fort and village.

It was the first taste of combat for Captain John L. Piotrowski and his fellow air commandos, with much more to come. As they quickly learned, counterinsurgency warfare was different. Besides total secrecy, every mission involved major political as well as military considerations.

At the time, our government claimed American forces were not in the Republic of South Vietnam—only a training cadre to teach the ARVN military skills. To support this facade, before launching on a combat mission, each air commando pilot had to be accompanied by a host-country national. Then, if the airplane was shot down, the American airman's presence could be justified as a "training flight." Typically, the "trainee" was a young and recalcitrant enlisted trooper. His only training consisted of a briefing on the bailout procedure and when to pull the D-ring to deploy his parachute.

When sitting ready alert, if the klaxon sounded for an immediate scramble, both crewmen were to run to their assigned aircraft and strap in for immediate takeoff. But after a couple of missions in the back seat of an AT-28, the terrified passenger would run the other way and have to be chased down and strapped in the airplane.

Because their operations were covert, the pilots could not receive credit for either combat missions or the coveted combat flight time. Instead, each flight was logged as "combat support" or "training sortie." For Capt. Piotrowski it was the beginning of an almost continuous clandestine presence in Southeast Asia.

Background

The son of Polish immigrants, he had graduated as class valedictorian from Detroit's Henry Ford Trade School (HFTS). This unique high school not only taught teenage students marketable toolmaker skills, which upon graduation typically led to well-paying jobs at Ford Motor Company, but the academic curriculum prepared them for admission to a university. Upon graduating, Piotrowski was only seventeen years old, which was too young to be hired by Ford. Instead, he continued his apprenticeship as a draftsman and toolmaker.

On February 17, 1952, his eighteenth birthday, he registered for the draft. With the Korean War raging, his induction into the army was a certainty. A close friend, who was a couple years older and who had led the way to the HFTS, had already enlisted in the air force. He repeatedly extolled the virtues of air force technical training and the potential for follow-on job opportunities.

Since education was young Piotrowski's goal, on September 2, 1952, he enlisted in the US Air Force. But before being officially sworn in as a recruit, he was administered mental and aptitude tests to determine his acceptability and best technical career field. After his tests were scored, a master sergeant called him aside and said he had scored 100 percent on the tests—the first perfect score in the history of that recruiting station. From there it was south to San Antonio, Texas, and twelve weeks of basic training at Lackland Air Force Base.

Despite his apprentice training as a toolmaker and two years as a draftsman, the air force needed radar technicians. Thus he was assigned to Keesler AFB, Mississippi, to a basic electronics course. This was to be followed by radar repair school. Being new to electronics, he found the discipline fascinating. The ground radar technician's course involved a lot of practical learning, which he relished. Because of his outstanding grades in both courses, he was awarded a second stripe.

Then one day while checking the weekend duty roster, Piotrowski noticed a letter requesting volunteers for flight training as a pilot or navigator. To qualify, the applicant had to pass a college equivalency test and a Stanine psychomotor test. Better yet, the minimum age had been lowered to nineteen. Upon graduation, the successful applicant would be commissioned a second lieutenant and awarded the silver wings of a pilot or navigator.

During his brief time in the service, he had become aware that officers were paid more money, dated prettier women, and lived in better quarters. Thus he volunteered, and easily passed all the required tests. Then, during an interview with a major, he was informed that he had qualified for any of six aeronautical programs—pilot, navigator, bombardier, etc. Piotrowski quickly responded that he wanted pilot training. But the major needed navigators; he told Piotrowski that he faced a two-year delay getting into a pilot training class and that in the meantime he would continue in his present career field. He must have looked crestfallen, as the major followed with, "But I can have you in a navigator class in just a couple weeks." Airman Second Class Piotrowski quickly responded, "Sir, you just got yourself a navigator."

Still, there was a downside to leaving Keesler AFB. He had been promoted to airman second class because of his exceptional academic performance. Now that he was departing, the squadron commander, a captain, summoned him to the office. On the pretext that Piotrowski was improperly dressed, he took away that second stripe—busting him to airman third. The captain wanted to preserve the stripe for some other deserving airman. But to Airman Third Piotrowski it was a humiliating experience.

As a navigation cadet, his previous electronics and radar training proved to be an ideal background. During the final phase of the program, he was sent back to Keesler AFB for electronic-warfare officer training. When it became obvious the basic radar instructor didn't know the subject, Cadet Piotrowski volunteered and taught the course. Subsequently, the instructors encouraged him to just take the rest of the course subject exams, which allowed him to finish the entire program quickly.

On August 11, 1954, as one of five distinguished graduates, twenty-year-old John L. Piotrowski was awarded the silver wings of an air force navigator and commissioned a second lieutenant. Although distinguished graduates were eligible for regular commissions, at the time he didn't understand the significance. As a result, he was commissioned as a reserve officer.

His entire navigator class was assigned to the Sixty-Seventh Tactical Reconnaissance Wing, flying RB-26s on nighttime electronic ferret missions along the borders of North Korea. Later Piotrowski volunteered to fly on the eight-hour weather reconnaissance sorties that provided the Korean peninsula's weather pattern for the next few days. This, along with night college courses, kept him occupied through the two-year Far East assignment.

During the course of his Far East tour, he was promoted to first lieutenant. Then, after contemplating his imminent return to the United States, he made two requests of his squadron commander. The first was for pilot training, and the second was for a regular air force commission. Ultimately, he got both.

B-26 navigator Second Lieutenant Piotrowski is shown preparing for yet another weather reconnaissance mission off the North Korean coast.

Back in the United States, he reported to Marana AFB, Arizona, where as a member of Pilot Training Class 58M he learned to fly the tandem-cockpit T-34 Mentor. This training went fast, and soon he was headed to Bainbridge, Georgia, for more advanced instruction in the NAA-made T-28A. There Piotrowski found that, "The routine was about the same as Marana, except everything was bigger—the town, the airfield, and the airplane." From Bainbridge it was on to Bryan AFB, Texas, for advanced training in the Lockheed T-33A, a two-seat version of the F-80, which had been the air force's first operational jet fighter.

Once again he excelled in the jet phase of training, ultimately graduating as top pilot of Class 58M and receiving the Commanders Trophy. Concurrently, he was awarded a regular commission and given first choice in assignments. He quickly chose combat crew training in the F-86F Sabre at Williams AFB, Arizona. This assignment proved fortuitous, as it led to a very beneficial redirection of his career.

Upon graduating from the F-86F crew training course, his entire class was assigned to Strategic Air Command (SAC) to become copilots on B-47 bombers. This was a major downer for the newly minted fighter pilot, and he went to the wing commander to appeal the assignment. Although initially reminded that air force needs came first, because of his electronics and radar background, he was offered an opening at Williams AFB for an electronics maintenance officer. With the F-86F slated to be around for a while, and the arrival of the new F-100 Super Sabres now imminent, he quickly agreed to the career change.

The job proved a good fit for the industrious lieutenant. He excelled at improving the fighters' fire-control and radar systems, while concurrently averaging ninety hours a month flying jet fighters along with the base C-47 and C-45 transports. In his spare time, he continued taking college courses at night, in a determined effort to earn a degree. Meanwhile, he was promoted to captain.

Then the air force announced the impending closure of Williams AFB, and the F-86F crew training operation was transferred across town to Luke AFB. Soon, at the new base, Piotrowski was again flying maintenance test flights in both the T-33 and F-86F.

Then, out of the blue, came an unusual interview for a special assignment. In an interrogation-like setting, a general officer speaking to him from the shadows asked the captain three questions: "Are you willing to fly obsolete airplanes?" Since he was already doing just that, he responded, "Yes, sir! The second question was, "Are you willing to fly combat?" Because he was a military pilot, again the obvious answer was, "Yes." The final question was unusual: "If sent into combat and captured, are you willing to be disowned by the government?" This required more thought. But if captured, he reflected, no one came home until the war ended anyway, so what did it matter? Again his answer was, "Yes, sir!"

With that the general rose and said, "That completes the interview. You'll hear from us if we need you." Shortly thereafter he received secret orders to Project Jungle Jim, forerunner to the First Air Commando Group, which later became the First Air Commando Wing. The project had begun gestating in the spring of 1961, with the new clandestine organization formally authorized by President Kennedy in National Security Action Memorandum No. 104, (para. 4) on October 13, 1961, "for the initial purpose of training Vietnamese forces."

Captain Piotrowski was to report by May 7, 1961, to Eglin Auxiliary Field Number 9, Hurlburt Field, Florida. The new unit would be outfitted with the T-28B and A-26 light attack bombers (later redesignated B-26). The T-28B, with its Wright R1820-86, 1,425-horsepower engine turning a three-bladed propeller, proved to be a trainer on steroids—essentially a tri-gear P-47. The lethality of the World War II–era A-26 was equally impressive. Yet despite experience flying both aircraft, he was assigned as an armament and munitions officer rather than fighter pilot. Still, he felt certain there would be flying involved.

This 1962-era photo, taken at Bien Hoa, shows the AT-28B being loaded with weapons. The aircraft proved to be a trainer on steroids.

Before leaving Luke AFB, Piotrowski went to his boss and expressed concern that he was being assigned as a munitions maintenance officer but didn't know anything about real bombs, fuzes, and bullets. His total experience was with training ammunition. Fortuitously his boss, a World War II veteran, just happened to have in his desk copies of two important Army Air Corps Field Manuals, "Bombs for Aircraft" and "Ammunition for Aircraft." He generously gave both to Captain Piotrowski, and on the long overland trip to Hurlburt Field he memorized the contents of both manuals. Thus, upon arriving at his new assignment, he proved to be a jet-age munitions officer with in-depth knowledge of World War II weapons.

At Hurlburt Field he quickly became known as the go-to guy to make things happen, a tag that would follow him the rest of his career. It started at the end of his first week at Hurlburt Field, when the wing commander made an uncharacteristic visit to the weekly Friday night happy hour at the base's officers club. He was looking for the newly assigned armament/munitions officer.

When Captain Piotrowski introduced himself he was crisply ordered to be in the colonel's office at 0700 hours the next morning. The Saturday meeting proved to be short and brusque. In a one-sentence order the colonel stated: "Captain, I will fly an A-26 early Monday morning, and I expect it to be a gunnery mission, dropping [practice] bombs, firing rockets, and strafing with the .50-caliber machine guns—all six or eight of them; that is all, Captain!"

The colonel had thrown down the gauntlet, but there were no tools, no ammunition account, and no enlisted armament technicians to do the work. Because Saturday was a regular air commando workday, Piotrowski was able to find armament technician Technical Sergeant Dennis Premeaux, who turned out to be a godsend. Sergeant Premeaux not only was trained on the bombs, guns, and rockets with which they would be working but also had friends at Eglin AFB who could provide them with .50-caliber ammo and rockets for Monday's mission. But the small twenty-five-pound practice bombs were unavailable.

The captain's first action was to taxi an A-26 to the old World War II gun harmonization pit. Because there were no aircraft tugs or tow-bars available to move the three large aircraft jacks and a power cart for electricity that were needed to get the ship's guns working and harmonized, Capt. Piotrowski towed them out to the aircraft using his automobile.

For a target, he purchased white bed sheets, then he and T. Sgt Premeaux pinned them together and painted an eight-foot circle with an alignment cross in the center. With the aircraft on jacks, the target was hung at a distance of one thousand feet in the center of the firing-in pit.

To lubricate the guns and save time, he used motor oil he kept in the trunk of his auto. By sunset Saturday afternoon, they had successfully harmonized all eight guns. Then the rockets were loaded. That left only the practice bombs.

During their lunch break they had dined at the Hurlburt Marina Snack Bar. While eating lunch they noticed that the weights tied to ropes holding the boats centered in the docks were rusty twenty-five-pound practice bombs. Since the small bombs were not available from base supply, they quickly decided to retrieve this government property at midnight and replace them with bricks.

By their calculations, the colonel would be happy with four dive-bomb and four skip-bomb passes, so they purchased eight bricks. In addition, they bought sandpaper, metal primer, and blue spray paint to get the rusty bombs looking new.

Sunday morning found them refurbishing the practice bombs and testing them in the aircraft's bomb-bay racks to be sure they released properly. To protect the newly refurbished bombs, the innovative munitions officer used the mattress from his bed in the bachelor officers' quarters (BOQ) to catch them, with T. Sgt Premeaux in the bomb bay to watch for hang-ups.

Because there were no smoke charges in the bombs, Capt. Piotrowski would explain to the colonel that the range was very wet and he would be unable to see their impact, but the range officer would call out the score. Then he prepared a mission briefing and typed up a checklist so the colonel could arm the guns, rockets, and bombs.

Next day the mission went as planned, and when the colonel taxied in, T. Sgt. Premeaux and Capt. Piotrowski were awaiting his debriefing on the armament systems. The colonel deplaned clearly happy. Piotrowski relates, "He walked over to us smiling, returned our salutes and shook my hand. Then he said, 'Pete, you SOB, I didn't think anyone could get the job done.'" With that, Piotrowski introduced T. Sgt. Premeaux and said, "Colonel, this is the man who got it done."

From that day on, Capt. Piotrowski became the man to call for any "mission impossible." And T. Sgt Premeaux was the captain's go-to guy for all the years they were in the Air Commandos.

In early September 1961, Capt. Piotrowski proposed marriage to his sweetheart from the Phoenix area, Sheila Fredrickson, and they decided on early-December nuptials. Alas, later that month their plans were dashed by a sudden clandestine assignment to Southeast Asia—so secret he couldn't tell his betrothed where he was going or whether he would be able to write or call. But all was not lost: with their pastor's indulgence, they managed a late-December wedding via telephone from Taiwan and Fort Walton Beach. The honeymoon would come later.

His secret assignment was to take six B-26s from storage at the CIA's Air Asia facility at Tainan, Taiwan, and get them combat ready and in place for the budding air commando detachment at the then primitive South Vietnamese air base of Bien Hoa. The aircraft had been loaned to the French in their fight with the Viet Minh in Indochina and had been in storage since the French defeat at Dien Bien Phu in the spring of 1954.

It was during this refurbishing and overhaul process that Capt. Piotrowski's idea of wing-mounted weapon pylons for the B-26 was finally realized. As configured, the B-26 they had received could carry only certain size bombs in the internal bomb bay. But the thin-skinned napalm tanks, which were one of the air commandos' primary weapons, couldn't be safely dropped from a bomb bay, nor could rocket pods be mounted on the wing. However, using Piotrowski's idea, the Chinese engineers and technicians installed wing pylon stations, and the aircraft could now carry rockets pods, bombs, and napalm.

The pylons represented a major increase in the airplane's lethality. This project and subsequent assignments with the air commandos showed that a captain in the organization had unprecedented authority—equal to officers of much higher rank in the regular air force.

The addition of wing pylon stations greatly expanded the weapons-carrying capability of the B-26.

Once the six bombers were delivered to Bien Hoa, Capt. Piotrowski followed in a C-47, landing on the hastily built thirty-three-hundred-foot perforated-steel planking (PSP) runway. The rudimentary air base was supported by a tent city of ARVN and a cadre of air commandos. From this primitive environment, Capt. Piotrowski would be in and out of combat over the next three years, all the while developing new and more effective weapons.

Because of his in-depth involvement in air commando operations, he was asked to testify before the US Army's Howze Board, which was evaluating the air force's close air support of engaged ground forces. This was followed by his selection to testify regarding the reliability and utility of COIN (counter insurgency) aircraft, before Mississippi Senator Stennis's Senate Armed Services Subcommittee on Preparedness.

In 1965, thanks to Operation Boot Strap, he enjoyed a six-month sabbatical to finish his college degree at the University of Nebraska's Omaha campus. He studied hard and graduated with honors and a perfect 4.0 grade point average. Then it was back to the First Air Commando Wing, this time as an instructor pilot rather than armament officer.

Teaching experienced air force pilots to fly the armed version of the navy T-28B trainer—now designated the AT-28B—was easy. Soon, the wing commander elevated Capt. Piotrowski to the position of wing weapons officer. His job was to keep the pilots informed about new ordnance, fuzing, and tactics. Thus, flying as an instructor became the way he relaxed.

Later the same year, he was off to the Fighter Weapons School for more education, studying the F-100 fire-control system, radar, and twenty-millimeter M-39 cannon. When he arrived, phase one of the course had begun a week earlier. Yet for the forthcoming phase test he was to be held responsible for all the material covered. With the course materials in hand he burned the midnight oil studying. Soon it became obvious that not much had changed since his days as an electronics maintenance officer at Williams AFB. Upon taking the phase test he scored 100 percent, and was immediately accused of cheating. Because he had missed the first week's lectures and had never flown the aircraft, his instructors couldn't believe his perfect score. After an hour's verbal quiz on the F-100 fire control system by a cadre of FWS instructors, they finally acknowledged Capt. Piotrowski's expertise. He went on to prove it by scoring 100 percent on all subsequent tests.

Back at Hurlburt Field, he, his wife, and young daughter were just getting settled in their newly purchased house when yet another covert combat assignment arrived. Operation Waterpump was a clandestine operation based in Thailand, very near the Laotian border. The mission was to train Thai Air Force pilots to US standards in the AT-28 and to interdict the North Vietnamese supply trucks and troop reinforcements moving along the Ho Chi Minh trail.

This assignment was trumped, however, by a sudden, almost overnight transfer to Nellis AFB and the Fighter Weapons School (FWS). There, he was made part of team that would conduct a series of one-week training programs in conventional weapons, tactics, and employment for air force general officers being assigned to Vietnam. It was during this assignment that Piotrowski fathered night interdiction and close air support by jet fighters, using flares suspended by parachute, a technique that had been perfected by the air commandos in their AT-28s and B-26s. Better yet, the assignment put him back in a modern jet fighter—the F-4C Phantom II.

Once qualified in the Phantom, he had a full plate of duties because he was simultaneously appointed Chief of the FWS Academics. Now he was responsible for not only the senior officers' course but also classroom instruction on weapons and weapon systems, along with flying with students as instructor pilot (IP) in the Phantom.

In June 1966, Captain Piotrowski's IP duties in the F-4C were curtailed, and he was teamed with a major to devise techniques for employing the navy-developed AGM-62 Walleye electro-optical-guided glide (bomb) weapon. When their development work was completed, they were sent to the Eighth TFW at Ubon Air Base, Thailand, to introduce the Walleye and the procedures for employing it in combat. Using the newer avionics of the F-4D, the weapon proved very effective.

Meanwhile, in his spare time, the newly promoted major completed the career-enhancing Command and Staff College by correspondence. He theorized that this would prevent his being removed from a choice flying job to attend the nine-month residence course at the Air University, after which a headquarters staff assignment was likely.

Still, shortly thereafter he was selected to attend the five-month course of the Armed Forces Staff College with a starting date of early February 1968. By now, numerous senior colonels and generals knew Piotrowski well from his briefings on conventional weapons and his pacesetting work in the Fighter Weapons School. Upon graduation in August 1968, he was assigned to Headquarters US Air Force—the Pentagon. There, as an action officer under the director of plans for force development, his expansive weapons-systems knowledge, combined with his extensive and varied combat experience and abetted by an affable personality, set the course for his rapid progression in rank and responsibility. It was during this assignment that he also attended Harvard University's program for management development.

Following a year and a half in the Pentagon, from December 1970 until July 1971, he was a student at the Royal Air Force College of Air Warfare. Promoted to colonel, from there he became deputy commander of operations of the Thirty-sixth Tactical Fighter Wing. However, this assignment was short lived, and he was reassigned as commander of the Fortieth Tactical Fighter Group at Aviano, Italy. After two years of his leadership, the organization was rated "Best in the Air Force" by Lieutenant General Louis L. Wilson Jr., the air force inspector general.

In April 1974, Colonel Piotrowski was assigned as chief of a six-man group of colonels conducting special studies for the Air Force Chief of Staff. Then, in March 1975, he became vice commander of the Technical Training Center at Keesler AFB, Mississippi—ironically, the place he had left years before as an airman third.

In May 1976, he was given command of the newly reactivated 552nd Airborne Warning and Control Wing at Tinker AFB, Oklahoma. The E-3A Sentry was a specially modified Boeing 707 airliner, conceptualized for use in the continental US air defense early warning system. Because of cost overruns, Congress was debating the efficacy of this highly sophisticated weapons system, when the new commander (now promoted to brigadier general) recognized the E-3A as having much greater mission potential than that initially espoused by General David C. Jones. He wanted to expand the E-3A system's concept and deploy it to control the available air assets in any tactical warfare situation. To prove his point he filled the sophisticated aircraft with observers and took them on deployments worldwide—particularly in Europe and South Korea—where he demonstrated the aircraft's usefulness in tactical missions as well as air defense. Subsequently, the E-3A air-borne command and control concept became an integral part of air force doctrine.

Brigadier General Piotrowski briefs Vice President Mondale of the mission capabilities of the E-3A.

During this period, the commander of Tactical Air Command, General Dixon, decided the new brigadier general should be current in the F-15 too. Subsequently, General Piotrowski logged over three hundred hours in the new aircraft. This included an overseas deployment to Jordan and Somalia with the First Tactical Fighter Wing.

In the fall of 1979, and now as a major general, he became deputy commander of Tactical Air Command (TAC) for Air Defense at Peterson AFB, Colorado. Then, in April 1981, he was appointed TAC's deputy chief of staff for operations, based at Langley AFB, Virginia. During this assignment, he checked out in the F-16 and subsequently logged over six hundred hours in the aircraft.

In August 1982, after promotion to lieutenant general, he was appointed vice commander, TAC. Then in October 1982 he assumed command of Ninth Air Force at Shaw AFB, South Carolina. It was during this challenging assignment that he was again called on to perform several "mission impossible" assignments.

A classic example occurred shortly after he assumed command. While visiting his worldwide units in Europe and the Middle East, one of the stops included Port Sudan on the Red Sea coast of Sudan. His visit was intended to check on the air force detachment of five noncommissioned officers who were maintaining prepositioned US military equipment and war reserve assets used in the first Gulf War (Operation Desert Storm)—vehicles, field hospitals, tents—stored in warehouses leased from the Sudanese government. As in Desert Storm, these assets would greatly accelerate the prosecution of a war in the Middle East, since their immediate availability saved time and transportation requirements.

About midday of the first day of his visit, he was approached by the Sudanese Army region defense commander, who informed him that he was to depart immediately for Khartoum to meet with the Sudanese First Vice President Tyiebe. With the request subsequently sanctioned by the US embassy, he departed in his T-39 Sabreliner. After landing, as the copilot slowly taxied to terminal, he quickly dressed into a business suit then deplaned and entered the open door of one of the waiting black limos. Once in the limo, and seated beside the US chief of mission, the visiting general was informed that Ethiopia had attacked Sudan that morning and was overwhelming Sudanese forces near the border. Thus, the embassy staff in concert with the Sudanese leadership decided to have General Piotrowski meet publically with the first vice president for the TV cameras. This involved a salute, handshake, and embrace before entering the palace. Following thirty minutes of conversation indoors, the departure routine outside would be a repeat of the arrival scenario.

That night, on the country's only TV channel, the English subtitles announced to the world, "American general with responsibility for the defense of Sudan visits the area to look over the situation and take necessary action." Later that night, the "one-day war" was over, as Ethiopian forces withdrew behind their own border.

Promoted to general in August 1985, Piotrowski became vice chief of staff of the air force in Washington, DC. In February 1987, he became commander of the North American Aerospace Defense Command (NORAD), which later combined with Strategic Command to become US Space Command.

A command pilot with seven thousand hours, during his career the "Warrior General" flew thirty-one types of military aircraft, with extensive combat experience in the AT-28, B-26, and F-4C and D models. As a tribute to his contribution to counterinsurgency warfare, he was inducted into the Air Commando Hall of Fame.

His military decorations and awards include Defense Distinguished Service Medal, Air Force Distinguished Service Medal, Legion of Merit, Meritorious Service Medal with two oak leaf clusters, Air Medal with two oak leaf clusters, Air Force Commendation Medal with oak leaf cluster, Presidential Unit Citation and Air Force Outstanding Unit Award with three oak leaf clusters, and the Eugene M. Zuckert Management Award for 1979.

His life story represents a classic example of the American experience, wherein with intelligence, drive, and courage this son of Polish immigrants progressed from the lowest rank of airman basic to the peak of rank and authority in the US military. His success should serve as an example and challenge to young airmen of future generations.

General and Mrs. Piotrowski are shown while visiting various command locations.

Chapter 30

The Last Jet Ace of the Korean War

It took fifty-five years, but in January 2008 the air force finally confirmed the Korean War's fortieth jet ace.

THE DATE WAS JULY 11, 1952, and the fighting in the Korean War was still intense, but stalemated by seemingly futile peace talks. They were flying F-86E Sabrejets and the engagement with a MiG-15 was the newly minted flight commander's first as a flight leader. First Lieutenant Charles R. Cleveland remembers: "It was late afternoon. The weather around the Yalu [river] was forecast to be socked in, and my wingman, John 'Red Dog' Hager and I, flying a weather recce [recon-naissance], were the only two F-86s in the area…There was a scattered to broken deck underneath us and a large thunderstorm just north of the Yalu. We were at about 35,000 feet when [our island based radar site] Dentist Charlie called a bandit heading northeast over Antung [China].

"We dropped our [external fuel] tanks, went buster [full throttle] and headed southwest along the Yalu [river]. I sighted a lone MiG at about six to eight miles at our altitude, dead ahead, on a reciprocal heading. Seconds later, we passed about 100 feet apart and turned for each other's tail…I must say I felt very confident as we entered the most exciting five minutes of my life. The fight was high-G, round and round, up and down—about five or six turns with me gaining a little every time we passed.

"I finally settled into his six o'clock position, very close. We were down to probably 15,000 feet, and very much slower than when we started. Before I could fire, he bunted [stick forward] and throttled back, and I lost sight of him momentarily. It surprised me as I had never seen that maneuver before. I rolled on my back, and he was practically under-neath me with the obvious intention of slipping into my six o'clock; but with flaps [extended], speed brakes [out] and throttle [at idle] I got behind him again. Hager did a great job staying with me the whole time.

"The MiG started a right climbing turn, and I pulled lead on him at about 300–400 feet range…I put the [gunsight] pipper on his tailpipe and fired a long burst [with] immediate strikes up the tailpipe and along the right side of the fuselage up to the canopy area. He did a slow roll to the left, past 90 degrees left bank, to his back. The [aircraft's] nose went down and he started a long leisurely descent, which I took to be a death throes maneuver.

"We followed him down, but he disappeared going straight down into low clouds extending from the thunderstorm at I guess, [an altitude of] about 3,000–4,000 feet…I know he never got home. I hit him hard from close range, and he went into a vertical dive into the roll cloud of a towering thunderstorm, and MiGs just didn't do that."

Although both Cleveland and John Hager, his wingman, felt certain it was a kill, neither one had actually seen the enemy pilot eject or the MiG explode or crash. And because his gun camera failed to work, Lt. Cleveland declined to claim a kill and listed it as a "probable" (Trest 2012, 80–81).

Cleveland's feeling of confidence and skillful maneuvering in his first actual dogfight was the byproduct of the training that new flight commanders received in the 334th Fighter Interceptor Squadron. Thanks to the squadron's new operations officer, Major Fredrick C. "Boots" Blesse, a new aggressive training program had been initiated. To be scheduled for a combat mission, each pilot was required to have logged three practice dogfights a week. He would gleefully tell his pilots, "No guts, no glory, men!" (Blesse 1987). Blesse likened it to golf, as a pro wouldn't play a tournament "if he hadn't played in two weeks. Those guys practice all the time." In addition, it was Blesse's policy that any wingman who lost contact with his leader in combat was grounded for a week and given extra chores.

At the time of this first engagement, Lt. Cleveland had already flown eighty-five missions as wingman, whose sole job was to "check six" and keep the enemy off his element leader's tail. Firing your guns without your leader's permission was a sure ticket to a new job in the food-service squadron or base motor pool. Blesse had relieved several older flight commanders who had flown numerous missions but had few engagements or no kills. He specifically promoted Lt. Cleveland to flight commander because of his demonstrated flying skill and aggres-siveness. He later said, "Chick was the best of my flight commanders."

Thanks to Fifth Air Force Commander, Lieutenant General Glenn O. Barcus, the United Nations' sanctuary policy for enemy aircraft while in Chinese airspace had been unofficially canceled. Now Sabre pilots could attack MiGs where they operated. Consequently, Cleveland's first *confirmed* kill began very near the Chinese airfield at Antung, with the action ending up over the mouth of the Yalu River.

That engagement occurred on August 5, 1952. His flight had reached the Yalu River at thirty-five thousand feet—very near the Chinese air-base of Antung. Dutifully he turned the flight east, flying parallel to the river. Then he looked down at their Antung airbase, and saw a flight of four MiGs in the landing pattern and immediately decided to shoot down the number four aircraft. In a diving attack, with his Sabre indi-cating 550 knots and the MiG on final approach at about 150 knots, he quickly caught up and began firing. Unfortunately, his aim was off, although he still got some strikes on the MiG's left wing.

First Lt. Charles R. Cleveland of the 334th Fighter Interceptor Squadron, 4th Fighter Interceptor Wing.

The antiaircraft fire over the enemy airfield was fierce, but by staying low he and his wingman managed to reach the Yellow Sea west of Antung. Then eight MiGs were scrambled to counter the two Sabres. "One of the pictures stamped in my mind was that of a MiG-15 firing at me head-on, all three cannons throwing tracers and his whole nose lit-up a bright orange. But he missed me by a good ways," said Cleveland.

He damaged another MiG-15 with a high angle-off shot, then spotted a pair of MiGs at his two o'clock position, flying level at seven thousand feet. But instead of turning left to engage, the two aircraft turned away from the F-86s—probably to avoid going over the Yellow Sea, with the chance of being captured if shot down.

Cleveland chased them to around eleven thousand feet, then one of the MiGs made a hard left climbing turn. "I hit him with a burst from 1,200 feet. He reversed his turn to the right and I hit him again hard from 800 feet—then he pulled straight up, and as I closed to 500 feet for my final burst, he blew his canopy. Simultaneously, his engine exploded and he ejected—his opened chute didn't go twenty feet over my canopy." The action ended almost directly over the mouth of the Yalu River. Cleveland's wingman, Lt. Ken Elston transmitted, "Nice going." Then, being low on fuel, they headed for home (Trest 2012, 86–87).

Lt. Cleveland scored another probable on September 14, and the next day was credited with his second confirmed kill. Flying an older model F-86A, he described the event as, "not a terribly exciting him-or-me dogfight." After a couple of turns, the MiG pilot saw he was about to lose and attempted to break off the engagement and go home. He started climbing toward the Yalu River, but at a range of about one thousand feet, Cleveland got some strikes on the aircraft and the pilot ejected.

On September 21 he got another probable, which, at the time, his wingman Lt. Don Pascoe insisted was a kill. His squadron was flying high cover for F-84s striking targets in the extreme northwest corner of North Korea, very near the Yalu River and the MiGs' home base at Antung. As they approached the Yalu at thirty-five thousand feet,

Cleveland spotted two MiGs at his one o'clock position, crossing in front of his two-ship element. The Sabres promptly dropped their external pylon tanks, and because of the rarified atmosphere, made a gentle, wide sweeping turn to get behind them.

Rolling out about two thousand feet astern, Cleveland felt they were too far back. After a five-minute tail chase at full power the slightly faster F-86Es slowly closed to eighteen hundred feet. Then Pascoe reported more MiGs way back at about forty-five thousand feet and descending. This forced Cleveland to shoot early. His first burst went low, so he moved the gunsight's pipper above the MiG's large tail and fired. This time he saw hits on the aircraft's tailpipe, the engine area, and right wing. Following a second burst, there was an explosion, with the MiG now on fire. Cleveland continued shooting and got a couple more hits. Then instead of climbing away to disengage from the Sabrejets, the damaged MiG-15 began descending.

Ominously, Pascoe reported the other MiGs closing the distance. In a classic display of element integrity, Cleveland had total faith in his wingman and didn't look back. Instead, he continued his pursuit and told Pascoe to call a break when he felt it was absolutely necessary. Finally Pascoe called "BREAK," and Cleveland didn't hesitate. They had learned a lesson when Major George Davis, the revered 334th squadron commander, had been killed a few months earlier. He had been shooting a MiG and had it burning, with yet another MiG on his tail. Despite his wingman's frantic calls to "BREAK," he had continued pressing his attack, ultimately taking a cannon hit in the cockpit. Then Cleveland and Pasco headed south and returned to Kimpo AB.

Lt. Cleveland's third confirmed aerial victory occurred on September 26th—a fight he describes as one-sided. Two MiGs had taken off from China's Feng-cheng airfield. But instead of first climbing north to high altitude in supposedly "politically protected" Chinese airspace, they turned south and crossed the Yalu into North Korea. Their mission was likely to intercept the slower F-80s and F-84 fighter bombers attacking targets in North Korea. The two Sabrejets dived from high altitude and got close behind the MiG element leader. Cleveland recounts: "He saw us and dropped his [external fuel] tanks, somewhere at an altitude around 1,500 to 2,000 feet. I hammered him really good and there was a huge explosion and black smoke. Then he pulled straight up and ejected." Cleveland's wingman saw the ejection and confirmed his aerial victory.

Two days later he made his fourth confirmed kill while leading a flight of four F-86Es. They were escorting slower F-84s that were attacking an ammo dump and troop concentrations about thirty miles south of the Yalu River boundary with China. At an altitude of seven thousand feet he had his flight busily S-turning over the slower F-84s, when without any warning from our coastal radar site, Dentist Charlie, "a flight of four MiG-15s suddenly dived out of the clouds to attack the fighter-bombers." Cleveland quickly had his flight drop their tanks and "go buster!" Then he latched onto the MiG leader who had slowed down behind an F-84.

Even today, he recalls the scene vividly, with an F-84 out front strafing a convoy, and a MiG-15 behind him shooting and hitting its right wing. Cleveland was the third aircraft in line, locked onto the MiG and shooting—getting hits all over the enemy aircraft.

Suddenly the MiG pilot pulled up to the left and started to climb, but then slowed down rapidly and the aircraft began to burn. Lt. Cleveland pulled up and over to the right and looked down at the enemy fighter. It was shredded with .50-caliber bullets, with the canopy smashed and the pilot slumped over the control stick. He then resumed firing, and the MiG crashed into the side of a hill (Trest 2012, 91–92).

In order to get his fifth victory, he had extended his combat tour for the second time and was flying his 135th combat mission. One morning, Major Boots Blesse said, "Chick, I'm going to get you that [fifth] MiG if it kills me. I know where the MiGs are, and I'll take you where you need to go." And away they went deep into mainland China. Unfortunately, the MiGs weren't flying, and they stayed north until Cleveland's fuel level got dangerously low. He said later it was probably the dumbest thing he had ever done in an airplane. After climbing to fifty thousand feet, he shut down his engine, and with Blesse guiding him, glided home.

He made it back to Kimpo Air Base then restarted his engine and landed normally—but flamed out upon clearing the runway - alas, directly in front of wing commander Colonel Harrison Thyng's office window. Colonel Thyng saw the activity and asked "Who is that?" When his ops officer replied "Lt. Cleveland," the colonel recognized the potentially fatal obsession and responded with, "Send his ass home!" Thus with 135 combat missions, four confirmed aerial victories, two probables, and four damages, Lt. Cleveland was sent home (Trest 2012, 94–95).

Over the years, his career blossomed as he was promoted to positions of ever greater responsibility. On July 27, 1984, after thirty-five years of service, he retired as a lieutenant general and commander of the Air University. It wasn't until a 1999 West Point Class of 1949 reunion at Hilton Head, North Carolina, during a discussion of his aerial victories with classmate Dolphin D. Overton—himself a jet ace—that he described his two probables. Overton felt certain they both should have been confirmed kills and immediately went to work, first tracking down the pilots who had been Cleveland's wingmen on the missions in question. Don Pascoe was the only one living; and he told Overton that the second probable, claimed on September 21, 1952, should have been claimed as a kill.

Overton got a statement from Pascoe, and together with retired double ace Major General Boots Blesse—who had been the 334th FIS operations officer at the time—they submitted the claim to the Victory Confirmation Board of the American Fighter Aces Association. The board reviewed the documentation and agreed, then recognized Cleveland as a fighter ace. He was then inducted into the association. The next step was to correct the official air force record.

Correcting the military record proved more problematic. The Air Force Historical Research Agency said the action was too long ago and that they were not qualified to credit the victory in the absence of any official record. Then in 2004, Overton heard that under Glasnost, the Russian government had opened its military records from the Korean War, including every MiG-15 sortie flown. In fact, our National Archives had disk copies available. Both Overton and Cleveland drove to the Silver Springs, Maryland, facility where an archivist provided a disk containing the Russian records. One of their two losses on April 21, 1952, was across the Yalu River in China, and the time and coordinates closely matched those of Cleveland's engagement that day. But the Historical Research Agency remained disinclined to make changes.

Their only recourse was to petition the Air Force Board for Correction of Military Records to change Cleveland's record. With his friends' urging, General Cleveland (reluctantly) put the evidence together, and in March 2007 submitted the package to the Air Force Board for Corrections. In a formal hearing that included the testimony of both Overton and Blesse, the five-member board was thorough. It wasn't until January 2008 that he received a call saying that correction of his records had been approved and signed by the Secretary of the Air Force (Trest 2012, 238–241).

Thanks to his determined friends Overton and Blesse, General Cleveland had steadfastly upheld West Point's Code of Honor, and had belatedly become a revered member of the 1,450 aces among World Wars I and II, Korea and Vietnam, approximately 150 of whom were still living. His honesty, integrity and military competence will serve as a benchmark paradigm for generations of air force warriors yet to come.

Epilogue

Until the early 1960s, justification for air force accidents had been that "in big military operations you've got to expect losses." But as the Cold War heated up, and the cost of modern jet fighters and the training of their pilots increased, accidents caused by the mindless aggressiveness and flamboyant and reckless aerial customs of the military fighter pilot culture became problematic.

For the first decade after World War II, the threat of creeping communism and the danger of yet another world war seemed to justify the continual high loss rate. Ultimately, the number of aircraft accidents and fatalities in the newly christened US Air Force became unsustainable. The cost in hardware and loss of human life finally forced the air force leadership to begin demanding strict discipline to stem the losses.

General Curtis Lemay, who took over the air force in 1961, began the process of professionalizing military aviation: And he was (justifiably) brutal. He had already succeeded with Strategic Air Command (SAC), and as air force chief he promptly began the process of "Sac-um-sizing" Tactical Air Command (TAC). It took a while, but ultimately his efforts succeeded. With an astounding rate of 19.5 major accidents per one hundred thousand flying hours in the 1950s, under General Lemay's leadership in the 1960s, the mishap rate declined steadily to 4.8 accidents per one hundred thousand hours and continued downward over the years to 1.3 mishaps per one hundred thousand flying hours in the first decade of the twenty-first century. This was thanks to not only better discipline but improvements in aircraft design, use of computerized systems, sophisticated simulators used for the more hazardous training events, and greater application of electronic warfare. In today's air force, the military pilot can be reasonably assured of not only surviving that first year out of flight school but also flying to the magic twenty-year retirement or beyond.

What you have read illustrates the learning curve the US Air Force experienced during the Cold War era. The stellar accident record of today shows the result of discipline, dedication, professionalism, futuristic design, and realistic training. And as General Piotrowski's story shows in chapter 29, the US military services offer unmatched career opportunities to every American citizen. I know of no career path offering young men and women a more adventurous and interesting professional life.

Bibliography

"4th Fighter-Interceptor Group, Operations in MiG Alley—Tactical Doctrine," Colonel Thomas De Jarnette, Commanding. June 17, 1953. (declassified April 30, 2004)

"AA-2 Atoll," accessed April 22, 2008. GlobalSecurity.org.

"AII POW-MIA KW Accounting 2000" "Authentication and Discussion on the '1205' Document," US Senate, April 8, 1993. 9 (www.aiipowmia.com/sea/1205.html)

Anton, Frank. *Why Didn't You Get Me Out?* Arlington, TX: Summit, 1997.

Associated Press, "Missing Korea War POWS—New Report." *San Francisco Chronicle*, A-3, January 18, 1994.

Barnhill, Gary, "SAM Hunter – Killer Missions," MiG Sweep, Volume 128, Winter 2004.

"Battle of Khe Sanh." Wikipedia. Accessed Aug 13, 2009. http://en.wikipedia.org/wiki/Battle_of_Khe_Sanh.

Baugher, Joe. "Invaders for Covert Operations in the Congo." 2000. www.joebaugher.com/usattack/a26_30.html., Accessed September 11, 2008..

Benge, Michael D. "War Crimes: The Cuban-Vietnam Connection." Paper presented to the National Alliance of Families. February 10. 1997.

"Benge, Michael Dennis, Bio," Department of Defense Loss/Capture report, January 31, 1968.

Benge, Michael D. "The Cuban Torture Program." Testimony before the House International Relations Committee, chaired by the Honorable Benjamin A. Gilman. November 4, 1999.

Berger, Carl, et al. *The United States Air Force in South East Asia, 1961–1973.* Washington, DC: Office of Air Force History, 1977.

Blesse, Frederick C. M/General USAF, Ret. *Check Six.* Mesa, AZ: Champlin Fighter Museum Press, 1987.

Boyne, Walter J. "The Berlin for Munch Bunch." *Air Force* magazine, July 2012.

Cole, Paul M. 1993. *POW/MIA Issues: Volume 1, The Korean War.* Santa Monica, CA: RAND Corporation AND MR-351/1-USDP.

Cole, Paul M. "*POW/MIA Issues,*" Volume 1, *The Korean War.* 1994.

Daily Operational Summaries, 12 April 1953, Soviet 64th Fighter Aviation Corps.

. Davies, Peter E. *USAF F-4 Phantom II MiG Killers 1965–68.* Oxford, UK, Osprey Publishing Limited, 2004.

Davies, Peter E. *USAF F-4 Phantom II MiG Killers 1972–73.* Oxford, UK: Osprey Publishing Limited, 2005.

Davis, Larry. *F-86 Sabre In Action.* Carrollton, TX: Squadron/Signal, 1978.

Davis, Larry. "The Unknown Ace, Manual J. Fernandez." *Sabre Jet Classics,* 2004.

Defense Intelligence Agency. "Have Doughnut (U), Tactical, FTD-CR-20-13-69-INT." Vol. II, August 1, Washington, DC, 1969.

Defense Intelligence Agency. 1986. "The Tighe Report." May 27, ,

DFI International. "Moscow Report," June 20, 1996.

Dorr, Robert F. *F-86 Sabre.* Hong Kong: Motorbooks International, 1993.

Eger, Christopher. "Secret MiGs Flown by the USAF.". Air Force, April 2007Escalle, James D. *Unforgotten Hero.* Seattle, Traylor House, 2013.

Ethell, Jeff. "The Roger Locher Rescue." *Flight Journal,* August 1997.

Federal Aviation Regulation 25, Appendic C, Atmospheric Icing definitions. Date unknown.

Gal, Tamas. "The Desertion of the MiG-21." *Eastern Wings.* 08/1966.

Glazov, Jamie. "The Torture of American Soldiers." Frontpagemag. vom, May 6, 2009.

Government Accounting Office. 1992. Report, GAO/IMTEC-92-31. Feb.19.

Haas, Michael E., Colonel, USAF (Ret). *Apollo's Warriors.* Maxwell AFB, AL: Air University Press, 1997.

Hammel, Eric. *Aces at War, Vol. 4,* October 1997

Haney, Eric L. *Inside Delta Force.* New York: Dell, 2003.

Hemming, Gerald Patrick. "Soldier of Fortune get 35-year Term," The Miami Herald, June 4, 1982.

Hendon, Bill, and Elizabeth A. Stewart. *An Enormous Crime.* New York: St. Martin's, 2007.

Hoar, William P. "America's POW Secrets Exposed." *Periscope* (US Naval Institute), February 7, 1998.

Hoffsommer, Alan. *Flying With Floats*. North Hollywood, CA: Pan American Navigation Service Inc., 1966.

Holder, William G. "The Mysterious Curse of the Lady Be Good." *Air University Review*, n.d.

Jensen-Stevenson, Monica, and William Stevenson. *Kiss the Boys Goodbye, How the United States Betrayed Its Own POWs in Vietnam*. New York: Penguin Dutton, 1990.

Jolidon, Laurence. *Last Seen Alive*. Austin, TX: Inkslinger Press, 1995.

Krings, Jack. "Better Stability through Fuel Management." *Phantoms Phorever*, St. Louis, MO. (McDonnell Douglas), October 1980.

Krings, Jack. "Controlling the Phantom." *Phantoms Phorever*, McDonnell Douglas, October/November, 2000.

Marrett, George. *"Don't Kill Yourself."* Flight Journal, June 2008.

McMaster, H. R. *Dereliction of Duty*. New York: HarperPerennial, 1997.

Miller, Robert S. *America's Abandoned Sons*. Bloomington, IN: Xlibris Corporation, 2012.

Momyer, William W., General USAF (Retired). 1978. "Air Power in Three Wars." Government Printing Office. January 1978.

Myles, Bruce, *The Amazing Story of Russia's Women Pilots in World War II,* June 1, 1990

NASA, "McDonnell Douglas F-4 Phantom II—Highlights of Research by Langley for the F-4." April 20, 2008.

No, Kum-Sok, (with J. Roger Osterholm). *A MiG-15 to Freedom*. Jefferson, NC: McFarland, 1996.

Report of Investigation, "Final Search for the Lady Be Good," Headquarters US Army Quartermaster Mortuary System, Europe, June 20, 1960.

Ritchie, Steve, Brigadier General. "Leadership That Inspires Excellence." Unit 012, Air War College, n.d.

Royal Air Force Museum, 1999, 9

Rutan, Dick. "The Fiery Loss of Strobe 01," *Flight Journal.* February 2002.

Sayers, William A. "The Red Baron Reports; What They Really Said." *Airpower History.* Fall 2008.

Schanberg, Sydney H. "Senator Covered Up Evidence of P.O.W.s Left Behind." *Village Voice Media* Inc., February 2004.

Schanberg, Sydney. "McCain and the POW Cover-up." (PDF). *The American Conservative,* July 1, 2010..

Sherman, Stephen. 2000. "Lt. Guy Bordelon." Acepilots.com/korea. updated 04/20/2012.

Stuck, Don. "Spin, Crash and Burn…but…WHY?" Phantoms Phorever St. Louis, McDonnell-Douglas), October1980.

"The Night Witches." mysite.pratt.edu/~rsilva/witches.htm., Accessed December 8, 2004.

"The Tighe Report," Defense Intelligence Agency, 27 May 1986.

Tamayo, Juan O. "Former US POWs detail Torture by Cubans in Vietnam." *The Miami Herald.* August 22, 1999.

Trest, Warren A. *Once a Fighter Pilot.* Montgomery, AL: River City Publishing, 2012.

"US Air Force Oral History Interview, Roger F. Brodman, Volume II." November 1986 and June 1987, Maxwell AFB, AL, USAF Historian.

USAir Force Unit history, USAF, "The 334th Fighter Interceptor January 1953 through 30 June 1953." Maxwell AFB, AL, USAF Historian.

United Airlines Flight 736, midair collision April 21, 1958, Nellis AFB, NV. F-100F 56-3755A. Wikipedia.**org/wiki/United_Airlines_flight 736.**

USAF Manual 160-5. 1969. *Physiological Technical Training Manual.* February 27, 5-1–5-11.

USAF. "Report of Aircraft Accident, F-86F, SN 52-4980." July 8, 1955.

USAF. "Report of Aircraft Accident, F-86E, SN 52-5053." July 18, 1955.

USAF. "Report of Aircraft Accident. F-86F-30, SN 52-4990." August 22, 1956.

USAF. "Report of Aircraft Accident, F-100F, SN 56-3755." April 21, 1958.

USAF. "Report of Aircraft Accident, JF-106A, SN 57-0242." October 27, 1958

USAF. "Report of Aircraft Accident F-4C, 22-NC, SN 64 0733." March 31, 1967.

USAF. "Report of Aircraft Accident F-104C, SN 56-922." November 22, 1968.

USAF. "Report of Aircraft Accident, F-105D, SN 60-459." January 16, 1969

USAF. "Report of Aircraft Accident, Report F-4C, SN 64-0721." July 11, 1973.

United States Senate, memo for record, "The 1205 or Quang Document," April 8, 1993.

Wagner, Ray. *The North American SABRE*. New York: Doubleday, 1963.

Weiss, Reuven. "The Blue Bird Legend." *Israel News*. May 29, Y Net news.com. Access April 2009..

Werrell, Kenneth P. *Sabres over MiG Alley*. Annapolis, MD: Naval Institute Press, 2005.

Wetterhahn, Ralph. "Nguyen Van Bay and Aces from the North." *Air & Space Magazine*, November 2000.

Wetterhahn, Ralph. "The Unreturned." *The Retired Officer*. November 2002.

Wolfe, Tom. *The Right Stuff*. New York: Bantam, 1979.

Wright, Donald C. "The Last Flight of the Lady Be Good." *The Retired Officer*, September 1977.

Zampini, Diego F. "North Vietnam Aces." Acepilots.com, November 2002, revised March 22, 2012.

Made in the USA
Lexington, KY
30 April 2017